# OFF THE BOOKS

## SUSTAINABLE INFRASTRUCTURE SERIES

Sustainable infrastructure is a key enabler of economic and social development, as well as environmental sustainability. Quality infrastructure enhances productivity and competitiveness, contributing to economic growth and employment as well as facilitating international trade. Broad coverage of infrastructure services promotes social inclusion and equity and supports the formation of human capital. Green infrastructure safeguards local environmental quality, while contributing to the global decarbonization process. The challenge of delivering sustainable infrastructure services is a complex one that goes far beyond "bricks and mortar" to encompass good policy, sound planning, efficient procurement, smart regulation, transparent governance, affordable finance, and functional markets. The Sustainable Infrastructure Series covers a wide range of policy topics relating to network infrastructure services, including energy, multimodal transportation, information and communications technology and digital development, water and sanitation, and urban and rural infrastructure, as well as irrigation and flood management.

### Titles in This Series

*Beyond The Gap: How Countries Can Afford the Infrastructure They Need while Protecting the Planet*

*Lifelines: The Resilient Infrastructure Opportunity*

*Rethinking Power Sector Reform in the Developing World*

*Laying the Foundations: A Global Analysis of Regulatory Frameworks for the Safety of Dams and Downstream Communities*

*Off the Books: Understanding and Mitigating the Fiscal Risks of Infrastructure*

**All books in the Sustainable Infrastructure Series are available for free at https://openknowledge.worldbank.org/handle/10986/31290.**

SUSTAINABLE INFRASTRUCTURE SERIES

# OFF THE BOOKS

## Understanding and Mitigating the Fiscal Risks of Infrastructure

*Matías Herrera Dappe, Vivien Foster,
Aldo Musacchio, Teresa Ter-Minassian,
and Burak Turkgulu*

# Contents

**Boxes**

**Figures**

# Foreword

Worldwide more than 700 million people lack access to electricity, and about 1 billion people live more than two kilometers from an all-season road. By 2050, the number of people living in cities will increase by 2.5 billion, with most of the increase occurring in developing countries. All of these people need access to reliable electricity networks and dependable transport alternatives, lack of which hampers economic and social development in low- and middle-income countries (LMICs) by constraining private sector investments, the integration and efficiency of goods and labor markets, and access to educational opportunities and health care services.

A recent report in this series (*Beyond the Gap*) estimates that LMICs will need to invest at least 3.5 percent of their GDP per year in the electricity and transport sectors to close the infrastructure gap and achieve the Sustainable Development Goals while staying on track to keep the rise in global temperature to 2°C. Undertaking this level of investment—and the related operations and maintenance expense—will require governments to mobilize massive resources through all means available, including on-budget spending and off-budget vehicles, namely state-owned enterprises (SOEs) and public-private partnerships (PPPs).

Especially given the strong headwinds currently facing LMICs, governments will need to use their fiscal space efficiently and sustainably. As evidenced by the January 2023 edition of the *World Economic Prospects* report, developing economies are now facing the triple challenge of heavy debt burdens, the global tightening of financial conditions, and declining growth rates, all of which put pressure on infrastructure sector budgets. Combined with the needs to invest in infrastructure as part of the postpandemic recovery and to finance resilience to climate change and the transition to cleaner fuels, these global challenges increase the urgency of creating sustainable fiscal space for infrastructure.

To do so, LMIC governments need to improve their understanding of the fiscal risks of infrastructure, which often arise because significant swathes of infrastructure spending take place "off the books," through a variety of extra-budgetary vehicles. Realization of such risks can present countries with large unanticipated demands on the public purse—through either a steady drain or an occasional major liability—that increase the life-cycle cost of infrastructure provision.

Experience shows that such risks can be mitigated when governments account for and manage them properly. Doing so requires improved planning and implementation of infrastructure projects regardless of the financing method used. Governance reforms to improve the financial sustainability of SOEs and clarify their mandate are also essential to make infrastructure spending and management sustainable. Mobilizing private capital will be increasingly important to access additional expertise and promote efficiency gains, but governments should not ignore the explicit and implicit fiscal risks PPPs pose when projects do not go according to plan.

This report takes a comprehensive look at the fiscal risks of infrastructure. It provides a conceptual framework for understanding the risks based on the modality of provision, presents quantitative evidence on the risks, and proposes concrete reforms for managing them. The powerful conceptual framework proposed, and the evidence (based on rigorous analytical work) presented, are accessible to policy makers and a general audience familiar with the infrastructure sector.

Good governance of infrastructure can help governments deliver infrastructure to the billions of people for whom it is currently inadequate. By targeting reforms to areas in which they can be expected to have the greatest impact in ensuring sustainable infrastructure for all and recognizing the unique situations every country faces, this report presents policy makers with a realistic roadmap to success.

**Guangzhe Chen**
Vice President for Infrastructure
The World Bank

# Acknowledgments

This report was prepared by a team led by Matías Herrera Dappe and Yadviga Semikolenova. Matías Herrera Dappe, Vivien Foster, Aldo Musacchio, Teresa Ter-Minassian, and Burak Turkgulu wrote the report. Its wide scope meant that a large team of experts, including many World Bank specialists complemented by external consultants, undertook the underlying research and data collection.

- On direct public provision, a team led by Vivien Foster, comprising Nisan Gorgulu, Massimo Mastruzzi, and Anshul Rana, conducted original research. Teresa Ter-Minassian contributed to the conceptual framework and policy reform agenda.
- On state-owned enterprises, a team led by Matías Herrera Dappe and Aldo Musacchio, comprising Jonathan Barboza, Carolina Pan, Yadviga Semikolenova, and Burak Turkgulu, conducted original research. Teresa Ter-Minassian contributed to the conceptual framework and policy reform agenda.
- On public-private partnerships, a team led by Matías Herrera Dappe, comprising Eduardo Engel, Martin Ferrari, Ronald Fischer, Alexander Galetovic, and Burak Turkgulu, conducted original research. David Duarte also contributed.
- A team led by Matías Herrera Dappe and Yadviga Semikolenova, comprising Castalia LLC, Carlos Centeno, David Duarte, Eduardo Engel, Martin Ferrari, Ronald Fischer, Alexander Galetovic, Timothy C. Irwin, Fernando Lecaros, Giancarlo Marchesi, Vasile Olievschi, Andres Ricover, Teresa Ter-Minassian, and Burak Turkgulu, prepared the country case studies.
- A team led by Matías Herrera Dappe, Stephen Nash, Yadviga Semikolenova, and Burak Turkgulu, comprising Antonella Bonacina, Hugues Boulnois, Maria Cabrera Escalante, Ivan Kokoureen, Dmitry Lesnichiy, Abhishek Malhotra, and Frank Ngoussome, collected the financial data on state-owned enterprises.

The report's peer reviewers provided valuable guidance. They included Ani Balabanyan, Cecilia Briceño-Garmendia, Sudarshan Gooptu (Millennium Challenge Corporation), Fernanda Ruiz Nunez, Binyam Reja, Eivind Tandberg (International Monetary Fund), and Genevieve Verdier (International Monetary Fund). The report also benefited from comments and suggestions from Luis Andres, Richard Damania, Clive Harris, Martin Melecky, Alvaro Pedraza Morales, Gerardo Ruiz-Tagle (Inter-American Development Bank), Tomas Serebrisky (Inter-American Development Bank), Siddharth Sharma, Jevgenijs Steinbuks, Mikel Tejada Ibañez, Fatouma Toure Ibrahima, Robert Johann Utz, and Maria Vagliasindi. Guangzhe Chen, Makhtar Diop, Pablo Fajnzylber, Imad Fakhoury, and Riccardo Puliti also provided helpful guidance.

This report would not have been possible without generous funding provided by the Energy Sector Management Assistance Program (ESMAP) and the Public-Private Infrastructure Advisory Facility (PPIAF).

Barbara Karni edited the report, Bill Pragluski designed it, and Datapage typeset it.

# About the Authors

**Matías Herrera Dappe** is a senior economist in the Infrastructure Vice-Presidency of the World Bank, where he leads policy research programs on infrastructure. He has published extensively on a wide range of topics, including infrastructure economics, economic development, trade and logistics, public-private partnerships, state-owned enterprises, competition, auctions, and fiscal policy. Before joining the World Bank, he worked for consulting firms and think tanks, advising governments and companies in Latin America, North America, and Europe. He holds a PhD in economics from the University of Maryland, College Park.

**Vivien Foster** is chief economist for the Infrastructure Vice-Presidency of the World Bank. Over the past 20 years, she has advised the governments of more than 30 developing countries on a wide range of infrastructure policy challenges. Her policy-oriented research has been extensively published, including titles such as *Water, Electricity, and the Poor* (2005); *Africa's Infrastructure* (2009); *Building Bridges* (2009); *Tracking SDG7: The Energy Progress Report* (2013–18); *Regulatory Indicators for Sustainable Energy (RISE)* (2016, 2018); and *Rethinking Power Sector Reforms* (2020). She was co-director of the *World Development Report 2021: Data for Better Lives*. She holds a PhD in economics from University College London.

**Aldo Musacchio** is a professor of management and economics at the Brandeis International Business School and a faculty research associate at the National Bureau of Economic Research. Before joining Brandeis, he was an associate professor and Marvin Bower Fellow at the Harvard Business School. Together with Sergio G. Lazzarini, he has written academic papers and *Reinventing State Capitalism: Leviathan in Business, Brazil and Beyond* (Harvard University Press, 2014), which examines the performance implications of different governance arrangements in state-owned enterprises (SOEs) and the effects of investments and loans from development banks on the performance of private and state-owned firms. He has also edited two books for the Inter-American Development Bank that provide new sets of best practices to improve the reporting and performance of SOEs. He holds a PhD in the economic history of Latin America from Stanford University.

**Teresa Ter-Minassian** is an international economic consultant and the former director of the Fiscal Affairs Department of the International Monetary Fund (IMF). At the IMF, she led missions to several countries, including Greece, Italy, and Spain, and program negotiations with Argentina, Brazil, and Portugal. She currently works on fiscal issues, particularly in Latin America. She has published more than 40 papers and books on fiscal issues, especially on macro-fiscal and intergovernmental fiscal relations. She holds a law degree from the University of Rome and an MA in economics from Harvard University.

**Burak Turkgulu** is a consultant in the Infrastructure Vice Presidency of the World Bank. He has contributed to numerous empirical research projects in infrastructure economics and finance and maintains the World Bank Infrastructure SOEs Database. His other research focuses on institutional economics, human capital valuation, growth and development, and the political and economic history of Türkiye. He holds an MA in economics from the University of Maryland, College Park.

# Main Messages

Developing countries face significant infrastructure needs—and rising debt levels and tightening fiscal and monetary conditions are increasing pressure on the funds available for infrastructure. Whether governments spend directly on budget, spend at arm's length through state-owned enterprises (SOEs), or delegate spending via public-private partnerships (PPPs), the risks of fiscal surprises—infrastructure costing more than projected—are high. It is therefore critical that governments tackle the governance challenges undermining the efficiency of infrastructure spending and absorbing scarce fiscal space.

This report quantifies the magnitude and prevalence of fiscal risks from electricity and transport infrastructure, identifying their root causes across a range of low- and middle-income countries and putting forward policy options to tackle fiscal risks from infrastructure in a comprehensive and cohesive manner. By providing policy makers with a deeper understanding of the fiscal risks of infrastructure, it can help them understand just how much is at stake in the good governance of infrastructure and target reforms to areas in which those efforts can be expected to have the greatest impact.

Three main findings stand out from the analysis:

- **Off-budget modalities drain public finances more often and on a larger scale than usually assumed.** Infrastructure SOEs require average annual fiscal injections of 0.25 percent of gross domestic product (GDP) to remain afloat. In 57 percent of the cases studied, SOEs received net fiscal injections, with the injections reaching as high as 3 percent of GDP in some cases. One reason the full extent of fiscal dependency is not always clearly understood is that governments use a wide range of fiscal instruments to support infrastructure SOEs, including operations subsidies, equity injections, and loans from government and other SOEs. As a result, assessing the full extent of the problem is challenging.

  A large share of PPP contracts is renegotiated, leading to a small but frequent drain of fiscal resources. The annual fiscal cost of renegotiation averages about 0.2 percent of GDP in the countries studied (this figure should be viewed as a lower bound, because these countries are among the best in the world in terms of PPP governance). Early termination of PPPs is less frequent than renegotiation, but terminations can be costly, because multiple terminations often occur at the same time. The predicted fiscal risks from early termination in a sample of developing countries are 0.1–2.8 percent of 2020 GDP.

- **Inefficiencies in public provision lead to fiscal surprises in the near, medium, and long term.** Developing countries executed only about 70 percent of infrastructure investment budgets in 2010–18, indicating a potentially significant risk of project delay and cost overruns. There is also evidence of a pronounced capital bias in infrastructure expenditure, especially in the road sector. Coupled with expenditure that is not as productive or efficient as it could be, this bias leads to growing investment liabilities because of asset deterioration, which extreme weather events can exacerbate. In addition, public infrastructure spending has been low and investment has declined in recent years, falling well short of normative estimates of what is required to meet development goals.
- **When it rains, it pours.** On-budget spending on infrastructure was procyclical in 2005–20, suggesting that public infrastructure spending is a soft target for budget cuts. During economic downturns, SOEs can weaken a country's overall fiscal situation and amplify the negative macroeconomic shock, because SOEs need fiscal injections precisely when governments are under pressure from the fall in total tax revenues. A profound macroeconomic crisis also increases the fiscal risks from early termination of PPPs by an order of magnitude immediately after the shock.

Vulnerability to exogenous shocks and the prevalence of perverse incentives faced by government officials, SOE managers, and private partners (which, in turn, lead to moral hazard and principal–agent problems) explain the prevalence of fiscal risks in the provision of infrastructure service. A reform agenda to mitigate the fiscal risks from infrastructure should be grounded in an effort to build government capacity and include the following four building blocks:

- **Robust integrated public investment management (PIM)** leads to projects being selected because they are aligned with a country's development goals and yield the highest net benefits and provision modalities being selected based on value for money and fiscal affordability. Robust integrated PIM requires consistent assessment of all potential projects and consistent fiscal treatment of all implemented projects (projects delivered through direct public provision, PPPs and, in some cases, SOEs). Such management is needed to ensure that projects and modalities are not selected because of differential fiscal treatment. Countries should also adopt rolling medium-term fiscal frameworks that include PPPs, in order to ensure alignment of investment plans with available funding. The effectiveness of integrated PIM rests on granting the ministry of finance final authority to approve projects and contract renegotiations and modifications.
- **Effective fiscal and corporate governance of SOEs** allows and incentivizes boards and managers to operate SOEs efficiently, thereby mitigating fiscal risks. It requires clearly specifying the SOEs' mandates and avoiding government interference in SOEs' operations, particularly through the imposition of policy mandates or quasi-fiscal operations. If interference cannot be avoided, SOEs should be compensated in a commensurate, timely, and transparent manner. Where an independent sector regulator exists, it should work with the ministry of finance to determine appropriate compensation. SOEs' access to financing should be based on their debt-servicing capacity and approved by the ministry of finance in a nondiscretionary manner. To mitigate the need for fiscal injections, the government should establish clear requirements for financial management and monitoring.

- **A robust PPP preparation, procurement, and contract management framework** that allocates risk optimally and limits opportunistic behavior is needed to mitigate the risks from renegotiation and early termination of PPPs. A robust framework should avoid allocating demand risk to the private partner when it has no or minimal control over demand. Flexible-term contracts, such as present-value-of-revenue contracts, are a good option for allocating the demand risk to the government in such cases. Measures to reduce financing risk can help reduce the risk of early termination. Clearly regulating contract renegotiations, modifications, and early terminations and establishing alternative dispute resolution mechanisms are important measures for mitigating fiscal risks.
- **Integrated fiscal risk management** leads to the most efficient outcomes, because of potential interactions among different risks and portfolio effects. It requires a central institutional structure, within the ministry of finance or chaired by the minister, that is responsible for managing all fiscal risks. It also requires comprehensive disclosure of fiscal information. A risk mitigation strategy should start with sound macroeconomic and debt management. Risks from natural disasters, for example, particularly disasters related to extreme weather events, affect different types of infrastructure and noninfrastructure assets, requiring integrated approaches to mitigate those risks.

# Abbreviations

| | |
|---|---|
| CEM | coarsened exact matching |
| EBIT | earnings before interest and taxes |
| EBITDA | earnings before interest, taxes, depreciation, and amortization |
| ESA | European System of Accounts |
| EU | European Union |
| GDP | gross domestic product |
| ICSID | International Centre for Settlement of Investment Disputes |
| IPSAS | International Public Sector Accounting Standards |
| IRR | internal rate of return |
| MTEF | medium-term expenditure framework |
| MTFF | medium-term fiscal framework |
| O&M | operations and maintenance |
| PFRAM | PPP Fiscal Risk Assessment Model |
| PIM | public investment management |
| PPI | Private Participation in Infrastructure |
| PPP | public-private partnership |
| PVR | present value of revenue |
| QFO | quasi-fiscal operation |
| ROAA | return on average assets |
| SOE | state-owned enterprise |

All dollar amounts are US dollars unless otherwise indicated.

# Overview: Key Findings and Policy Recommendations

Electricity and transport infrastructure is an important driver of inclusive economic growth and development; it can also increase resilience to shocks and help countries meet global climate targets. Electricity and transport infrastructure allows firms to produce and trade and people to access economic and social opportunities. Resilient infrastructure allows areas to remain connected and receive needed support in the event of shocks. Electricity and transport systems together account for over half of global greenhouse gas emissions. If the right infrastructure investments in these sectors are made, both sectors can contribute significantly to the reduction of greenhouse gas emissions.

**Governments play a key role in providing infrastructure, because of its socioeconomic and environmental implications and because infrastructure investments tend to be large, risky, and affected by market failures.** Investments in highways, railways, ports, and power plants require hundreds of millions of dollars in site-specific and long-lived assets that are exposed to significant risks. The network characteristic of electricity and transport infrastructure means that coordinated planning and development is needed to maximize their benefits and reduce the risk of "bridges to nowhere." Some infrastructure assets, such as power transmission networks, are natural monopolies, which require some level of government involvement.

**Governments provide infrastructure directly (through line ministries or public authorities) and indirectly (through off-budget provision modalities such as state-owned enterprises [SOEs] and public–private partnership [PPPs]).** Capital spending on electricity and transport through direct public provision declined from a peak of 1.8 percent of gross domestic product (GDP) in 2012 to 1.2 percent of GDP in 2018. Between 2009 and 2018, average spending on infrastructure by SOEs and PPPs in a sample of developing countries represented 37–53 percent of total capital spending through the three modalities (figure O.1).

**Developing countries face significant infrastructure needs, and rising debt levels and tightening fiscal and monetary conditions are increasing pressure on the funds available for infrastructure.** Recent estimates put the electricity and transport infrastructure investment needed in the developing world to deliver on the Sustainable Development Goals and the Paris Climate Agreement at 3.5 percent of GDP a year through 2030

**FIGURE O.1**  Share of capital spending on infrastructure in developing countries, by modality, 2009–18

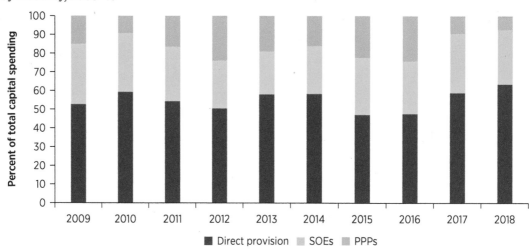

*Source:* Original figure for this publication, based on data from the BOOST, World Bank Infrastructure SOEs, and PPI databases.
*Note:* Capital expenditures in PPPs were distributed over a five-year period beginning in the investment year indicated in the PPI Database. Expenditures through direct public provision are expenditures by the general government. When spending through direct public provision in the power sector was not available for a country in the BOOST data, total energy spending was used. Countries include Albania, Argentina, Bhutan, Bulgaria, Burundi, Ethiopia, Georgia, Indonesia, Kenya, Kosovo, Peru, Romania, Solomon Islands, South Africa, and Ukraine. PPP = public-private partnership; SOE = state-owned enterprise.

(Rozenberg and Fay 2019). Government debt has grown to critical levels for developing countries since 2010, exacerbated by the pandemic (Kose and others 2021). Fiscal deficits are projected to remain above their pre-pandemic levels, putting further pressure on public debt. The cost of borrowing, in both global and domestic markets, is increasing as central banks tighten monetary policy in response to inflationary pressures. Rising interest rates may make current levels of debt unsustainable for many developing countries (World Bank 2022), hindering their ability to invest in needed infrastructure.

**Governance challenges undermine the efficiency of spending and absorb scarce fiscal space.** Whether governments spend directly on budget, spend at arm's length through SOEs, or delegate spending via PPPs, the risk of fiscal surprises—infrastructure costing more than projected—is high.

**Closing the infrastructure gap while supporting the postpandemic recovery requires the creation of sustainable fiscal space for infrastructure.** Fiscal risks must be mitigated in order to increase the value for money from existing resources and additional capital that will need to be mobilized to close the gap. Because of current macroeconomic conditions, developing countries will try to increase private capital mobilization through PPPs and likely call on their SOEs to increase investments and help implement social and employment generation programs, heightening the need to mitigate the fiscal risks associated with these channels.

**This report quantifies the magnitude and prevalence of fiscal risks from electricity and transport infrastructure and identifies their root causes across a range of low- and middle-income countries.** Drawing on important new sources of evidence, such as the World Bank Infrastructure SOEs Database, and compiling many others, the report quantifies the magnitude of different types of risks and examines how risks vary across contexts.[1] The results make it possible to answer several important questions: How much of an ongoing fiscal drain do off-budget infrastructure vehicles like SOEs and PPPs routinely represent? How frequent and large are major bailouts? How do major macroeconomic shocks affect SOEs and PPPs? What fiscal surprises are associated with on-budget spending? How does the magnitude and profile of fiscal surprises differ across types of infrastructure, such as electricity and transport?

A deeper understanding of the fiscal risks of infrastructure can help policy makers understand how much is at stake in the good governance of infrastructure and target reforms in areas in which they can be expected to have the greatest impact. **This report contributes to the debate on creating sustainable fiscal space for infrastructure by putting forward policy options to tackle fiscal risks from infrastructure in a comprehensive and cohesive manner.**

The report begins by presenting a conceptual framework for assessing fiscal risks from infrastructure, focusing on direct public provision, SOEs, and PPPs (chapter 1). It then provides new empirical evidence on the prevalence, magnitude, and sources of fiscal risks in developing countries from direct public provision (chapter 2), SOEs (chapter 3), and PPPs (chapter 4). The last chapter presents a reform agenda for mitigating fiscal risks from infrastructure. The rest of this overview presents the main findings and policy recommendations.

## WHAT ARE THE MAIN SOURCES OF FISCAL RISKS FROM INFRASTRUCTURE?

**Fiscal risks from infrastructure manifest themselves in different ways, depending on the modality of provision (figure O.2).** Direct public provision of infrastructure can lead to fiscal surprises through unanticipated additional expenditures caused by cost

**FIGURE O.2** Sources of fiscal costs and risks associated with provision of infrastructure

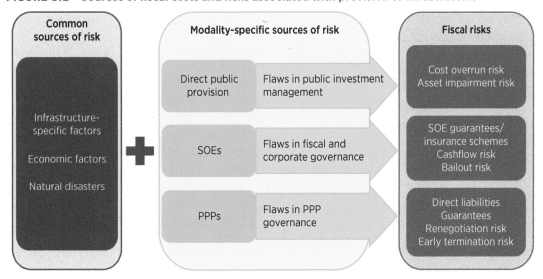

*Source:* Original figure for this publication.
*Note:* PPP = public-private partnership; SOE = state-owned enterprise.

overruns or asset deterioration. Infrastructure SOEs can create substantial risks for public finances through explicit guarantees, public insurance schemes, and cashflow and bailout risk. Cashflow risk stems from the volatility of SOE net income, which requires fiscal transfers to cover occasional and modest losses associated with exogenous shocks and inefficiencies related to soft budget constraints. Bailout risk refers to the risk associated with having to recapitalize an SOE; help it avoid default or bankruptcy; or cancel its liabilities because it had insufficient capital buffers to deal with large, unexpected shocks and the continuous write-off of losses.

**Involving the private sector in the provision of infrastructure through PPPs changes the nature of the fiscal risks.** Direct liabilities, such as upfront capital subsidies and availability payments, can lead to fiscal surprises if PPPs are kept off the fiscal balance sheet and the budget. Guarantees of minimum revenue or demand, the foreign exchange rate, and debt (provided by the government to ensure the commercial feasibility and bankability of PPPs) can lead to fiscal surprises. Infrastructure PPP contracts themselves create contingent liabilities from renegotiations and early terminations that can also lead to fiscal surprises.

**No matter how good government plans and projections are, uncertainties exist; when realized, they can put financing pressure on the fiscal authorities.** Most of these uncertainties are common to all provision modalities. Some are specific to infrastructure projects; others are related to economic factors or natural disasters. Infrastructure projects tend to be technically complex and involve large budgetary outlays, including substantial sunk costs. Infrastructure is site specific, which makes its cost depend on the availability and geological characteristics of the land it is built on as well as on environmental regulations. The fact that infrastructure investments are typically long-lived increases the uncertainties associated with both construction and operations and maintenance costs as well as demand for their services, leaving them vulnerable to unforeseen exogenous shocks, including macroeconomic cycles or crises, exchange rate fluctuations, and natural disasters. The complexity and long-term nature of infrastructure greatly complicates both forecasting and provisioning for risks.

**Governance challenges can create and increase the magnitude of fiscal risks.** Significant social and political pressures may distort governments' decisions regarding the selection of projects and provision modalities. Especially in low-income countries, public administrations may have limited technical skills and data to undertake integrated transport and electricity planning and select the optimal provision modality for each project.

**Weaknesses in public investment management (PIM) can lead to fiscal risks.** Lack of coordination across and within levels of government in planning and budgeting lead to projects being only partially implemented. The political benefit of new infrastructure and low capacity often create incentives to prioritize capital spending over maintenance spending (capital bias) and underestimate the likelihood and impact of possible adverse shocks. Flaws in contract and asset management can lead to inefficient spending. All these weaknesses can lead to inadequate maintenance and poor-quality construction, eventually requiring additional spending on maintenance to avoid asset impairment, which disaster and extreme weather events can exacerbate. The fact that public spending on infrastructure tends to be the first victim of fiscal crises adds to the risk of asset impairment.

**Flaws in fiscal and corporate governance that create soft budget constraints are the main SOE–specific source of fiscal risks.** Soft budget constraints arise whenever a government is unable to credibly commit not to provide unjustified financial support.

Soft budget constraints hurt SOEs by encouraging them to take excessive risks and sapping their incentive to be efficient.

**One of the main causes of soft budget constraints are quasi-fiscal operations (QFOs)—the imposition of public policy objectives and practices on SOEs.** Examples of QFOs include the pricing of goods and services below cost-recovery levels (to moderate the headline inflation rate or prevent social discontent, for example) and the imposition of labor market policies that constrain SOEs' ability to adjust their workforces. Other causes of soft budget constraints are the excessive extraction of resources by their owner governments, the granting of preferential access to financing, information asymmetries between SOEs and their owners, and flaws in corporate governance that exacerbate information asymmetries and allow government interference in the selection of SOE boards and management.

**Flaws in PPP governance—including inadequate fiscal treatment of PPPs, the uncertainty around infrastructure. and the long-term contractual nature of PPPs— can give public authorities and private partners incentives to behave opportunistically, creating fiscal risks.** Governments have incentives to deliver projects through PPPs rather than directly because of the fiscal implications rather than because of value for money. The off-budget nature and information asymmetries between different government authorities may give awarding authorities the incentive to behave strategically and use renegotiations to fulfill policy and political objectives. When the government is unable to commit not to renegotiate a PPP or there is significant uncertainty regarding the return on investment of a PPP, strategic and opportunistic behavior by the private partner can lead to renegotiations and even early termination.

## OFF-BUDGET MODALITIES DRAIN PUBLIC FINANCES MORE OFTEN AND ON A LARGER SCALE THAN USUALLY ASSUMED

It has long been known that infrastructure SOEs and PPPs can lead to extreme fiscal surprises (tail risk) (Bova and others 2019; Musacchio and Pineda Ayerbe 2019; Schwartz and others 2020). This report shows that during good times SOEs and PPPs represent a more frequent and much larger drain on public finances than usually assumed.

### Fiscal risks from SOEs

**Infrastructure SOEs require average annual fiscal injections of 0.25 percent of GDP to remain afloat.** In 57 percent of the 187 country-year observations captured for the period 2009–18, infrastructure SOEs received fiscal injections (net of asset increases).[2] These injections included 4 events with fiscal injections of more than 1 percent of GDP, 38 with fiscal injections of 0.2–1.0 percent of GDP, and 64 with fiscal injections of less than 0.2 percent of GDP (figure O.3). Fiscal risk from SOEs should therefore be thought of as a series of small to medium-size deviations from budgeted figures requiring frequent fiscal injections.

**One reason why the full extent of fiscal dependency is not always clearly understood is that governments use a wide range of fiscal instruments to support infrastructure SOEs—including operations subsidies, equity injections, and loans from government and other SOEs—which make assessing the full extent of the problem challenging.** The type and extent of fiscal injections used to support infrastructure SOEs varies across countries (figure O.4). During 2009–18, for example, Bulgaria supported its infrastructure SOEs with average annual fiscal injections of 0.8 percent of GDP, using operations subsidies and loans from SOEs as the main instruments. In Bhutan and Croatia, average

**FIGURE O.3**    Distribution of fiscal injections to infrastructure SOEs

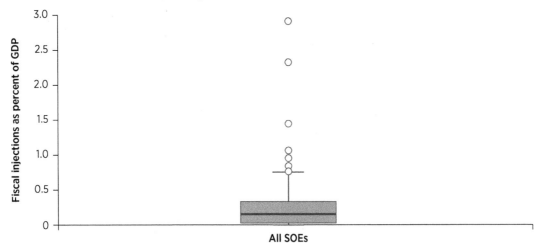

*Source:* Original figure for this publication, based on data from the World Bank Infrastructure SOEs Database.
*Note:* Data are from 2009–18. Box shows interquartile variation (25–75 percent) of fiscal injections to GDP. Horizontal line across the box shows the median. Whiskers show the maximum and minimum, capped at 1.5 times the interquartile range. Dots represent outliers. Distribution is over positive fiscal injection events. GDP = gross domestic product; SOE = state-owned enterprise.

**FIGURE O.4**    Average annual fiscal injections to infrastructure SOEs, 2008–19, by country

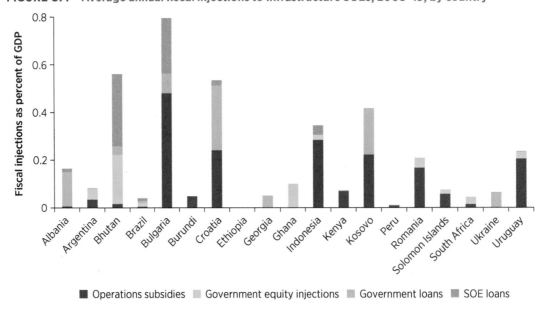

*Source:* Original figure for this publication, based on data from the World Bank Infrastructure SOEs Database.
*Note:* Government loans and SOE loans capture the annual increase in long-term debt or loans. Figure was constructed by adding operations subsidies, government equity injections, and increases in government loans and SOE loans and subtracting change in assets from the previous year by SOE for each year to determine whether there was a fiscal injection (that is, a positive difference). Fiscal injections by sector were then added in each country for each year and the resulting figure was divided by GDP, which was then averaged over years. GDP = gross domestic product; SOE = state-owned enterprise.

annual fiscal injections to infrastructure SOEs amounted to about 0.5 percent of GDP, with Bhutan using mostly SOE loans and government equity injections and Croatia using mostly operations subsidies and government loans.

**The negative return on assets of infrastructure SOEs shows that governments provide an implicit subsidy to them on top of their explicit fiscal injections.** The average adjusted return on average assets (ROAA) of infrastructure SOEs once operations subsidies are netted from net income is –5.1 percent. The average ROAA when operations subsidies are considered is –0.14. Both the ROAA and the adjusted ROAA are significantly lower than those of comparable private firms (2.4 and 5.2 percentage points lower, respectively, on average), revealing the extent of the implicit subsidy provided by the government.

**The underperformance of infrastructure SOEs is associated with state ownership and QFOs.** SOEs underperform similar private firms, with the former yielding lower return on assets gross and net of operations subsidies than the latter. The difference in the ratios of employee costs to total expenses between SOEs and private companies is 20.5 percentage points (Herrera Dappe and others 2022). One of the QFOs SOEs undertake on behalf of governments is generating employment, often paying salaries that are at least as high as in the private sector. The larger share of employment expenses relative to revenues is likely a consequence of the role SOEs play as employers. QFOs that cap tariffs can lead to net losses, which in many cases are not adequately compensated by the government.

**The magnitude and likelihood of fiscal risks from power and transport SOEs present interesting differences** (box O.1). Transport SOEs are more likely to have received

---

**BOX O.1     Sectoral features affecting the size and profile of fiscal risks from SOEs**

On average, SOEs in the power sector absorb the most fiscal resources, with annual fiscal injections representing 0.25 percent of GDP (figure BO.1.1). They are followed by SOEs in the road, rail, and airline and airport sectors, with average annual fiscal injections of 0.24, 0.12, and 0.04 percent of GDP, respectively. In the power sector, average annual fiscal injections are equivalent to 10 percent of average assets; in the transport sectors, they are equivalent to 20–35 percent of average assets. Fiscal support to SOEs therefore provides significant recapitalization, most of it through operations subsidies. Loans from government and other SOEs are also important for power and road SOEs.

Transport SOEs were more likely to have received fiscal injections, but the power sector was more likely to have received larger injections. In the 156 country-year observations captured in this report for the transport sector, there were 77 instances of fiscal injections (49 percent). In the 180 country-year observations captured for the power sector, there were 59 instances of fiscal injections (33 percent). The share of injections that exceeded 0.2 percent of GDP was 36 percent in the transport sector and 34 percent in the power sector. In the transport sector, only 1 percent of the injections exceeded 0.6 percent of GDP; in the power sector, 17 percent did so (figure BO.1.2).

Power SOEs had a modest positive rate of return on average assets (ROAA). The average adjusted ROAA was 1.0 percent and the average ROAA 1.9 percent (figure BO.1.3). Power SOEs

*(continued)*

**BOX O.1**   *Continued*

**FIGURE BO.1.1**   Fiscal injections to infrastructure SOEs by sector, 2009–18

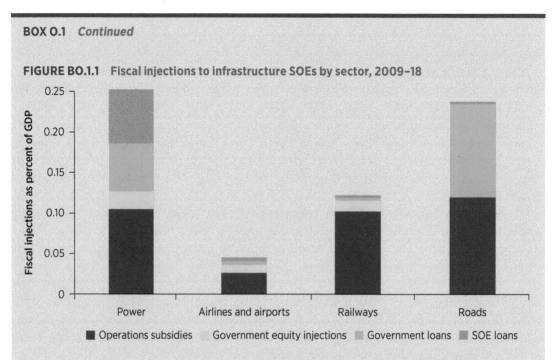

■ Operations subsidies    Government equity injections    Government loans    ▨ SOE loans

*Source:* Original figure for this publication, based on data from the World Bank Infrastructure SOEs Database.
*Note:* Government loans and SOE loans capture annual positive increases in long-term debt or loans. Figure was constructed by adding operations subsidies, government equity injections, and increases in government loans and SOE loans and subtracting the change in assets from the previous year by SOE for each year to determine whether there was a fiscal injection (that is, a positive difference). Fiscal injections by sector in each country were then added for each year and the resulting figure was divided by GDP. All country-year observations of positive fiscal injection events were then averaged by sector. GDP = gross domestic product; SOE = state-owned enterprise.

**FIGURE BO.1.2**   Size distribution of fiscal injections in the transport and power sectors

■ Transport    Power

*Source:* Original figure for this publication, based on data from the World Bank Infrastructure SOEs Database.
*Note:* GDP = gross domestic product.

*(continued)*

**BOX O.1**   *Continued*

**FIGURE BO.1.3**   Return on average assets of infrastructure SOEs, with and without adjustment for operations subsidies, by sector

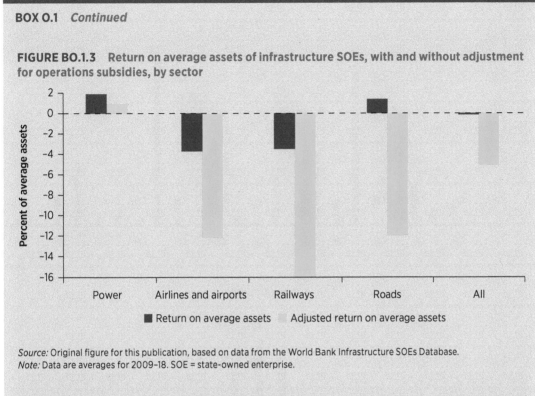

*Source:* Original figure for this publication, based on data from the World Bank Infrastructure SOEs Database.
*Note:* Data are averages for 2009–18. SOE = state-owned enterprise.

have manageable payroll costs (17 percent of revenues on average) but are highly exposed to fluctuations in fuel prices, which account for a significant share of revenues (40 percent on average) and affect their profitability. Several governments cap electricity tariffs at below cost-recovery levels, one of the main reasons for the underperformance of SOEs. In some cases, SOEs are properly compensated for QFOs through operations subsidies.

Transport SOEs performed worse financially than power SOEs. The average adjusted ROAA of rail, road, and airline and airport SOEs ranged between –16 and –12 percent; the average ROAA was 1.4 percent for road SOEs and about –4.0 percent for rail and airline and airport SOEs. These differences partly reflect the fact that payroll expenses tend to absorb the bulk of revenues in roads (62 percent) and airlines and airports (91 percent), and substantially exceed revenues in railways (188 percent).

*Note:* SOE = state-owned enterprise.

fiscal injections, but the power sector is more likely to have received larger injections. SOEs in the power sector therefore absorb the most fiscal resources. Power SOEs had a modest positive rate of return on average assets and performed better financially than transport SOEs.

### Fiscal risks from PPPs

**PPP renegotiations represent a small but frequent drain on fiscal resources.** Evidence on the fiscal costs of PPP renegotiations is scarce. Data from Chile and Peru collected for this study indicate that the annual fiscal costs of transport PPP renegotiations tend to be less than 0.54 percent of GDP. Renegotiations in both countries have been frequent (figure O.5), with average annual fiscal costs of 0.14 percent of GDP in Chile and 0.2 percent in Peru.[3] The high

**FIGURE O.5**  Costs of renegotiation of PPPs in Chile and Peru

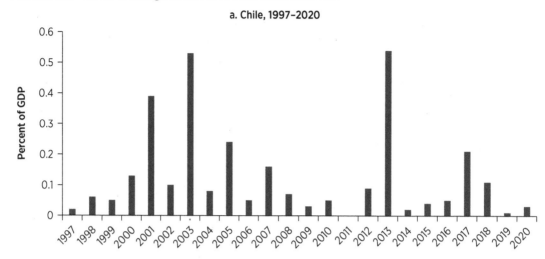

a. Chile, 1997–2020

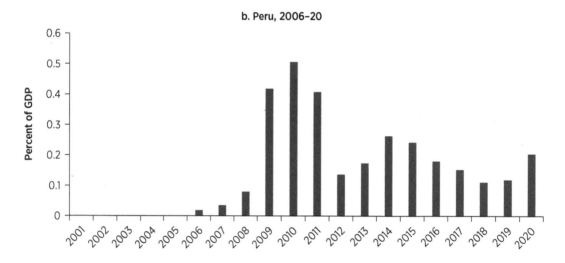

b. Peru, 2006–20

*Sources:* (a) Engel and others 2022; (b) Original figure for this publication, based on data from Marchesi 2022.
*Note:* Peru incurred no renegotiation costs between 2001 and 2005, although there were PPPs. GDP = gross domestic product; PPP = public-private partnership.

frequency of renegotiations in Chile and Peru is consistent with global evidence showing that 42–91 percent of transport PPPs are renegotiated.

**Early termination of PPPs is less common than renegotiations, but the fiscal costs tend to be higher.** Almost 3 percent of electricity and transport PPPs in developing countries (151 PPPs) were terminated early between 1990 and 2020. Cancellations are costly because three-quarters of them occur in clusters. The number of cancelled power and transport PPPs was 25 in India in 2012–14, 15 in Mexico in 1996–97, 9 in China in 2002–04, 6 in Brazil in 2004–06, 5 in China in 1999–2001, and 5 in Malaysia in 2001–02 (figure O.6). In Mexico, the cancellations of toll roads imposed a significant cost on the Treasury, including a 1.6 percent of GDP debt assumption in 1997 (Bova and others 2019).

**Developing countries need to set aside significant resources to be prepared to cover the fiscal costs from early termination of infrastructure PPPs.** Using the

**FIGURE O.6**    Number of early terminations of PPPs in developing countries, 1990–2020

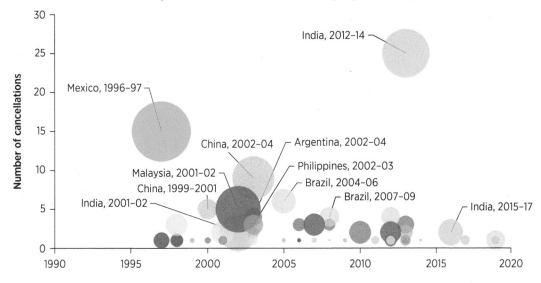

*Source:* Original figure for this publication, based on data from the PPI Database.
*Note:* The size of the bubbles represents total investment in the cancelled PPPs, and each color represents a country. The bubbles that cover several years are centered at the middle of the period (the second year if only two years are covered). Only the largest bubbles have been labeled. PPP = public-private partnership.

value-at-risk approach, this report estimates the maximum expected loss from early termination of PPP portfolios with 99 percent confidence—99 percent value-at-risk—for 17 developing countries under three scenarios. The value-at-risk from early termination of active PPPs over their lifetime is highest in Brazil (0.89–2.82 percent of 2020 GDP), Peru (0.47–1.25 percent), and Albania (0.39–1.02 percent) (figure O.7). These figures represent the amount each government needs to set aside in a contingency fund to cover the maximum expected loss, with 99 percent confidence, over the entire contract period. The amount in the contingency fund needs to be adjusted every year, because projects age, changing their probability of early termination; some PPPs reach the end of their contract; and new PPPs are awarded.

**The risk allocation in PPP contracts affects the likelihood of renegotiation and early termination.** In general, PPP contracts that shift market-related risks, such as demand risk, to the private partner are more susceptible to renegotiation if the private partner has limited or no control over demand. Evidence from Chile indicates that variable-term highway PPPs are renegotiated less frequently and have much lower renegotiated costs than fixed-term highway PPPs (Engel and others 2022). Measures that reduce the financing risk of a project, such as the provision of support through capital grants, revenue subsidies, or in-kind transfers, can reduce the rates of early termination (Herrera Dappe, Melecky, and Turkgulu 2022).

**Governance features are also associated with the likelihood of renegotiation and early termination, as they can affect the incentives to renegotiate or terminate PPPs.** Limiting the causes for renegotiation and requiring competitive procurement for any additional work reduce the private partner's bargaining power and the incentives of both the private partner and the government to renegotiate (Engel and others 2022). In countries with better bureaucratic quality and an independent PPP regulatory body, PPP contracts tend to be

**FIGURE O.7**    Fiscal risks from early termination of PPPs in selected countries

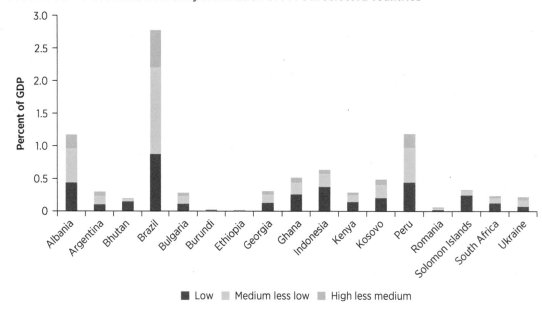

Source: Original figure for this publication, based on data from PPI Database, Polity IV Project, World Development Indicators Database, and Laeven and Valencia 2020.

Note: Fiscal risks are the maximum expected loss over the entire contract period with 99 percent confidence, expressed as a percent of GDP of a single year. The low scenario assumes that 79.3 percent of the PPP's debt (the average ultimate recovery rate of debt to PPPs estimated by Moody's Investor Service [2019]) is covered by the government in the event of early termination and no private equity is covered. The medium scenario assumes that the government covers all debt and private equity. The high scenario assumes that on top of the debt, the government compensates the private party for 150 percent of the equity it invested in the project. The estimations for Ukraine do not consider the impact of the Russian invasion. GDP = gross domestic product; PPP = public-private partnership.

renegotiated less often (Guasch, Laffont, and Straub 2008), because such institutions allow less opportunistic behavior by the government and the private partner (Guasch and Straub 2009). In countries with stronger constraints on executive power, PPPs have lower probability of early termination, because the constraints limit the government's incentive to terminate PPPs or unilaterally change the economic and financial balance of the contract (Herrera Dappe, Melecky, and Turkgulu 2022).

**Fiscal risks from demand guarantees tend to be smaller than those from renegotiations and early termination, particularly when guarantees are used prudently.** Both Chile and Peru have been conservative in providing guarantees to attract private investment; the fiscal costs from guarantees were therefore low. In Chile, the annual fiscal costs from traffic demand guarantees on toll road PPPs were as high as 0.04 percent of GDP during 2003–21. The highest cost was incurred in 2020, during the COVID-19 pandemic. Peru paid a guarantee just once, costing the government only $2.6 million. Chile and Peru's experience differs markedly from that of Türkiye, which initiated an ambitious program of highway and bridge PPPs in the late 2000s. It provided generous minimum revenue guarantees in hard currency to attract the private sector. The fiscal cost of these guarantees ranged from 0.04 percent of GDP in 2017 to 0.21 percent of GDP in 2021.

**Most countries do not have a robust framework for the fiscal treatment of PPPs, which creates a fertile ground for fiscal risks.** If the cost of PPP projects is not accounted as public investment in the budget and the debt to the concessionaire is not recorded, only when fiscal commitments and contingent liabilities materialize is the true cost of PPPs recognized. According to the World Bank's *Benchmarking Infrastructure Development 2020* report, only 17 of the 140 surveyed economies had provisions for the budgetary, reporting, and accounting treatment of PPPs, and only 9 had adopted the International Public Sector Accounting Standards (IPSAS), which require PPPs to be consolidated in the public sector's balance sheet. In 101 of the 140 economies surveyed, the ministry of finance has the authority to approve PPPs, but in only 22 economies it has the authority to approve renegotiations. The lack of such authority can lead to opportunistic renegotiations and fiscal surprises.

**The magnitude and likelihood of fiscal risks from power and transport PPPs present interesting differences** (box O.2). Transport PPPs have a higher rate of renegotiation, are renegotiated sooner, and are more likely to result in direct fiscal transfers than power PPPs. Transport PPPs are more likely to be terminated early and lead to higher fiscal risks from early termination than electricity PPPs.

---

**BOX O.2    Sectoral features affecting the size and profile of fiscal risks from PPPs**

The power sector attracted more private capital through PPPs than the transport sector did. More than 50 percent of all PPPs (transport, energy, water, and information and communications technology) and investments through PPPs in developing countries were in the power sector. Twenty-eight percent of all PPPs and 38 percent of all investments through PPPs were in the transport sector.

Transport PPPs have a higher rate of renegotiation, are renegotiated sooner, and are more likely to result in direct fiscal transfers than power PPPs. The share of PPPs that is renegotiated is 42–91 percent in the transport sector and 24–41 percent in the power sector, depending on the country. In developing countries, the first renegotiation takes place about a year after signing in the transport sector and about 1.7 years after signing in the power sector. Renegotiation of PPPs in the power sector tends to lead to minimal, if any, fiscal transfers, because electricity tariffs paid by final consumers are regulated and can be readily adjusted to maintain the profitability of electricity PPPs, even transmission and generation PPPs. In Peru, for example, transmission projects are awarded on the basis of required payments for investment and maintenance of the infrastructure, but concessionaires are compensated through electricity tariffs that are routinely adjusted to make the concessionaire whole (Marchesi 2022). In contrast, the revenues of transport PPPs come from direct users or government payments, and it is usually politically difficult to increase tolls or railway fares.

Transport PPPs are more likely to be terminated early and lead to higher fiscal risks from early termination than electricity PPPs. Airport, rail, and road PPPs are about five times more likely to be terminated early than electricity PPPs; port PPPs are as likely to be terminated early as electricity PPPs. The higher likelihood of early termination and the larger average size of transport PPPs lead to higher fiscal risks from early termination of transport PPPs than electricity PPPs. The average fiscal risks are 6–14 percent of the portfolio size in the transport sector and 2–4 percent in the power sector. As a share of the portfolio, the fiscal risks from early termination are larger for transport PPPs than for electricity PPPs in almost all countries studied (figure BO.2.1).

*(continued)*

**BOX O.2**  *Continued*

**FIGURE BO.2.1**  **Fiscal risks from early termination of electricity and transport PPPs**

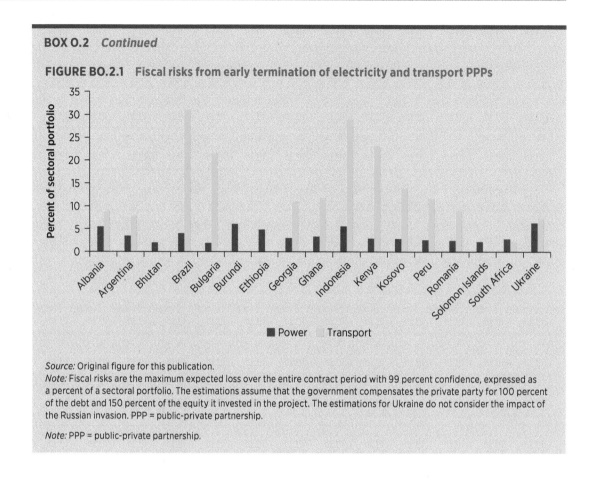

*Source:* Original figure for this publication.
*Note:* Fiscal risks are the maximum expected loss over the entire contract period with 99 percent confidence, expressed as a percent of a sectoral portfolio. The estimations assume that the government compensates the private party for 100 percent of the debt and 150 percent of the equity it invested in the project. The estimations for Ukraine do not consider the impact of the Russian invasion. PPP = public-private partnership.

*Note:* PPP = public-private partnership.

## INEFFICIENCIES IN PUBLIC PROVISION LEAD TO FISCAL SURPRISES IN THE NEAR, MEDIUM, AND LONG TERM

**Low budget execution, particularly in transport, indicates a potentially significant risk of project delays and cost overruns.** In transport, 82 percent of capital spending is made through direct public provision (on budget), 11 percent through SOEs, and 7 percent through PPPs. In electricity, just 9 percent of capital spending is on budget; SOEs and PPPs represent 60 percent and 31 percent of total capital spending, respectively (figure O.8). Underexecution of infrastructure investment budgets, which may signify delays in project implementation and translate into cost overruns, is observed in more than 80 percent of the 65 developing countries in the World Bank's BOOST Database (Foster, Rana, and Gorgulu 2022). The budget execution rate is much higher for road projects (about 69 percent) than for power projects (about 37 percent).

**A strong capital bias in road and electricity expenditure leads to growing investment liabilities because of asset deterioration.** A regime of undermaintenance and periodic rehabilitation leads to a much higher present value of costs than a regime of prudent preventive maintenance (Labi and Sinha 2003; Burningham and Stankevich 2005). Road spending is strongly skewed toward capital expenditure, with almost all of the

**FIGURE O.8**   Share of capital spending in the power and transport sectors, by modality, 2009–18

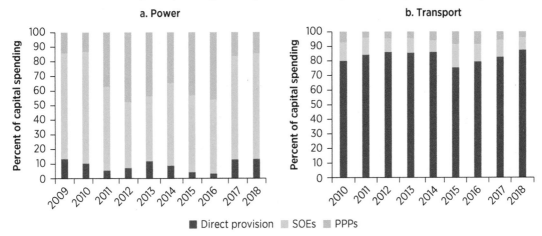

*Source:* Original figure for this publication, based on data from the BOOST, World Bank Infrastructure SOEs, and PPI databases.
*Note:* Capital expenditures in PPPs were distributed over a five-year period beginning in the investment year indicated in the PPI Database. Expenditures through direct public provision are for the general government. When data on spending through direct public provision in the power sector were not available for a country in the BOOST data, total energy spending was used. Countries include Albania, Argentina, Bhutan, Bulgaria, Burundi, Ethiopia, Georgia, Indonesia, Kenya, Kosovo, Peru, Romania, Solomon Islands, South Africa, and Ukraine. PPP = public-private partnership; SOE = state-owned enterprise.

46 countries for which data were available spending more on capital expenditures than on maintenance. Indeed, capital bias is so marked that countries spend about seven times as much on investment as maintenance. Countries with road funds spend more on maintenance than their peers, but they still allocate more resources to investment than maintenance (Foster, Rana, and Gorgulu 2022). Power utility SOEs generally handle maintenance. Foster, Rana, and Gorgulu (2022) find that the ratio of capital to maintenance expenditure in electricity exhibits a capital bias in almost all of the countries they study. The bias is less pronounced than for roads.

**Road sector expenditure became less productive and more inefficient over the 2006–18 period in many developing countries.** Ten of the 18 countries analyzed saw a decrease in the productivity of their road spending—that is, they built fewer kilometers of roads per dollar spent (at constant prices) in 2018 than in 2006.[4] In some countries, more stringent social and environmental requirements may have driven the change. However, more than half of the countries analyzed experienced a decline in the efficiency of road expenditure, delivering fewer kilometers of roads than comparable countries (countries with the same technology and level of spending) and fewer in 2018 than in 2006. Inefficiency in spending leads to road deterioration, which puts further pressure on growing investment liabilities in many developing countries.

## WHEN IT RAINS, IT POURS: FISCAL RISKS FROM INFRASTRUCTURE DURING BAD TIMES

**New evidence reveals that on-budget spending on infrastructure was procyclical in 2005–20, suggesting that public infrastructure spending is a soft target for budget cuts.** During an economic downturn, on-budget infrastructure spending is expected to be particularly vulnerable to spending cuts, given that it is less socially sensitive than other types of spending; the damage from spending cuts may take years to materialize. Spending cuts can weaken the economic recovery from a recession, including the recession caused by the COVID-19 pandemic. Following the developing country debt crisis of the 1980s, East Asian countries rebounded more quickly than Latin American ones, because East Asia was better able to sustain infrastructure investment than Latin America (Kaminsky and Pereira 1996).

SOEs are sometimes thought to be able to act as countercyclical spending vehicles during a crisis or a severe negative shock, by increasing spending using their own resources. However, **a systematic exploration of the effects of negative macroeconomic shocks on infrastructure SOEs' performance undertaken for this report shows that SOEs can increase fiscal risk and amplify negative macroeconomic shocks.** Because infrastructure SOEs use most of their revenues to cover payroll, fuel, and maintenance expenses, they have little left over to buffer negative shocks. As a result, a significant negative shock that leads to a deterioration in financial performance prompts affected SOEs to ask for sizable fiscal injections and cut their capital spending.

**SOEs that faced a negative shock received increases in fiscal injections as a percent of average assets of 3.5 percent the year after the shock.** The increase in fiscal injections is almost 30 percent of the average capital ratio of these infrastructure SOEs—the equivalent of a significant recapitalization the year after the shock. SOEs need fiscal injections precisely when governments are under pressure from the decline in total tax revenues. Probably because of the narrowing fiscal space, fiscal injections take the form of loans from the government and state-owned financial enterprises. As a result, government loans as a percent of SOEs' assets increased by 5.5 percentage points one year after the shock and 4.0 percentage points two years after the shock.

**Capital expenditure as a percent of average assets in fully owned infrastructure SOEs decreased by 3.5 percentage points the year after the negative shock.** This decline is equivalent to 40 percent of average capital expenditure as a percent of average assets, implying that even after receiving additional fiscal injections, fully owned SOEs cannot keep up with their regular physical investment requirements after a shock. The finding also implies that there may be persistent effects after a shock, at least in the medium term, because a reduction in capital expenditures of fully owned SOEs in affected countries likely leads to a decrease in productivity and operational performance.

**A profound macroeconomic crisis also increases the fiscal risks from early termination of PPPs by an order of magnitude immediately after the shock.** Early terminations of PPPs are procyclical, because negative macro-financial shocks increase the probability of early termination, which increases fiscal risks. Analysis conducted for this report simulates the impact of a negative macro-financial shock. The simulation assumes a 48.3 percentage point depreciation shock and the occurrence of both a banking and a debt crisis in year 0. Such a profound macroeconomic crisis is similar to some crises in emerging markets and developing economies that led to the early termination of many PPPs.[5] In the simulation, the year after the shock, the fiscal risks are 11.7–19.2 times the fiscal risks without a shock, depending on the country, with an average ratio of 15.9 (figure O.9).

**FIGURE O.9**  Increase in fiscal risks from early termination of PPPs associated with a profound macro-financial shock

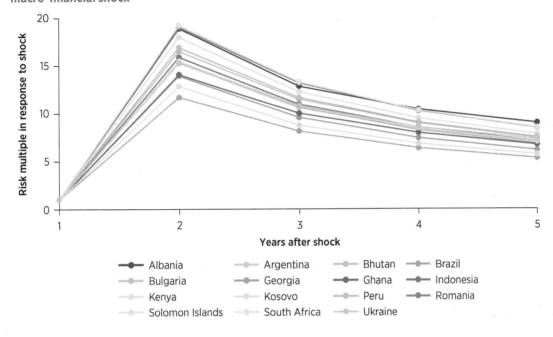

Source: Original figure for this publication, based on data from PPI Database, Polity IV Project, World Development Indicators Database, and Laeven and Valencia 2020.
Note: Each data point represents the ratio of fiscal risk from PPPs where there is a severe adverse shock to the fiscal risk when there is no shock. Fiscal risk is measured as the maximum expected losses with 99 percent confidence level from early termination of the PPP portfolio over the period starting in year 0 and ending in the corresponding year. The estimations for Ukraine do not take into account the impact of the Russian invasion. PPP = public-private partnership.

## IMPLEMENTING A REFORM AGENDA CAN CREATE SUSTAINABLE FISCAL SPACE FOR INFRASTRUCTURE

**Closing the infrastructure gap requires creating sustainable fiscal space for infrastructure. Doing so entails mitigating the fiscal risks from infrastructure** to increase the value for money from existing resources and additional capital that need to be mobilized to close the gap. In some countries, it also entails raising additional budget revenues. The reform agenda proposed in this report focuses on mitigating fiscal risks.

The report shows that a combination of vulnerability to exogenous shocks and the prevalence of perverse incentives faced by government officials, SOE managers, and private partners, which lead to moral hazard and principal–agent problems, explain the prevalence of fiscal risks in infrastructure service provision. **A reform agenda to mitigate the fiscal risks from infrastructure should aim to create good incentives and mitigate the risks that cannot be eliminated or that the government is best placed to deal with.** Creating good incentives requires transparency to observe and control the actions of agents and accountability of government officials, SOE boards and managers, financial institutions, and private partners in PPPs.

All countries are different; the content and pace of implementation of each reform agenda therefore needs to be tailored to the sources of risk and the institutional and socio-political characteristics of each country, as well as the government's capacity. Country-specific strategies will involve different mixes of the preventive and corrective actions presented in this report. **However, all reform agendas include four building blocks—integrated public investment management (PIM); effective fiscal and corporate governance of SOEs; robust PPP preparation, procurement, and contract management framework; and integrated fiscal risk management—and grounded in an effort to build adequate government capacity (figure O.10).**

The reform agenda includes both macro-fiscal and infrastructure-specific reforms, with some reforms tied to a particular provision modality and others covering all modalities. Most reforms are broadly applicable to both the electricity and transport sectors, with reforms specific to a provision modality being more relevant to the sector that relies more heavily on that modality.

### Integrated public investment management

Mitigating the fiscal risks from infrastructure starts with selecting the right projects and provision modalities. In robust integrated PIM, projects are selected because they are aligned with the country's development goals and yield the highest net benefits; the provision modality is selected based on value for money and fiscal affordability (table O.1), not differential fiscal treatment. Robust integrated PIM requires consistent assessment of all potential projects and consistent fiscal treatment of all projects delivered through direct public provision and PPPs— and in some cases also projects delivered by SOEs. To ensure consistent fiscal treatment,

**FIGURE O.10**    **Building blocks of a reform agenda to mitigate fiscal risks from infrastructure**

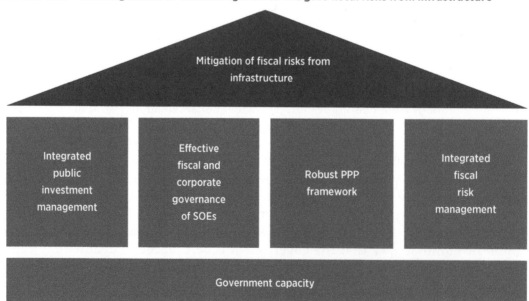

*Source:* Original figure for this publication.
*Note:* SOE = state-owned enterprise; PPP = public-private partnership.

**TABLE O.1    Actions for strengthening public investment management**

| High-level action | Detailed actions |
| --- | --- |
| Implement robust integrated public investment management | • Identify, appraise, and select all public infrastructure investment projects together, in accordance with integrated infrastructure plans and strategies and based on robust appraisal methodologies.<br>• Select the best provision modality for each project based on value for money and affordability.<br>• Apply IPSAS as the normative accrual accounting framework, and comply with the IMF's *Government Finance Statistics Manual 2014* (IMF 2014) and the 2011 *Public Sector Debt Statistics: Guide for Compilers and Users* (IMF 2011).<br>• To guide the annual budget process, prepare rolling MTFFs and MTEFs that are sufficiently disaggregated.<br>• To strengthen asset management, implement appropriate asset management systems and create dedicated maintenance funds, such as road funds.<br>• Strengthen project implementation process, from procurement to monitoring of the physical and financial execution of projects.<br>• Give the ministry of finance a gatekeeping role in the selection of projects, the provision modalities, and renegotiations and modifications of PPP. |

*Source:* Original table for this publication.
*Note:* IMF = International Monetary Fund; IPSAS = International Public Sector Accounting Standards; MTEF = medium-term expenditure framework; MTFF = medium-term fiscal framework; PPP = public-private partnership.

the government should apply IPSAS as the normative accrual accounting framework for financial reporting.

Countries should also adopt rolling medium-term fiscal frameworks (MTFFs) and medium-term expenditure frameworks (MTEFs) that include PPPs, in order to ensure proper alignment of investment plans with available funding. Doing so helps reduce the risk that overambitious infrastructure investment plans end up not being implemented and projects are delayed for lack of adequate budgetary resources. Such frameworks also help ensure that funds are available to meet PPP payment obligations.

Adoption of sufficiently disaggregated MTFFs and MTEFs also helps reduce the risks that capital investments are chosen over maintenance spending under direct public provision. Establishing appropriate asset management systems and dedicated maintenance funds, such as road funds, and strengthening project implementation processes, from procurement to monitoring of the physical and financial execution of projects, helps mitigate the risks of asset deterioration and cost overruns under direct public provision.

The effectiveness of integrated PIM rests on granting the ministry of finance the authority to approve investment projects, PPP contracts, and renegotiations and modifications. The ministry of finance is best positioned to decide whether public investment decisions are fiscally sustainable and act as a counterbalance to spending agencies, which usually act as procuring authorities.

### Effective fiscal and corporate governance of SOEs

Effective fiscal and corporate governance allows and incentivizes SOE boards and managers to operate the enterprises efficiently, mitigating fiscal risks. Good governance clearly specifies the SOEs' mandates and avoids government interference in the operation of SOEs, particularly through the imposition of policy mandates or QFOs (table O.2). If, for political reasons, the imposition of QFOs cannot be avoided, SOEs should be compensated in a commensurate, timely, and transparent manner. When there is an independent sector regulator, the ministry of finance and the regulator should work together to determine the appropriate compensation.

Sound financial management systems are key to the good operational and financial performance of SOEs—and therefore to reducing the fiscal risks posed by these enterprises. Accordingly, shareholder governments should take proactive steps to ensure that such systems are in place in their SOEs, regardless of the model of corporate governance and control chosen. Governments should establish clear requirements for their SOEs on all aspects of financial management, including preparation of multiyear business plans and annual budgets; monitoring of the execution and, if needed, revision of both; accounting and reporting; internal and external auditing; and asset-liability management. Governments should also monitor and enforce SOEs' compliance with such requirements.

Many of the considerations regarding the management of public investments also apply to investments by SOEs, particularly regarding project appraisal and selection and the maintenance of existing infrastructure. Sound corporate and fiscal governance is key to generating the right incentives for SOEs to adopt and consistently use strong investment management systems and practices.

To mitigate fiscal risks, it is essential that SOEs' access to financing be contained within limits consistent with their debt-servicing capacity, in both the short and the long term. For this purpose, governments should eliminate preferential channels or terms of access of SOEs to financing and introduce transparent, nondiscretionary, and effective systems of control of

**TABLE O.2  Actions for improving the effectiveness of the fiscal and corporate governance of SOEs**

| High-level actions | Detailed actions |
|---|---|
| Reduce the risk from quasi-fiscal activities | • Avoid the imposition of quasi-fiscal burdens on SOEs.<br>• When quasi-fiscal activities cannot be avoided, quantify them and compensate the SOE from the budget for undertaking them. |
| Strengthen SOEs' financial management and monitoring | • Establish clear requirements for SOEs on the preparation of multiyear business plans and annual budgets, the monitoring of execution of both, accounting and reporting, and internal and external audits. |
| Limit SOEs' access to financing based on their debt-servicing capacity | • Introduce transparent, nondiscretionary systems of control of SOE borrowing, focused primarily on solvency and liquidity criteria.<br>• End policies that give SOEs preferential access to financing.<br>• Limit the granting of explicit guarantees to SOEs to the financing of investment projects of clear public interest. |
| Avoid excessive and discretionary resource extraction from SOEs | • Subject SOEs to the same tax regime as other enterprises in the same sector.<br>• Provide guidance on SOEs' expected rates of return and the distribution of dividends and reinvestment in the firm. |

*Source:* Original table for this publication.
*Note:* SOE = state-owned enterprise.

SOEs' borrowing, focused primarily on solvency and liquidity criteria. The granting of explicit guarantees to SOEs should be strictly limited to the financing of investment projects of clear public interest, subject to an aggregate ceiling and granted based on the SOE's capacity to service the debt.

To reduce the risks from excessive extraction of resources from their SOEs—which is often dictated by short-term budgetary pressures—governments should subject them to the same tax and royalty regimes as other enterprises operating in the same sector. They should also provide guidance about expected rates of return and the distribution of dividends and reinvestment in the firm.

### A robust PPP framework

A PPP framework that optimally allocates risk and limits opportunistic behavior is needed to mitigate the risks from renegotiation and early termination of PPPs. A robust preparation framework should avoid allocating demand risk to the private partner when it has minimal or no control over demand (table O.3). Flexible-term contracts, such as present-value-of-revenue contracts, are a good option for allocating demand risk to the government in such cases. Measures to reduce financing risk—such as providing support through capital grants, revenue subsidies, or in-kind transfers—can help reduce the risk of early termination.

A procurement process that awards the PPP to the private partner that can deliver the highest value for money can help mitigate fiscal risks. Because of the uncertainties around infrastructure projects, and PPPs in particular because of their long-term nature, it is important that the government provide as much information as possible on the project. Low transactions costs, clarity, fairness, and transparency of the procurement process can also help attract competition and ensure an efficient outcome.

**TABLE O.3  Actions for developing a robust framework for PPPs**

| High-level actions | Detailed actions |
| --- | --- |
| Implement a robust preparation framework | • Avoid allocating demand risk to the private partner when it has minimal or no control over demand. |
| | • Consider reducing the financing risk of PPPs by, for example, providing support through capital grants, revenue subsidies, or in-kind transfers. |
| Implement an efficient procurement framework | • Provide as much information as possible on the project to reduce uncertainty about the value of the project and ensure an efficient outcome. |
| | • Reduce transactions costs, and ensure clarity, fairness, and transparency of the procurement process. |
| Implement an effective contract management framework | • Establish alternative dispute-resolution mechanisms. |
| | • Regulate contract renegotiations and modifications. |
| | • Regulate causes that justify early termination and its associated consequences. |

*Source:* Original table for this publication.
*Note:* PPP = public-private partnership.

Properly managing the implementation of a PPP contract is key to ensuring that the project delivers the expected value for money and fiscal risks are properly managed. Modification and renegotiation of the contract should be regulated, with only a narrow set of reasons allowed as justification for renegotiation. It is advisable that when renegotiations exceed specific thresholds or the scope of work is increased, a new tendering process be implemented to support competition and reduce incentives for renegotiation. Specific circumstances that may arise during the life of the contract should also be regulated, and mechanisms should be in place that allow the parties to resolve disputes without adversely affecting the project. To reduce the fiscal costs from early termination, the grounds for termination of the PPP contract and its associated consequences should be well defined (World Bank 2020).

### Integrated fiscal risk management

There are risks that cannot be eliminated or that the government is best placed to deal with. They must be properly managed. Because of potential interactions among different risks and portfolio effects, integrated risk management—the management of risk across government, sectors, and provision modalities—will increase the efficiency of outcomes. A well-functioning fiscal risk management system should provide the right information to the right people at the right time. Doing so requires a fiscal risk management system that can identify, analyze, and disclose fiscal risks; incorporate them in the budget; mitigate them; and monitor and review them. Most of these tasks are best handled in a centralized manner, by either the ministry of finance or a high-level interagency committee chaired by it (table O.4).

Transparency is a central tenet of proper fiscal management. Transparency on public spending, public debt, SOE operations and liabilities, and PPP fiscal commitments and contingent liabilities can create stronger incentives to ensure that all risks are identified, quantified, and carefully managed. Transparency allows civil society to keep the government accountable. Progress has been made in recent years, but there are still significant actions that governments can take to improve debt transparency and the disclosure of fiscal risks.

Mitigating fiscal risks entails reducing potential risks before they are taken on or materialize and reducing the cost once a risk materializes. Mitigating fiscal risks from infrastructure starts with sound macroeconomic and debt management to reduce a country's

**TABLE O.4    Actions for implementing integrated fiscal risks management**

| High-level action | Detailed actions |
|---|---|
| Implement integrated fiscal risk management | • Create a central institutional structure, within or chaired by the ministry of finance, in charge of managing all fiscal risks, including from infrastructure. |
| | • Improve debt transparency, including by publishing statistics on core public and publicly guaranteed debt annually, and disclose comprehensive information on fiscal risks. |
| | • Undertake sound macroeconomic and debt management. |
| | • Mitigate the fiscal impact of climate risk. |

*Source:* Original table for this publication.

vulnerability to crises and the need to support SOEs and cover explicit and implicit contingent liabilities from PPPs.

Mitigating risks from natural disasters, particularly disasters related to extreme weather events, requires integrated approaches. Sometimes the assets most at risk can be relocated or strengthened. Some climate risk can be insured against, either through explicit insurance policies for physical infrastructure or through national disaster funds. Because of the increased variability in weather patterns and severity of extreme events, some insurance mechanisms may be insufficient to cover unexpected costs, however, especially in countries with no disaster relief endowments. Fiscal planning should therefore incorporate assessments of the fiscal impact of climate change to mitigate it.

### Government capacity

Mitigating fiscal risks from infrastructure requires adequate government capacity. Governments need to develop the databases and staff capacities needed to appraise, select, procure, implement, and manage public investment projects, including PPPs (table O.5). In the case of SOEs, it is important to endow the oversight authority with adequate human resources and information systems to enable it to monitor and enforce compliance with budgeting and reporting requirements, analyze such budgets and reports, and request and enforce appropriate corrective actions. Governments must develop the capacity to structure and manage PPPs over their lifetime. Managing PPPs is different from managing typical construction contracts; not all emerging market and developing economies are able to do so. The contract management authority should be endowed with adequate human resources and systems to manage PPP contracts, including risk mitigation mechanisms.

The ministry of finance needs the capacity to analyze fiscal risks in an integrated manner in order to incorporate them into overall fiscal analysis. Approaches and tools to estimate the fiscal risks from contingent liabilities from PPPs and SOEs can be used as part of an integrated analysis. Examples include the value-at-risk method used in this report for contingent liabilities from early termination of PPPs (chapter 4), which can be used for other contingent liabilities as well; the Z" score for contingent liabilities from SOEs (chapter 3); and the PPP Fiscal Risk Assessment Model (chapter 4).

**TABLE O.5**  Actions for strengthening government capacity to mitigate fiscal risks

| High-level action | Detailed actions |
|---|---|
| Develop adequate government capacity | • Implement clear and robust project appraisal and selection methodologies for all public investment projects, including PPPs. |
| | • Invest in the development of the required databases, tools, and staff capacities to undertake appraisal, selection, procurement, implementation, and management of public investment projects, including PPPs. |
| | • Endow the SOE oversight authority with adequate human resources and information systems to monitor SOEs. |
| | • Invest in the development of the required databases, tools, and staff capacities to assess fiscal risks from infrastructure. |

*Source:* Original table for this publication.
*Note:* PPP = public-private partnership; SOE = state-owned enterprise.

## NOTES

1. See appendix A for a description of the databases used.
2. This measure of fiscal injections is intended to capture fiscal transfers that increase involvement in the financing of the operation of the SOE only rather than transfers that fund investments. SOEs can account for financial support from the government in other ways as well. For instance, governments can support SOEs through increases in trade payables payable to another SOE. As not all trade payables can be identified as government support, the methodology errs on the side of caution, underestimating fiscal injection ratios by leaving out trade payables from the calculations.
3. The figures from Chile are the cost of additional works agreed through renegotiation and so should be interpreted as lower bounds of the fiscal costs from renegotiations, as no concessionaire would agree to additional works unless it is compensated for the additional cost and it is possible that the government ended up overcompensating the concessionaire, given the stronger bargaining power of the latter. The figures from Peru are actual government payments, including payments to concessionaires and for land acquisitions because of changes in the scale and scope of PPP projects.
4. The sample includes Afghanistan, Bulgaria, Burkina Faso, Costa Rica, Ethiopia. Guatemala, Kenya, Kosovo, Macedonia, Mauritius, Mexico, Namibia, Niger, Paraguay, Peru, Senegal, Tanzania, and Tunisia.
5. The systematic banking crises dataset of Laeven and Valencia (2020) identifies 104 banking crisis episodes among the countries included in the PPI Database, 13 of which also involved sovereign debt and currency crises. During these 13 episodes, the maximum annual deviation in the depreciation rate from its long-run average ranged from 15.1 to 116.0 percentage points, with an average of 48.3 percentage points.

## REFERENCES

Bova, Elva, Marta Ruiz-Arranz, Frederik Giancarlo Toscani, and Hatice Elif Ture. 2019. "The Impact of Contingent Liability Realizations on Public Finances." *International Tax and Public Finance* 26 (2): 381–417.

Burningham, Sally, and Natalya Stankevich. 2005. "Why Road Maintenance Is Important and How to Get it Done." Transport Notes Series TRN 4, World Bank, Washington, DC.

Engel, Eduardo, Martín Ferrari, Ronald Fischer, and Alexander Galetovic. 2022. "Managing Fiscal Risks Wrought by PPPs: A Simple Framework and Some Lessons from Chile." Policy Research Working Paper 10056, World Bank, Washington, DC.

Foster, Vivien, Anshul Rana, and Nisan Gorgulu. 2022. "Understanding Public Spending Trends for Infrastructure in Developing Countries." Policy Research Working Paper 9903, World Bank, Washington, DC.

Guasch, J. Luis, Jean-Jaques Laffont, and Stéphane Straub. 2008. "Renegotiation of Concession Contracts in Latin America: Evidence from the Water and Transport Sectors." *International Journal of Industrial Organization* 26 (2): 421–42.

Guasch, J. Luis, and Stéphane Straub. 2009. "Corruption and Concession Renegotiations: Evidence from the Water and Transport Sectors in Latin America." *Utilities Policy* 17 (2): 158–90.

Herrera Dappe, Matías, Martin Melecky, and Burak Turkgulu. 2022. "Fiscal Risks from Early Termination of Public-Private Partnerships in Infrastructure." Policy Research Working Paper 9972, World Bank, Washington, DC.

Herrera Dappe, Matías, Aldo Musacchio, Carolina Pan, Yadviga Semikolenova, Burak Turkgulu, and Jonathan Barboza. 2022. "Infrastructure State-Owned Enterprises: A Tale of Inefficiency and Fiscal Dependence." Policy Research Working Paper 9969, World Bank, Washington, DC.

IMF (International Monetary Fund). 2013. *Public Sector Debt Statistics: Guide for Compilers and Users*. Revised second printing (original 2011). Washington, DC: International Monetary Fund.

IMF (International Monetary Fund). 2014. *Government Finance Statistics Manual 2014*. Washington, DC: International Monetary Fund.

Kaminsky, Graciela L., and Alfredo Pereira. 1996. "The Debt Crisis: Lessons of the 1980s for the 1990s." *Journal of Development Economics* 50 (1): 1–24.

Kose, M. Ayhan, Peter Nagle, Franziska Ohnsorge, and Naotaka Sugawara. 2021. "What Has Been the Impact of COVID-19 on Debt? Turning a Wave into a Tsunami." Policy Research Working Paper 9871, World Bank, Washington, DC.

Labi, Samuel, and Kumares C. Sinha. 2003. "The Effectiveness of Maintenance and Its Impact on Capital Expenditures." Publication FHWA/IN/JTRP-2002/27, Joint Transportation Research Program, Indiana Department of Transportation and Purdue University, West Lafayette, IN.

Laeven, Luc, and Fabian Valencia. 2020. "Systematic Banking Crises Database II." *IMF Economic Review* 68: 307–61.

Marchesi, Giancarlo. 2022. "Fiscal Cost and Risks of Electricity and Transport PPPs: The Case of Peru." Background paper prepared for this report. World Bank, Washington, DC.

Moody's Investor Service. 2019. *Default and Recovery Rates for Project Finance Bank Loans, 1983–2017.*

Musacchio, Aldo, and Emilio I. Pineda Ayerbe, eds. 2019. *Fixing State-Owned Enterprises: New Policy Solutions to Old Problems.* Washington, DC: Inter-American Development Bank.

Rozenberg, Julie, and Marianne Fay. 2019. *Beyond the Gap: How Countries Can Afford the Infrastructure They Need While Protecting the Planet.* Sustainable Infrastructure Series. Washington, DC: World Bank.

Schwartz, Gerd, Manal Fouad, Torben Hansen, and Geneviève Verdier, eds. 2020. *Well Spent: How Strong Infrastructure Governance Can End Waste in Public Investment.* Washington, DC: International Monetary Fund.

World Bank. 2020. *Benchmarking Infrastructure Development 2020: Assessing Regulatory Quality to Prepare, Procure, and Manage PPPs and Traditional Public Investment in Infrastructure Projects.* Washington, DC: World Bank.

World Bank. 2022. *Global Economic Prospects, January 2022.* Washington, DC: World Bank.

# A Conceptual Framework for Assessing Fiscal Risks from Infrastructure

1

## MAIN MESSAGES

1. Governments provide infrastructure through direct public provision and off-budget modalities, such as state-owned enterprises (SOEs) and public-private partnerships (PPPs).

2. Direct public provision of infrastructure gives rise to risks that weaken the fiscal position of the government, by creating unanticipated additional expenditures. The main sources of risk specific to direct public provision are weaknesses in public investment management.

3. Infrastructure SOEs can create substantial risks for public finances, through either explicit guarantees and public insurance schemes or the unanticipated need to provide financial support to SOEs. The underlying cause of SOE–specific fiscal risks is the widespread inability of governments to credibly commit not to provide unjustified financial support (through various explicit or implicit means) to the enterprises.

4. Inadequate fiscal accounting of liabilities, the uncertainty around infrastructure, and the long-term contractual nature of PPPs can create substantial fiscal risks if PPPs are not properly planned, designed, and managed.

## INTRODUCTION

Electricity and transport infrastructure is a driver of economic growth and development that can promote social inclusion and help address inequality. Roads, railways, ports, and other types of transport infrastructure connect markets and people, allowing firms to trade and people to access economic and social opportunities. Power plants and transmission and distribution networks allow firms and people to access electricity, a key production input and central to modern life.

If done right, transport and electricity infrastructure can increase resilience to shocks and help countries meet global climate targets. Resilient infrastructure allows affected areas to remain connected with main economic centers and receive needed support in the event of environmental and health shocks. Electricity and transport systems together account for more than half of global greenhouse gas emissions, and low- and middle-income countries will account for much of the projected increase in emissions in the coming years. If the right infrastructure investments in these sectors are undertaken, both sectors can contribute significantly to the reduction of greenhouse gas emissions.

Governments play a key role in providing infrastructure because of its socioeconomic and environmental implications and because infrastructure investments tend to be large, risky, and suffer from market failures. Investments in highways, railways, ports, and power plants require hundreds of millions of dollars in site-specific and long-lived assets that are exposed to significant risks. The network characteristic of electricity and transport infrastructure means that coordinated planning and development is needed to maximize their benefits and reduce the risk of "bridges to nowhere." Infrastructure such as power transmission networks are natural monopolies, which require some level of government involvement.

Governments provide infrastructure directly (through line ministries or public authorities) and indirectly (through off-budget provision modalities, such as SOEs and PPPs). The fiscal risks from infrastructure tend to be opaque and imperfectly understood, particularly because of the reliance on off-budget provision modalities and their opacity. This chapter presents a conceptual framework for studying fiscal risks from infrastructure from all three modalities and their root causes.

## FISCAL RISKS FROM INFRASTRUCTURE

Infrastructure spending can be planned and budgeted for. But no matter how good government plans and projections are, there are uncertainties that when realized can lead to financing pressures on the fiscal authorities through the realization of contingent liabilities. There are also obligations that are not contingent on any specific event—direct liabilities—that can lead to financing pressures on the fiscal authorities, particularly if they are kept off-budget.

Infrastructure is risky because of its intrinsic characteristics, economic risks, and natural disaster risks (figure 1.1). Most projects are technically complex and involve large budgetary

**FIGURE 1.1    Sources of fiscal costs and risks associated with the provision of infrastructure**

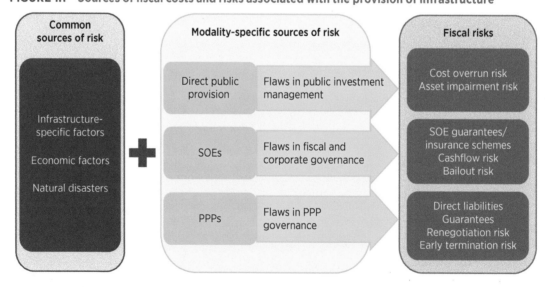

*Source:* Original figure for this publication.
*Note:* PPP = public-private partnership; SOE = state-owned enterprise.

outlays, with substantial sunk costs once begun. Infrastructure is site specific, which makes its cost dependent on the availability and geological characteristics of the land it is built on as well as on environmental regulations. The long-lived nature of infrastructure investments increases uncertainties regarding their construction and operations and maintenance (O&M) costs as well as the demand for their services, leaving them vulnerable to unforeseen exogenous shocks, including macroeconomic cycles or crises, exchange rate fluctuations, and natural disasters. The complexity and long-term nature of infrastructure assets complicates both forecasting and provisioning for them.

Not all sources of fiscal risks from infrastructure are exogenous to the government; some are the result of moral hazard. Infrastructure projects tend to be subject to significant social and political pressures that may distort governments' decisions regarding the selection of projects and provision modalities. Especially in low-income countries, public administrations may have limited technical skills to undertake integrated transport and electricity master planning and select the optimal provision modality for each project. Each of the three infrastructure provision modalities—direct public provision and indirect provision through SOEs and PPPs—faces specific sources of fiscal risks, all of them related to government decisions (see figure 1.1), which are discussed in the following sections.

Governments often lack a central institutional structure to identify, quantify, mitigate, and manage fiscal risks from infrastructure, leaving it to individual agencies to do so. As a result, the interactions among fiscal risks are likely to be ignored and the government is likely to be unprepared to absorb their overall potential budgetary impact.

## Fiscal risks from direct government provision of infrastructure

Fiscal risks from infrastructure under direct public provision include the risks from cost overruns and asset deterioration. Delays and cost overruns in public infrastructure projects are significant. Because of topographical and geological heterogeneity, cost drivers are often site specific and subject to significant uncertainty that can be resolved only during construction (Flyvbjerg and Bester 2021). In addition, limited competition among construction firms at the procurement stage introduces the possibility of strategic bidding, in which contractors lowball their bids in anticipation of contract renegotiation (Decarolis 2014; Hanák, Drozdová, and Marović 2021). Even when neither of these factors is present, limited institutional capacity to procure and oversee complex construction contracts often creates its own bottlenecks.

Inadequate maintenance of infrastructure, because of insufficient and inefficient spending, including capital bias, and poor-quality construction, eventually requires additional spending on recurrent and nonrecurrent maintenance to avoid asset impairment. Governments must make adequate budgetary provision for maintenance costs when they build new infrastructure assets. They often do not. The shortness of the electoral cycle incentivizes governments to prioritize capital spending on infrastructure, which yields significant visibility and political dividends, over maintenance expenditure, which offers no immediate payback beyond sustaining the status quo. Disaster and extreme weather events can magnify the fiscal implications of inadequate maintenance and poor construction, leading to higher than budgeted expenditures.

The wide and procyclical fluctuations in infrastructure spending over business cycles and the fact that public spending on infrastructure tends to be the first victim of fiscal crises add to the risk of asset impairment and lead to adverse effects on economic growth and, therefore, fiscal revenues. Given the delay before the consequences of infrastructure spending cuts are felt, infrastructure expenditure is particularly vulnerable during periods of fiscal austerity. This delay is in contrast to the effects on other budget lines, where a reduction in spending has an immediate adverse impact on livelihoods (Gupta, Liu, and Mulas Granados 2015; Kim 2022).

Many of the fiscal risks associated with direct government provision of infrastructure reflect weaknesses in the various phases of the public investment management process. At the planning stage, an important weakness is the lack of adequate coordination across and within different levels of government (national, regional, and local) and with the agencies involved in infrastructure projects, which may have conflicting priorities. Infrastructure plans tend to be drawn up by sectoral ministries, with little or no focus on intersectoral choices within limited fiscal resources envelopes. As a result, ministries often overestimate their funding possibilities, and projects end up being only partially implemented. In addition, especially in low-income countries, public administrations may lack the technical skills to appraise and prepare projects.

At the budgeting stage, the political benefits of new infrastructure often promote optimism bias in the estimates of the costs of, demand for, and funding and financing availability for projects and create incentives to underestimate the likelihood and impact of possible adverse shocks. Because of the visibility of new projects, political incentives tend to favor spending on them over spending on the O&M of existing ones, which may be a more cost-effective way to provide their services. The budget processes in most low- and middle-income countries have an annual time horizon; few countries use medium-term expenditure frameworks (MTEFs) to guide the allocation of their budgetary resources. This short-termism has consequences for the budgeting of infrastructure, facilitating the underestimation of the costs of construction beyond the first year of the project as well as the costs of O&M.

Flaws at the project implementation stage also create significant fiscal risks. Some of them affect procurement. Procurement laws and regulations may not require adequate transparency, allowing favoritism or corruption; they may privilege lowest-price bids, at the expense of better-quality bids; and they may not be adequately enforced. All these weaknesses are likely to result in poor value for money and/or significant cost overruns.

Poor project management is also a source of risks. Among the main weaknesses in this area are frequent changes in project requirements and the failure of contracting government agencies to closely monitor project execution, identify risks of delays or cost overruns, and take timely corrective actions.

### Fiscal risks from infrastructure SOEs

Empirical evidence indicates that SOEs have been the source of substantial risks for their government owners (Bova and others 2019; Musacchio and Pineda Ayerbe 2019; Schwartz and others 2020). These risks are especially evident when a country defines its fiscal targets in terms of the public sector as a whole (including SOEs), as many Latin American countries do. They also exist when targets cover only the general or central government, because SOEs' finances can, and often do, have adverse repercussions on the government's finances.

The fiscal risks from SOEs include the guarantees of SOE debt and PPPs in which an SOE is the public partner and the public insurance schemes for infrastructure assets of SOEs, cashflow risk, and bailout risk. Cashflow risk is the risk stemming from the volatility of SOE net income, which requires fiscal transfers to cover occasional and modest losses associated with exogenous shocks and inefficiencies. Such losses are often covered by operations subsidies; they can also be covered by other means, such as providing loans from other SOEs or state-owned banks.

Bailout risk refers to the contingent liability risk associated with having to disburse large fiscal transfers to recapitalize an SOE or help it avoid default or bankruptcy after it faces large, mostly unexpected shocks for which the SOE has insufficient capital buffers. It also arises when cashflow shortfalls erode the equity of the firm with uneven, continuous write-off of losses, eventually generating the need for a major recapitalization. Bailout risk also includes the contingent risk that governments face because SOEs may accumulate large liabilities for which the government is an implicit guarantor—which can become the responsibility of the government when large shocks occur.

SOEs are vulnerable to exogenous shocks, including macroeconomic shocks (cyclical fluctuations in demand and changes in international commodity prices, interest rates, credit availability, and exchange rates); natural disasters (droughts, hurricanes, earthquakes, pandemics); and civil strife. The main determinants of an SOE's vulnerability to exogenous shocks are the demand elasticity of its sales and the structure of its revenues, costs, financial assets, and liabilities. SOEs heavily dependent on imported inputs and with net liabilities denominated in foreign currencies are most exposed to the risk of a depreciation of their countries' exchange rates. SOEs that are net importers of the commodities are adversely affected unless they are able to promptly reflect the increased costs in their domestic prices under the applicable regulatory regime. A tightening of financial conditions adversely affects SOEs with debt at variable interest rates, unless they have commensurate financial assets that are also at variable rates. An exchange rate appreciation is likely to hurt SOEs for which exports represent a large share of sales, especially if they are price-takers in international markets (they benefit from the appreciation if they are net debtors in foreign currency).

The underlying cause of SOE–specific fiscal risks is the soft budget constraint on these enterprises. Kornai (1992) introduced the concept of a soft budget constraint to characterize the relations between governments and SOEs in socialist economies. It is applicable to such relations in market economies at all levels of development. A soft budget constraint arises whenever a government is unable to credibly commit not to provide unjustified financial support (through various explicit or implicit means) to enterprises over which it has sole or controlling ownership.

A soft budget constraint hurts performance by encouraging SOEs to take excessive risks and by sapping their incentive to be efficient. SOEs face the same risks of exogenous shocks that private enterprises operating in the same sector do. They may not have the same incentives to prepare to withstand such shocks, however, because they expect their owner (the government) to use its fiscal resources to bail them out should the shocks materialize. This expectation may also lead SOEs to accumulate excessive debt, especially as financial markets tend to exercise less discipline on SOEs than on comparable private enterprises.

Private enterprises operating in competitive markets can expect to go bankrupt if they incur protracted losses because of their inefficiency; SOEs typically do not face the threat of bankruptcy, especially if they provide socially sensitive goods and services or employ large numbers of workers. The absence of the threat of bankruptcy reduces their incentives to control costs and improve the quality of their output. It may also provide an incentive to SOE managers to try to increase the size of the enterprise, at the expense of its profitability.

A soft budget constraint can be the result of policies that adversely affect SOEs' finances and policies that unduly favor them. In the first case, SOEs put at a competitive disadvantage vis-à-vis comparable private firms by government policies without explicit and transparent compensation can understandably expect that the government will step in to bail them out if they came under financial stress. In the second case, market expectations of an eventual bailout and consequent easy access to credit may allow SOEs to incur protracted operating losses or undertake investments that they could not otherwise afford.

The main causes of soft budget constraints on SOEs are flaws in their fiscal and corporate governance. The former includes quasi-fiscal operations, excessive extraction of SOE resources by their owner governments, preferential access of SOEs to financing, and information asymmetries between SOEs and their owners. The latter includes weaknesses that exacerbate information asymmetries and flaws in the selection of the board and management. The following subsections describe the main potential sources of soft budget constraints.

### Quasi-fiscal operations

The imposition of public policy objectives and practices by the government that are not compensated through commensurate budgetary transfers can give rise to significant fiscal risks in SOEs. Over time, extensive use of such uncompensated quasi-fiscal operations (QFOs) tends to lead to recurring losses, underinvestment, and/or excess borrowing by the SOE. Even if SOEs are compensated by the government, the ad hoc nature of the fiscal relation between the SOE and the government creates moral hazard, incentivizing SOEs to request funds at unexpected moments in the middle of the budget cycle and in amounts that may or may not correspond to the size and value of the QFOs they perform or have performed for the government (Musacchio and Pineda Ayerbe 2019; Baum, Mogues, and Verdier 2020).

Main sources of quasi-fiscal burdens on SOEs are the (under-) pricing of SOEs' goods and services and interference in the commercial operation of the SOEs. Governments sometime set the prices of goods and services provided by SOEs (in particular, the prices of energy and transportation services) at levels that do not allow cost recovery at an adequate degree of efficiency or fail to update prices at regular and sufficiently short intervals. These policies are generally motivated by governments' desire to moderate headline inflation or avoid social discontent.

Governments also sometime require SOEs to undertake activities unrelated to their core business, such as various types of social expenditures. SOEs are also sometimes under pressure to tolerate payment arrears from national or subnational government units or other SOEs and/or distribution losses from unauthorized tapping of the network of services (such as electricity) provided by the SOEs.

Labor, procurement, and investment policies are also sources of quasi-fiscal burdens on SOEs. Labor market policies—including legislation or regulations constraining SOEs' ability to adjust their workforce to changing needs that reflect changes in demand, technology, or financial constraints—can impose a financial burden on SOEs. Requirements that SOEs use national suppliers and equipment, even if they charge more than foreign sources, and to use government procurement regulations and practices, which are typically more cumbersome than those of private enterprises, can impose significant financial burdens on SOEs. In addition, SOEs providing public services are often asked to undertake financially unviable investments to expand the coverage of such services, in particular to remote areas.

Politically motivated interference also occurs in SOEs' day-to-day operations, including in decisions on the location and types of investment, recruitment of staff, and procurement, among others. Such behaviors frequently reduce efficiency. By diluting the responsibilities and accountability of SOE management and boards, they justify expectations of being bailed out in case of financial difficulties. Risks in this area tend to be more significant when SOEs' governance arrangements (particularly the appointment, dismissal, and remuneration of boards and managers) provide scope for extensive discretion.

There are strong political economy incentives for governments not to compensate SOEs through budgetary subsidies for the quasi-fiscal burdens imposed on them. Subsidies are highly visible and may require offsetting cuts in other spending, especially in the presence of numerical rules constraining the government's budget balance, debt, or expenditures. In contrast, erosion of the SOEs' profitability, capacity to invest, and ultimately financial soundness resulting from the regulatory burdens may not become fully apparent for years, often beyond the time horizon relevant to politicians.

Eventually, the government needs to bail out the enterprises through ad hoc transfers, equity increases, and (in the most extreme cases) the assumption and restructuring of their debt, often at substantial cost. Even in the absence of financial crises, underinvestment by SOEs can adversely affect the economy's growth potential and the population's access to public services of acceptable quality.

### Excessive extraction of SOEs' resources by shareholder governments

To promote efficient use by SOEs of the capital invested in them, their shareholder governments should require them to generate rates of return that are comparable to those of national or international private firms operating in the same sector, provided that the SOEs have been adequately compensated for any public policy objectives imposed on their activities. The translation of this principle into practice is often complicated by the difficulty of fully separating commercial and quasi-fiscal activities of SOEs and thus estimating the appropriate compensation for the quasi-fiscal component of their operations.

In contrast to advanced economies, most low- and middle-income countries set no explicit rate-of-return requirements for SOEs, and dividend distribution policies tend to be dictated largely by short-term government budgetary needs, with adverse consequences for the capital structure of the enterprises and for their capacity to invest. The discretionary nature of annual dividend distribution decisions by the government also makes it difficult for SOEs to forecast the amount of self-financing available for investments and plan accordingly. In countries in which SOEs are grouped into one or more holding companies, the holding company may require full surrender of profits by its members, for subsequent redistribution within the group, with adverse effects on SOEs' managers' incentives to generate profits.

### Excessive borrowing by SOEs

Preferential access of SOEs to financing not only gives them a competitive advantage over their private counterparts, thereby reducing pressures for them to be efficient, it can also facilitate excessive recourse to debt and ultimately lead to financial crises. Such preferential access can take various forms. One is through direct lending by the government to SOEs, usually at below-market interest rates, or privileged access to financing by state-owned banks. Another is through provision of government guarantees to borrowing or to bond issues by SOEs. The expectation by financial market agents that governments stand behind their SOEs, even in the absence of explicit guarantees, and would not allow them to go bankrupt in the event of severe financial difficulties is another form of preferential access to financing.

To limit fiscal risks from excessive borrowing by SOEs, governments can control such borrowing through standing rules or administrative mechanisms. They may also rely on financial market discipline by, for example, requiring SOEs to obtain minimum credit ratings as a condition for medium- to long-term borrowing or bond issuance.

A number of emerging markets and countries in the Organisation for Economic Co-operation and Development have chosen the latter route. However, market discipline may be weakened by information asymmetries if transparency standards for SOEs are not sufficiently strict. More importantly, financial markets may treat SOEs' risk as equivalent to sovereign risk and therefore lend to large SOEs beyond prudent limits that reflect the enterprises' debt-servicing capacity, in the expectation of eventual government bailouts.

For this reason, many developing countries rely on administrative controls by the government on SOEs' borrowing. In these countries, SOEs are required to obtain authorization by the ministry of finance for every borrowing operation except short-term ones to finance working capital or meet other liquidity needs. Such authorizations are largely discretionary, although in many cases they are based on an evaluation of the purpose of the proposed increase in indebtedness and its financial sustainability.

Such administrative control systems can, however, give rise to soft budget constraints. They open scope for bargaining between the government and the SOEs, especially large and politically well-connected ones. Governments may find it difficult to resist demands for bailouts if loans or bond issues that they (or their predecessors) approved give rise to financial difficulties for the SOE in question. Financial markets would understandably see the government as standing behind the SOEs' loans or bond issues that it had approved.

### Flaws in corporate governance

Information asymmetries between SOEs and their stakeholders (the holding company, if there is one, and the government) are an important source of fiscal risks. Relations between a government and its SOEs are typically characterized by principal–agent problems. The objectives of the government (the principal) may not be fully aligned with those of the SOEs' boards and managers (the agents). These differences in objectives create incentives for SOE managers to exploit the information advantage they typically enjoy over their shareholder governments. Such asymmetries are likely to be exacerbated by corporate governance models that distribute the oversight of individual SOEs among different ministries that may also privilege different objectives, without putting in place effective coordination mechanisms. In such a context of multiple principals, SOEs may try to reduce the government's control by strategically restricting the information provided to each ministry.

Lack of clear and firmly enforced government guidelines and transparency exacerbate information asymmetries. When SOE managers are not required to follow clear guidelines on planning, budgeting, investment selection, risk management, and disclosure, it is more difficult for the government to oversee their actions and decisions. Especially in developing countries, published information on SOEs' finances is often fraught with weaknesses, including noncompliance with international standards for corporate accounts, a limited degree of detail, infrequent and/or irregular reporting, and lack of qualified external audits.

Limited and inadequate human resources at SOEs and in government oversight positions can increase fiscal risks. A high degree of government discretion and lack of transparency on the criteria guiding the decisions on selection and tenure of appointment of SOE boards and management can give rise to choices that are motivated by political objectives rather than technical competence and relevant experience, leading to underperformance. Even if guidelines and systems are adequate and SOE managers have relevant experience, limited human resources and/or capacities in the ministerial units charged with the monitoring and control of the SOEs can allow SOE managers and boards to conceal inefficiencies—and, in some cases, fraud—ultimately requiring bailouts by the government.

### Fiscal risks from PPPs

A PPP is a long-term contractual arrangement, usually for 20–40 years, between a public entity or authority and a private entity to provide a public asset or service in which the private party bears significant risk and management responsibilities. PPPs bundle several activities in the provision of public infrastructure and allocate the responsibilities and risks involved in each stage of a project between the parties. In general, the private party finances, builds, operates, and maintains the project.

PPPs entail fiscal commitments of a different nature. Some are direct liabilities that will arise in any event if the PPP proceeds. The most common direct liabilities include upfront capital subsidies such as "viability gap" payments, availability payments over the life of the project, or any other type of output-based payment. Contingent liabilities are commitments whose occurrence, timing, and magnitude depend on some uncertain future event related to its intrinsic characteristics, economic or market risks, and/or disaster and environmental risks. Explicit contingent liabilities are legal or contractual government commitments to make certain payments if a particular event occurs. Typical examples are guarantees provided by the government to ensure the commercial feasibility and bankability of PPPs, such as minimum revenue or demand, foreign exchange rate, interest rate, and debt guarantees. Implicit contingent liabilities are political or moral obligations of the government to intervene, typically in the event of a crisis or a natural disaster. Infrastructure PPP contracts themselves create contingent liabilities from renegotiations and early terminations.

Although private parties undertake and finance PPPs, the fiscal implications of direct liabilities of PPPs are similar to those under public provision. PPPs are funded by government transfers or user fees. When infrastructure is funded by government transfers—that is, through a standard availability contract—the government does not make an upfront payment to cover the construction cost but makes pre-specified payments over time to cover the construction cost and a return on investment for the concessionaire. In the case of PPPs funded by user fees, the government avoids upfront spending and debt by not procuring the project itself. In return, it relinquishes user fee revenue, which is used to compensate the concessionaire for its investment. Using a PPP is thus like issuing a government bond to cover the construction cost and paying interest and capital over time with tax or user fee revenues. The only difference is that with traditional provision, future governments use tax or user fee revenues to pay bondholders, whereas under a PPP, the revenues are used to compensate the concessionaire. The fiscal implications of PPPs and public provision are therefore identical, unless PPPs bring efficiency gains (Engel and others 2022).

In practice, the most commonly used fiscal accounting rules treat PPPs and public provision differently. The costs of PPP projects are not accounted as public investment in the budget, and the debt with the concessionaire is not recorded. As a result, PPPs can sometimes be perceived as a means of delivering infrastructure for free. The differential treatment gives policy makers and politicians the incentive to use PPPs because the investments do not count as contributing to the current debt or deficit, allowing them to avoid fiscal constraints and engage in politically attractive infrastructure spending through new PPPs or renegotiation of existing PPPs, particularly before elections (Engle, Fischer, and Galetovic 2006).

Keeping PPP investments off the fiscal balance sheet and off the budget leads to fiscal risks. In many countries, even if the ministry of finance wants to account for the direct liabilities from PPPs in fiscal sustainability analysis, it cannot do so, because these liabilities are not properly recorded and reported even in off-budget documents. The explicit contingent liabilities of PPPs, such as minimum revenue or demand guarantees, are not usually included in fiscal accounts, as most countries follow a cash-based accounting approach, a practice that exacerbates the fiscal risks from them. The accounting treatment of PPP investments can lead to projects being undertaken based on their explicit budget implications rather than their efficiency gains and governments providing significant subsidies to attract private interest.

The uncertainties around the costs and benefits of PPP projects are part of the reason why PPP contracts are incomplete and can create or exacerbate information asymmetry problems. Complete contracts depend on the availability of complete and verifiable data, to ensure that each party's obligations are comprehensively specified. Crafting such contracts is particularly difficult in infrastructure projects, because of the complexity of the projects. It is particularly difficult in low- and middle-income countries, where information tends to be scarce.

PPP project designs often lack sufficient detail, partly because preparing detailed designs takes time and governments want to move quickly. As a result, one party has more information than the other, which gives agents the incentive to carry out rent-seeking strategies and engage in opportunistic behavior at the planning, procurement, and operation stages, inevitably leading to renegotiations and fiscal surprises.

The off-budget nature of PPPs and the information asymmetries between different government authorities may give awarding authorities the incentive to behave strategically and use renegotiations to meet policy and political objectives. In countries in which the budget authority approves PPPs at some point during the planning, procurement, and awarding process but has no role in approving renegotiations, the awarding authority has the incentive to procure PPPs with limited scope and scale, in order to ensure that they are approved. After the award is made, the authority asks the concessionaire to renegotiate the PPP to expand the scope and scale, without having to go through the budgetary process. In return for additional requirements on the concessionaire, the government has to make generous fiscal transfers to it.

When renegotiation is expected to occur shortly after the contract is awarded or there is significant uncertainty regarding the return of a PPP, the PPP may create fiscal risks. An efficient procurement process awards the PPP to the concessionaire that can deliver the infrastructure at the lowest cost under the project's risk-sharing design. However, expectation of an early renegotiation encourages opportunistic behavior by the bidders; if any of the bidders believes that it has significant bargaining power vis-à-vis the contracting authority, it may bid an unrealistically optimistic amount just to obtain the contract and renegotiate its terms later. When a PPP is procured without detailed designs, even if there are no expectations for renegotiations, the uncertainty faced by bidders and the asymmetric information they have can lead to the most efficient bidder not being awarded the PPP (Goeree and Offerman 2002). In both cases, the government may find itself stuck with an inefficient concessionaire that needs to be compensated regularly through renegotiations to ensure provision of the public service.

PPP contracts that shift market-related risks such as demand risk to the concessionaire are generally more susceptible to renegotiations than other PPPs. Demand risk exposes the concessionaire to economy-wide shocks as well as idiosyncratic demand fluctuations. When the economy does not grow as expected or demand for a service turn outs to be lower than projected, the cost already sunk in the project may prove to be too high and the private partner may not be able to service the financing raised for the project. As a result, the concessionaire may ask to renegotiate the terms of the concession and ask for government support, and the government may agree to ensure provision of the service. Allocating demand risks to the concessionaire provides room for aggressive opportunistic bidding, which can be disguised as optimistic demand forecasts. Availability-payment or variable-term present-value-of-revenue PPPs, which allocate the demand risk to the government, provide less room for variation in the expected rate of return; bids in these mechanisms reveal the revenue the concessionaire expects (Engel, Fischer, and Galetovic 2014).

Most renegotiations are successful, because both parties are usually interested in reaching an agreement. However, sometimes agreement is not possible, because of the government's default or voluntary termination of the project, the private partner's default or breach of contract, or force majeure. When renegotiation between the government and the private partner fails, a PPP is terminated early. Government exposure in this case depends on the causes of termination; it can be sizable.

Lack of clear, robust, and firmly enforced PPP governance reinforce fiscal risks. Weaknesses in the identification, structuring, procurement, and management of PPP projects, including their fiscal management, create the perverse incentives discussed above that give rise to moral hazard and principal–agent problems. Even if there are no weaknesses in the governance framework, limited and inadequate human resources in the government can make governance ineffective. Shifting risks and responsibilities to the private sector through PPPs demands different and often more sophisticated skills than direct public provision of infrastructure, because PPP contracts are significantly more complex than construction contracts.

Managing PPP contracts is also challenging, because of the shocks that affect the contract during its long life and the better information the private party has regarding the operation of the infrastructure. Governments can hire external experts to support them in the design and transaction stages, sometimes supported by multilateral institutions; more difficult and expensive is ensuring the right skills are in place during project management. Lack of adequate skills in the government can tilt the playing field in favor of the private party.

## IN SUM

Governments play a key role in the provision of infrastructure because of its positive and negative externalities and the presence of other types of market failures. They do so either directly or indirectly, through off-budget mechanisms such as SOEs and PPPs. Both on- and off-budget mechanisms for infrastructure provision can put financing pressure on fiscal authorities, derailing fiscal performance and economic development. Identifying and managing the fiscal costs and risks from infrastructure is thus important.

Some sources of fiscal risks are common to all infrastructure projects; others are specific to a particular provision modality. Some risks (economic shocks, natural disasters, geological risks) are exogenous to the government; others stem from government actions or inactions, such as inadequate maintenance, imposition of QFOs on SOEs, and off-budget treatment of PPPs. It is important to identify and understand all sources of fiscal risks in order to be able to manage them.

## REFERENCES

Baum, Anja, Tewodaj Mogues, and Geneviève Verdier. 2020. "Getting the Most from Public Investment." In *Well Spent: How Strong Infrastructure Governance Can End Waste in Public Investment*, edited by Gerd Schwartz, Manal Fouad, Torben Hansen, and Geneviève Verdier. Washington, DC: International Monetary Fund.

Bova, Elva, Marta Ruiz-Arranz, Frederik Giancarlo Toscani and Hatice Elif Ture. 2019. "The Impact of Contingent Liability Realizations on Public Finances." *International Tax and Public Finance* 26 (2): 381–417.

Decarolis, Franceso. 2014. "Awarding Price, Contract Performance and Bids Screening: Evidence from Procurement Auctions." *American Economic Journal: Applied Economics* 6 (1): 108–32.

Engel, Eduardo, Martín Ferrari, Ronald Fischer, and Alexander Galetovic. 2022. "Managing Fiscal Risks Wrought by PPPs: A Simple Framework and Some Lessons from Chile." Policy Research Working Paper 10056, World Bank, Washington, DC.

Engel, Eduardo, Ronald Fischer, and Alexander Galetovic. 2006. "Renegotiation Without Holdup: Anticipating Spending and Infrastructure Concessions." NBER Working Paper 12399, National Bureau of Economic Research, Cambridge, MA.

Engel, Eduardo, Ronald Fischer, and Alexander Galetovic. 2014. *The Economics of Public-Private Partnerships: A Basic Guide*. New York: Cambridge University Press.

Flyvbjerg, Bent, and Dirk W. Bester. 2021. "The Cost-Benefit Fallacy: Why Cost-Benefit Analysis Is Broken and How to Fix It." *Journal of Benefit-Cost Analysis* 12 (3): 395–419.

Goeree, Jacob K., and Theo Offerman. 2002. "Efficiency in Auctions with Private and Common Values: An Experimental Study." *American Economic Review* 92 (3): 625–43.

Gupta, Sanjeev, Estelle Xue Liu, and Carlos Mulas Granados. 2015. "Politics and Public Investment." *Finance and Development* 52 (4): 42–45.

Hanák, Tomáš, Adriana Drozdová, and Ivan Marović. 2021. "Bidding Strategy in Construction Public Procurement: A Contractor's Perspective." *Buildings* 11 (2): 47.

Kim, Jiseul. 2022. "Don't Pass Deferred Maintenance Costs to the Next Generation! The Effects of Politics on State Highway Maintenance Spending." *Public Works Management & Policy* 27 (2): 127–51.

Kornai, János. 1992. *The Socialist System: The Political Economy of Communism*. Princeton, NJ: Princeton University Press.

Musacchio, Aldo, and Emilio I. Pineda Ayerbe, eds. 2019. *Fixing State-Owned Enterprises: New Policy Solutions to Old Problems*. Washington, DC: Inter-American Development Bank.

Schwartz, Gerd, Manal Fouad, Torben Hansen, and Geneviève Verdier, eds. 2020. *Well Spent: How Strong Infrastructure Governance Can End Waste in Public Investment*. Washington, DC: International Monetary Fund.

# Fiscal Risks Associated with Direct Public Provision of Infrastructure 2

**MAIN MESSAGES**

1. Developing countries executed only about 70 percent of planned infrastructure investment budgets between 2010 and 2018. The transport sector had higher rates of budget execution than the electricity sector (69 percent versus 37 percent). In several countries, expenditure became less efficient over time, particularly in the road sector, however. Both the execution rate and the low level of efficiency are related to weak governance of public investment management, which lead to project delays and cost overruns.

2. There is evidence of a pronounced capital bias in infrastructure expenditure, especially in the road sector, where the ratio of capital to operating spending is 7 times what it should be (it is 4 times in the electricity sector). There are also growing investment liabilities from damage from severe weather events. As a result of undermaintenance or underdesign, additional capital expenditures will be needed during project operation to sustain service.

3. Public infrastructure spending has been low, and investment has been declining in recent years, falling well short of normative estimates of what is required to meet development goals. Public infrastructure spending has been broadly procyclical, suggesting that it is a soft target for budget cuts, falling further short of what is needed to support development and fiscal sustainability.

## INTRODUCTION

Direct public provision of infrastructure is susceptible to multiple sources of fiscal risk (figure 2.1). Flaws in public investment management increase cost overruns and asset impairment risks through inefficient spending, capital bias, and insufficient funding. Because of the long lifespan of infrastructure assets and the intertemporal dynamics involved, these mechanisms operate over different time horizons. It is therefore helpful to analyze the near-, medium-, and long-term risks from direct public provision of infrastructure separately.

**FIGURE 2.1** Fiscal risks associated with direct public provision of infrastructure

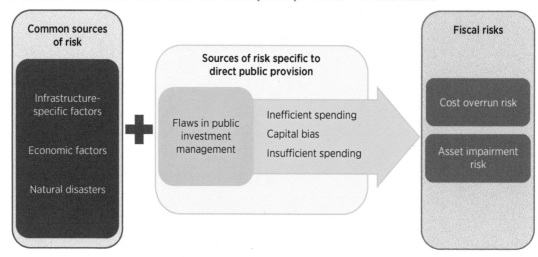

*Source:* Original figure for this publication.

The near-term, and most direct, fiscal risk is that the infrastructure project may cost the government more to deliver than anticipated during the construction phase. Even after the initial investment phase of the project has been completed, the risk remains that the project will continue to make further unplanned calls on the government's capital budget during its lifetime to sustain the capacity of the asset to deliver the intended stream of infrastructure services. Over the longer term, the vulnerability of infrastructure spending to budget cuts and its pronounced procyclicality raise the risk that infrastructure sectors may bear the brunt of fiscal adjustment. Such adjustment can squeeze investments below the levels needed for long-term economic growth, with detrimental consequences for the fiscal balance.

This chapter provides new empirical results illustrating the prevalence and magnitude of some of the fiscal risks from direct public provision in developing countries.

## NEAR-TERM RISK OF OVERSPENDING ON INFRASTRUCTURE PROJECTS

Delays and cost overruns in public infrastructure projects are significant. Flyvbjerg and Bester (2021) show that 78 percent of the more than 2,000 projects they studied experienced cost overruns. The magnitude differs across types of public investments, averaging 24 percent for roads, 36 percent for power plants, and 96 percent for dams. Across sectors, the average cost overrun was 40 percent, indicating substantial inaccuracy in cost estimates or mismanagement of the procurement process.

The size and complexity of infrastructure projects, the uncertainty around its costs, the strategic behavior of bidders, and inadequate institutional capacity may contribute to delays in project implementation, creating the potential for cost overruns. The inefficiency of public expenditure on infrastructure also raises the risk that the original budget may not be enough to deliver the intended objective.

### Low budget execution of public investment in infrastructure

When public investment management systems are weak, budget allocations for public investment projects in infrastructure may be inconsistent with the realities of the project-specific risks and the capacities of the implementing agencies. As a result, there is a significant risk that committed funds will not be spent during the annual cycle. In the short run, this practice leads to a waste of public resources that could potentially have been spent elsewhere and ties up fiscal space in subsequent budgets, where ongoing projects typically have a priority claim. Even when the budgetary resources can be redirected to other uses, underexecution of the budget may signify delays in project implementation, which usually translate into cost overruns (Rajaram and others 2014).

This phenomenon manifests itself in budget data as underexecution of infrastructure capital spending (Foster, Rana, and Gorgulu 2022), which is observed in over 80 percent of the 65 developing countries studied using the World Bank's BOOST Database. Underexecution is much more prevalent than overexecution, which is found in less than 20 percent of cases (figure 2.2, panel a). Exact budget execution is rare.

The average budget execution rate for public investment in infrastructure is 68 percent (table 2.1). The extent of underexecution depends on the type of infrastructure involved. Average budget execution rates are much higher for road projects (69 percent) than for the

**FIGURE 2.2**    Budget execution rates for public investment in infrastructure, 2010–18

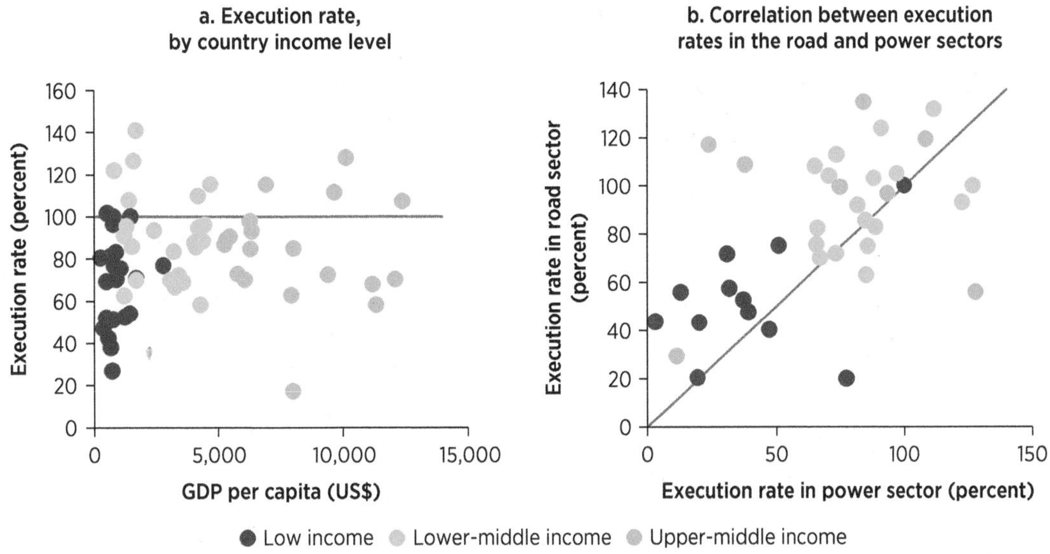

**a. Execution rate,
by country income level**

**b. Correlation between execution
rates in the road and power sectors**

● Low income    ● Lower-middle income    ● Upper-middle income

*Source:* Foster, Rana, and Gorgulu 2022.

**TABLE 2.1**    Mean budget execution rates for public investment on infrastructure, by country income level and sector (percent), 2010–18

| Country income level | Road sector | Power sector | Both sectors |
|---|---|---|---|
| Low | 63 | 25 | 57 |
| Lower-middle | 83 | 93 | 87 |
| Upper-middle | 71 | 27 | 52 |
| Total | 69 | 37 | 68 |

*Source:* Original table for this publication, based on data from the BOOST Database.

power sector (37 percent). Only a few countries have higher budget execution rates for power than for roads (see figure 2.2, panel b). This difference may reflect the fact that electricity projects tend to be larger and more idiosyncratic.

### Inefficient public expenditure on infrastructure

Inefficiency is another reason why infrastructure projects may end up costing more than originally projected. On average, a third of all public capital expenditures is wasted, according to an IMF study (Baum, Mogues, and Verdier 2020); in low-income countries, half of all public capital spending is wasted.

In the road sector, where inputs and outputs can be relatively easily defined, it is possible to gauge the efficiency of spending through standard data envelopment analysis, which compares the relationship between inputs (capital and maintenance expenditure per kilometer of road) and outputs (paved and unpaved kilometers of road in the national primary and secondary road network) across countries. Using data envelopment analysis on a sample of 18 developing countries for which data on road expenditure and the length of the network are available, Foster, Rana and Gorgulu (2022) find a very slight improvement in average productivity in the road sector between 2006 and 2018 (box 2.1).[1]

The aggregate results conceal wide variation in findings for individual economies. Ten of the 18 countries analyzed saw a decrease in the productivity of their road spending (blue dots in figure 2.3). In some countries, the change may have been driven by more stringent social and environmental requirements. However, more than half of the countries analyzed experienced an increase in the inefficiency of road expenditure (efficiency change score below 1). These countries delivered fewer kilometers of roads than countries with the same technology and level of spending, and they delivered even fewer kilometers of roads in 2018 than in 2006. Countries with technological change scores above 1 were using technologies that should have allowed them to build more kilometers of roads with the same level of spending, but in some countries the increase in inefficiency was stronger and led to a decrease in productivity. The increased inefficiency and lower productivity of spending reflect a waste of public resources.

### Weak governance of public investment and fiscal risks

Cost overrun risk and other inefficiencies can often be linked to poor governance arrangements in public investment management. Several normative frameworks for public investment

---

**BOX 2.1**   Using data envelopment analysis to assess the efficiency of spending

The data envelopment analysis input-oriented model minimizes inputs (defined as capital and operating expenditure on roads, in constant dollars per kilometer) while keeping outputs (defined as the change in kilometers of primary and secondary road networks) at their current level. The technique estimates a productivity Malmquist Index (Malmquist 1953), which decomposes the change in productivity into technological change and efficiency change, with the latter further decomposed into changes in pure efficiency and scale efficiency. The scale efficiency term captures economies of scale, recognizing that a process may become more efficient simply by increasing the scale of production. A Malmquist Index (or any of its components) greater than 1 indicates improvement in productivity; values less than 1 denote deteriorating productivity.

**FIGURE 2.3** Productivity and technological and efficiency change in road expenditure

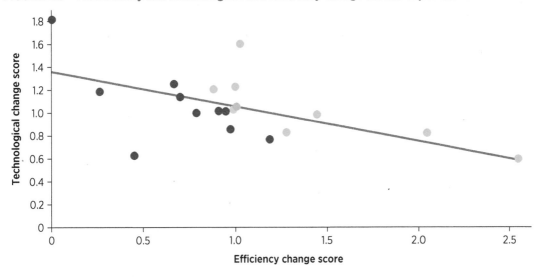

*Source:* Original figure for this publication, based on data from the BOOST Database.
*Note:* Yellow dots indicate countries that experienced increases in total factor productivity; dark blue dots indicate countries that experienced a decrease in total factor productivity; turquoise dot represents the mean of the sample.

management and infrastructure governance are available. They include the Quality Infrastructure Investment principles promulgated by the G20 under the Japanese presidency in 2019 (G20 2019), the Organisation for Economic Co-operation and Development's 10-dimensional framework for Getting Infrastructure Right (OECD 2017), the International Monetary Fund's Public Investment Management Assessment framework (IMF 2015), and the eight "must-haves" for public investment management put forward by the World Bank in 2014 (Rajaram and others 2014). These frameworks support the assessment of infrastructure governance arrangements as they exist on paper; they are not necessarily indicative of how closely they are adhered to in practice.

A 2020 cross-country assessment of public investment management systems by the World Bank measures public investment governance in infrastructure in 33 developing countries. It measures the adequacy of public investment management in the four stages of an infrastructure project's lifecycle: preparation, procurement, contract management, and asset management. The project preparation stage refers to the feasibility studies and impact assessments that need to be undertaken to guide the project selection and appraisal process. The project procurement stage refers to the steps associated with tendering large public works infrastructure contracts and finalizing the associated contractual arrangements. The contract management stage refers to the arrangements for supervising, monitoring, and adjusting the contract during the construction phase. The asset management stage refers to the arrangements that are in place to govern the operation and maintenance of the asset once it has been commissioned.

The assessment reveals that infrastructure governance falls well short of good practice and varies widely across countries. Average performance scores on project preparation, project procurement, and contract management are 58–75 out of 100, suggesting significant room for improvement. Deficiencies at these early stages of the project process readily translate into low budget execution and wider inefficiencies during implementation, as described above.

**FIGURE 2.4**   Distribution of governance scores for quality of public investment management of infrastructure projects across 33 developing countries

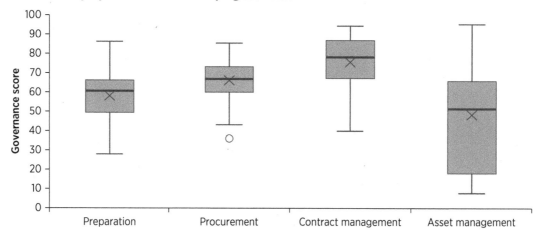

*Source:* Original figure for this publication, based on data from World Bank 2020.
*Note:* The lower and upper boundaries of each box represent the 25th and 75th percentiles, respectively. The horizontal lines inside the boxes represent the median. X represents the mean. The whiskers represent the minimum and maximum, capped at 1.5 times the interquartile range. The dot represents an outlier.

Performance is substantially worse, and even more heterogeneous across countries, in asset management, where the average score is just 48 out of 100 (figure 2.4). This finding reveals the lack of attention given to preserving assets after they are built. It is consistent with evidence of capital bias found in the infrastructure expenditure data, as reported below.

## MEDIUM-TERM RISK OF UNANTICIPATED CAPITAL EXPENDITURE ON INFRASTRUCTURE

Undermaintenance of infrastructure leads to the accumulation of rehabilitation obligations and the eventual deterioration of performance or collapse of service delivery. In recent years, climate change and the associated increasing frequency of extreme weather events has emerged as a significant threat that can wreak massive destruction on infrastructure assets part way through their useful lives. Violent conflict has a similar effect. Repairing such damage requires major unanticipated refurbishment and reconstruction by governments.

### Capital bias in public expenditure and the rehabilitation risk

Adequate maintenance can significantly increase the useful economic life of infrastructure. Over the lifecycle of an infrastructure asset, a regime of undermaintenance and periodic rehabilitation will lead to a much higher present value of costs than a regime of prudent preventive maintenance that avoids the need for rehabilitation (Labi and Sinha 2003). In South Africa, for example, the national road agency estimates that the cost of repairing roads is 6 times the cost of preventative maintenance after three years of neglect and 18 times after five years of neglect (Burningham and Stankevich 2005). An adequate maintenance regime is therefore essential to avoid both the physical risks associated with malfunction of infrastructure assets and the budgetary risks created by unanticipated rehabilitation costs.

The undermaintenance and government preference for capital expenditure can be gauged by examining capital bias in public expenditure patterns for infrastructure. High-level estimates provide a benchmark for the desirable level of capital and operating expenditures on infrastructure as well as the ratio of the two (Rozenberg and Fay 2019). Using these benchmarks, it is possible to evaluate whether infrastructure maintenance expenditure is adequate in absolute terms and whether countries are dedicating too large a share of infrastructure spending to capital investment (Foster, Rana, and Gorgulu 2022). In making these judgments about roads, it is important to include both infrastructure spending through direct public provision and road fund spending on maintenance, because many countries ringfence fuel tax revenues for road maintenance spending through off-budget road funds.

Figure 2.5 plots maintenance expenditure against capital expenditure, both expressed as percentages of gross domestic product (GDP), for a cross-section of developing countries. Countries in the green box are devoting adequate resources to both maintenance and investment, based on the spending needs estimated in the literature (Rozenberg and Fay 2019). Countries in the red box are devoting inadequate resources to either maintenance or investment. The diagonal blue line represents the optimal ratio of maintenance to capital expenditure. Countries below this line exhibit capital bias, irrespective of whether absolute spending levels are adequate.

Road spending is strongly skewed toward capital expenditure. Almost all of the 46 countries for which data are available appear below the diagonal line in figure 2.5. Capital bias is so marked that countries spend about seven times as much on investment as on maintenance. Countries with road funds (blue dots in figure 2.5) spend more on maintenance than countries without road funds (orange dots in figure 2.5), but most still dedicate more resources to investment than maintenance. Mozambique and Ethiopia—both of which have road funds—are the only countries in the sample reporting both adequate and balanced levels of expenditure between investment and maintenance of roads. Per-kilometer maintenance expenditure in most countries lies well below the engineering benchmarks of road maintenance adequacy (Foster, Rana, and Gorgulu 2022).

**FIGURE 2.5**   Capital bias in public expenditure on roads, 2006–18

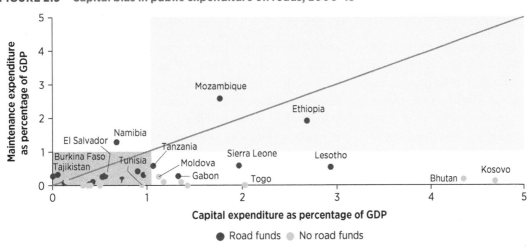

In the power sector, power utility state-owned enterprises (SOEs) usually handle maintenance. Therefore, to assess the extent to which undermaintenance can lead to unexpected capital costs, on-budget and off-budget spending must be combined. Foster, Rana, and Gorgulu (2022) find a similar pattern of capital bias in the power sector, where countries spend about four times as much on investment as on maintenance.

### The rising risks from extreme weather events and conflicts

Infrastructure is at growing risk of destruction from force majeure events. Because of climate change, the frequency and magnitude of extreme weather events increased over the last decade. In the first few months of 2022 alone, a tsunami severed the submarine communications cable connected to the Pacific Island of Tonga and Tropical Storm Anna destroyed almost half of Malawi's meager power generation capacity.

In countries experiencing armed conflict, strategic infrastructure, including power stations, communications towers, bridges, and ports, is deliberately targeted. During the civil war in Syria, for example, power infrastructure was targeted; following the destruction of two major power plants, generation capacity dropped by 30 percent (World Bank 2017). The war in Ukraine has already resulted in loss of physical infrastructure worth about two-thirds of the country's 2019 GDP, according to an early estimate (World Bank 2022).

The 2019 World Bank report *Lifelines*—the first study to systematically examine the economic impact of asset destruction from extreme weather events—estimated annual physical damage from such events at $18 billion, or 0.06 percent of 2019 GDP, in low- and middle-income countries (Hallegatte, Rentschler, and Rozenberg 2019). These costs will increase as natural hazards become more damaging and more likely because of climate change. The annual economic and social costs of asset destruction—estimated in the hundreds of billions of dollars—are many times higher than the costs sustained by asset owners. As a result, there is an incentive to underinvest in asset resilience despite high benefit–cost ratios.

## LONG-TERM RISKS OF ECONOMIC UNDERPERFORMANCE FROM THE SQUEEZING OF PUBLIC SPENDING ON INFRASTRUCTURE

In times of economic downturn, infrastructure spending may be particularly vulnerable to spending cuts, because it is less sensitive socially and the consequent damages may take some time to materialize. Following the debt crisis of the 1980s, for example, East Asian countries rebounded more quickly than Latin American countries, because East Asia was better able to sustain infrastructure investment whereas social pressures in Latin America arising from greater inequality meant that public investment had to be sacrificed to sustain consumption levels (Kaminsky and Pereira 1996). Such adjustment can squeeze investments below the levels needed for long-term economic growth, with detrimental consequences for the fiscal balance.

### Inadequate public expenditure on infrastructure

Developing countries face significant infrastructure needs if they are to deliver on the 2030 Sustainable Development Goals and the Paris Climate Agreement (Doumbia and Lykke Lauridsen 2019; Thacker and others 2019; World Bank 2019). A conservative estimate puts the annual electricity, transport, and water infrastructure investment needs for the developing world at 4.5 percent of GDP. Alongside investment, substantial operations and

**TABLE 2.2**  **Conservative estimates of annual infrastructure spending needs in developing countries, by percent of GDP**

| Sector | Investment needs | Operations and maintenance needs | Total expenditure needs |
|---|---|---|---|
| Electricity | 2.2 | 0.6 | 2.8 |
| Transport | 1.3 | 1.3 | 2.6 |
| Water | 1.0 | 0.8 | 1.8 |
| Total | 4.5 | 2.7 | 7.2 |

*Source:* Foster, Rana, and Gorgulu 2022.
*Note:* GDP = gross domestic product.

**FIGURE 2.6**  **Historic infrastructure spending and projected infrastructure investment financing gap, by region**

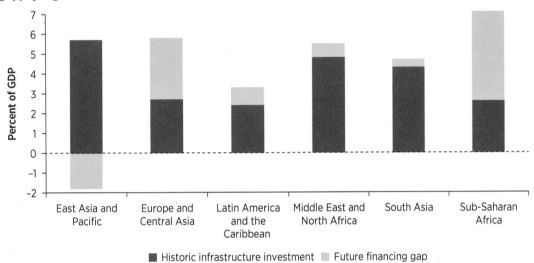

■ Historic infrastructure investment  ■ Future financing gap

*Source:* Foster, Rana, and Gorgulu 2022.
*Note:* GDP = gross domestic product.

maintenance (O&M) expenditures are needed, amounting to 2.7 percent of GDP a year under the conservative scenario. The transport and electricity sectors account for the lion's share of total spending requirements (table 2.2).

Evidence on how much countries are actually spending on infrastructure has been sparse. One of the first attempts to provide a comprehensive estimate put the infrastructure investments in low- and middle-income countries across all public and private sources at around 4.0 percent of their GDP in 2011 (Fay and others 2019). Variation across regions is substantial, ranging from around 2.5 percent of GDP in Sub-Saharan Africa, Europe and Central Asia, and Latin America and the Caribbean to 4–5 percent of GDP in South Asia and the Middle East and North Africa and 5.7 percent of GDP in East Asia and Pacific (3.5 percent of GDP if China is excluded). These figures suggest a sizable shortfall of infrastructure investment in Sub-Saharan Africa and Europe and Central Asia. In contrast, spending on infrastructure in East Asia and Pacific has been higher than future funding needs (figure 2.6). Two countries— China and India—account for almost 60 percent of the total infrastructure investment needs in developing countries as well as estimated historical spending. India has allocated reasonably adequate spending to infrastructure, and China's spending has been relatively high.

## Low budget expenditure on infrastructure in recent years

A more comprehensive picture of on-budget public expenditure on infrastructure over time can be constructed from the World Bank's BOOST Database, which covers over 70 economies for the 2010–20 period and is broadly representative of developing countries outside of China and India. The BOOST Database shows that average budget expenditure on infrastructure (defined to include only the power and transport sectors) was low, at about 1.9–2.7 percent of GDP in 2010–20 (figure 2.7, panel a). On-budget public investment on infrastructure was also

**FIGURE 2.7**   Government budgetary expenditure on infrastructure, by country income level and sector, 2010–20

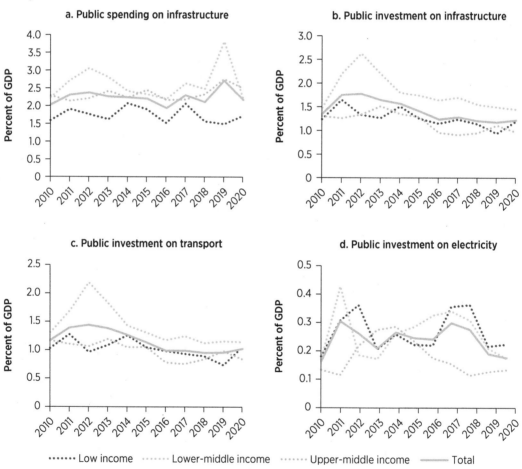

*Source:* Original figure for this publication, based on data from the BOOST Database.
*Note:* Countries include Afghanistan, Albania, Angola, Armenia, Bangladesh, Belarus, Benin, Bhutan, Bulgaria, Burkina Faso, Burundi, Cameroon, Cape Verde, Costa Rica, the Dominican Republic, Ecuador, El Salvador, Equatorial Guinea, Ethiopia, Fiji, Gabon, The Gambia, Georgia, Guatemala, Guinea, Guinea Bissau, Haiti, Indonesia, Jamaica, Jordan, Kenya, Kiribati, Kosovo, Kyrgyz Republic, Lebanon, Lesotho, Liberia, Macedonia, Malawi, Mali, Mauritania, Mauritius, Mexico, Moldova, Mongolia, Mozambique, Namibia, Niger, Papua New Guinea, Paraguay, Peru, Senegal, Sierra Leone, Solomon Islands, South Africa, St. Lucia, Tajikistan, Tanzania, Togo, Tunisia, Uganda, and Ukraine. GDP = gross domestic product.

low (1.2–1.8 percent of GDP) (figure 2.7 panel b), and it declined during this period. Lower-middle-income countries allocated the largest share of GDP to public spending on infrastructure (figure 2.7, panel a).

The decline in public investment on infrastructure was not consistent across sectors. The transport sector—historically one of the largest areas of budget expenditure on infrastructure—saw a smooth decrease in public investment, falling from 1.4 percent of GDP to about 1.0 percent of GDP in 2019 and 2020 (figure 2.7, panel c). In contrast, investment in electricity was volatile, ranging from 0.16 percent to 0.30 percent of GDP (figure 2.7, panel d).

The overall decline in infrastructure investment contrasts with relatively stable trends for aggregate public expenditure over the same period, indicating a lower priority for infrastructure rather than a decline in total government expenditure. Infrastructure typically accounts for just 5–10 percent of the government's overall budget and 15–20 percent of public investment. The share of infrastructure in total budget spending is relatively high in low-income countries, possibly because of the weak infrastructure endowment of these countries and the greater priority given to infrastructure.

### The weakly procyclical nature of public expenditure on infrastructure

One reason why infrastructure spending seems to have declined is the downturn of the economy in the years leading up to the global pandemic. The Keynesian approach to macroeconomic management entails countercyclical fiscal policy as a means of smoothing out economic fluctuations over time. This practice is prevalent in industrial economies. In contrast, aggregate government spending in developing countries has typically been procyclical, likely as a result of limited government access to capital markets (Alesina, Campante, and Tabellini 2008; Gavin and Perotti 1997; Kaminsky, Reinhart, and Végh 2004).

New evidence suggests that infrastructure spending in developing countries is also procyclical (Foster, Rana, and Gorgulu 2022). The synchronous movement of public spending on infrastructure with GDP is evident in figure 2.8 and confirmed by econometric analysis

**FIGURE 2.8**  **GDP per capita and total infrastructure expenditure per capita in low- and middle-income countries, 2006–20**

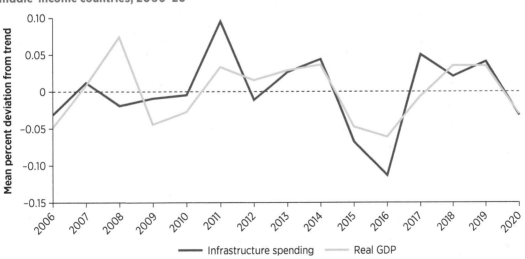

*Source:* Foster, Rana, and Gorgulu 2022.
*Note:* The dotted line is for reference to show when the deviation is above or below the trend. GDP = gross domestic product.

(Foster, Rana, and Gorgulu 2022). The extent of procyclicality in public spending on infrastructure varies across regions. It is particularly marked in Europe and Central Asia and the Middle East and North Africa.

## IN SUM

Most developing regions have massive infrastructure funding needs for capital and O&M spending. They are not being met, as public spending on infrastructure remains well below what is needed and was procyclical. Public investment on infrastructure also declined between 2010 and 2020 and half of all public capital spending in developing countries was wasted.

There are significant risks of delays and cost overruns on projects implemented through direct public provision. A clear warning sign of danger is the low budget execution rate (68 percent) observed on infrastructure investments in developing countries, which was as low as 25 percent for power investments in low-income countries. Low execution reflects widespread weaknesses in the governance frameworks for public investment in infrastructure across the project cycle, particularly in preparation, procurement, and contract management.

Inefficient capital and O&M spending in many developing countries leads to less and worse-quality infrastructure than could be achieved with the same spending levels if efficiency were higher. Capital bias is particularly pronounced in the road sector, where capital expenditure exceeds operating expenditure by a factor of 7:1 on average (where a ratio of 1:1 is advisable). Very few of the countries studied made adequate provision for maintenance.

Inadequate investment and maintenance significantly increase reconstruction risks and the need for asset rehabilitation. Exogenous events, such as extreme weather and armed conflict, which lead to premature destruction of assets, also increase such risks. Cuts to infrastructure spending during downturns further increase rehabilitation and reconstruction risks and may constrain the long-term performance of the economy, with fiscal implications for governments.

## NOTE

1. Their analysis was based on data from Afghanistan, Bulgaria, Burkina Faso, Costa Rica, Ethiopia, Guatemala, Kenya, Kosovo, Macedonia, Mauritius, Mexico, Namibia, Niger, Paraguay, Peru, Senegal, Tanzania, and Tunisia.

## REFERENCES

Alesina, Alberto, Filipe R. Campante, and Guido Tabellini. 2008. "Why Is Fiscal Policy Often Procyclical?" *Journal of the European Economic Association* 6 (5): 1006–36.

Baum, Anja, Tewodaj Mogues, and Geneviève Verdier. 2020. "Getting the Most from Public Investment." In *Well Spent: How Strong Infrastructure Governance Can End Waste in Public Investment*, edited by Gerd Schwartz, Manal Fouad, Torben Hansen, and Geneviève Verdier. Washington DC: International Monetary Fund.

Burningham, Sally, and Natalya Stankevich. 2005. "Why Road Maintenance Is Important and How to Get it Done." Transport Notes Series TRN 4, World Bank, Washington, DC.

Decarolis, Franceso. 2014. "Awarding Price, Contract Performance and Bids Screening: Evidence from Procurement Auctions." *American Economic Journal: Applied Economics* 6 (1): 108–32.

Doumbia, Djeneba, and Morten Lykke Lauridsen. 2019. "Closing the SDG Financing Gap: Trends and Data." *EMCompass* 73, International Finance Corporation, Washington, DC.

Fay, Marianne, Hyoung Il Lee, Massimo Mastruzzi, Sungmin Han, and Moonkyoung Cho. 2019. "Hitting the Trillion Mark: A Look at How Much Countries Are Spending on Infrastructure." Policy Research Working Paper 8730, World Bank, Washington, DC.

Flyvbjerg, Bent, and Dirk W. Bester. 2021. "The Cost-Benefit Fallacy: Why Cost-Benefit Analysis Is Broken and How to Fix It." *Journal of Benefit-Cost Analysis* 12 (3): 395–419.

Foster, Vivien, Anshul Rana, and Nisan Gorgulu. 2022. "Understanding Public Spending Trends for Infrastructure in Developing Countries." Policy Research Working Paper 9903, World Bank, Washington, DC.

G20. 2019. *G20 Principles for Quality Infrastructure Investment*. Osaka. https://www.mof.go.jp/english /international_policy/convention/g20/annex6_1.pdf.

Gavin, Michael, and Roberto Perotti. 1997. "Fiscal Policy in Latin America." *NBER Macroeconomics Annual* 12: 11–61.

Hallegatte, Stephane, Jun Rentschler, and Julie Rozenberg. 2019. *Lifelines: The Resilient Infrastructure Opportunity*. Sustainable Infrastructure Series. Washington, DC: World Bank.

IMF (International Monetary Fund). 2015. *Making Public Investment More Efficient*. IMF Staff Report. Washington, DC: International Monetary Fund.

Kaminsky, Graciela L., and Alfredo Pereira. 1996. "The Debt Crisis: Lessons of the 1980s for the 1990s." *Journal of Development Economics* 50 (1): 1–24.

Kaminsky, Graciela L., Carmen M. Reinhart, and Carlos A. Végh. 2004. "When It Rains, It Pours: Procyclical Capital Flows and Macroeconomic Policies." *NBER Macroeconomics Annual* 19: 11–82.

Labi, Samuel, and Kumares C. Sinha. 2003. "The Effectiveness of Maintenance and Its Impact on Capital Expenditures." Publication FHWA/IN/JTRP-2002/27, Joint Transportation Research Program, Indiana Department of Transportation and Purdue University, West Lafayette, IN.

Malmquist, Sten. 1953. "Index Numbers and Indifference Surfaces." *Trabajos de Estatistica* 4 (2): 209–42.

OECD (Organisation for Economic Co-operation and Development). 2017. *Getting Infrastructure Right: A Framework for Better Governance*. Paris: OECD Publishing.

Rajaram, Anand, Tuan Minh Le, Kai Kaiser, Jay-Hyung Kim, and Jonas Frank, eds. 2014. *The Power of Public Investment Management: Transforming Resources into Assets for Growth*. Washington, DC: World Bank.

Rozenberg, Julie, and Marianne Fay. 2019. *Beyond the Gap: How Countries Can Afford the Infrastructure They Need While Protecting the Planet*. Sustainable Infrastructure Series. Washington, DC: World Bank.

Thacker, Scott, Daniel Adshead, Marianne Fay, Stéphane Hallegatte, Mark Harvey, Hendrik Meller, Nicholas O'Regan, Julie Rozenberg, Graham Watkins, and Jim W. Hall. 2019. "Infrastructure for Sustainable Development." *Nature Sustainability* 2 (4): 324–31.

World Bank. 2017. *The Toll of War: The Economic and Social Consequences of the Conflict in Syria*. Washington, DC: World Bank.

World Bank. 2019. *The 2030 Sustainable Development Agenda and the World Bank Group: Closing the SDGs Financing Gap, 2019 Update*. Washington, DC: World Bank.

World Bank. 2020. *Benchmarking Infrastructure Development 2020: Assessing Regulatory Quality to Prepare, Procure, and Manage PPPs and Traditional Public Investment in Infrastructure Projects*. Washington, DC: World Bank.

World Bank. 2022. "War in the Region." *Europe and Central Asia Economic Update* (Spring). Washington, DC: World Bank.

# Fiscal Risks and Costs of State-Owned Enterprises

3

## MAIN MESSAGES

1. The drain on public resources of infrastructure state-owned enterprises (SOEs) is more frequent and larger than regularly assumed. Infrastructure SOEs require average annual fiscal injections of 0.25 percent of gross domestic product (GDP) to remain afloat and reach as high as 3 percent of GDP, with fiscal injections observed in 57 percent of the country-years studied.

2. Power SOEs tend to perform better financially than transport SOEs, with a modest positive average rate of return on average assets compared to a negative average rate of return for transport SOEs. However, power SOEs absorb the most fiscal resources, with average annual fiscal injections of 0.25 percent of GDP, followed by road SOEs (0.24 percent of GDP), railway SOEs (0.12 percent of GDP) and airline and airport SOEs (0.04 percent of GDP).

3. During crisis periods, SOEs can weaken the overall fiscal situation and amplify the negative macroeconomic shock. During macroeconomic shocks, total fiscal injections to SOEs as a percent of average assets rise by 3.5 percent the year after the shock, the equivalent of a significant recapitalization. Even after receiving the fiscal injections, fully owned SOEs reduce their capital spending as a percent of average assets by an amount equivalent to 40 percent of the average ratio right after the negative shock, which can amplify the impact of the shock.

4. Comprehensive measures of fiscal injections to SOEs and simple tools from the finance literature can help governments foresee and prevent fiscal risk. Governments use a wide range of instruments to support SOEs, including operation subsidies, equity injections, and loans from government and other SOEs. The $Z''$ score developed by Altman (2000, 2018) can be used to monitor SOE performance and predict the need for fiscal injections.

## INTRODUCTION

Governments often rely on SOEs to execute and operate infrastructure projects. The 19 developing countries in the World Bank Infrastructure SOEs Database have 154 SOEs in the power, airline, airport, railway, and road sectors.[1] Their investments averaged 0.77–1.60 percent of GDP in 2009–18. In the 15 of these countries for which data are available on investments through direct public provision and public-private partnerships (PPPs), SOEs' investments represented 23–32 percent of total infrastructure investments (figure 3.1, panel a).[2] Total operating and capital expenditures of SOEs represented 55 percent of total spending through direct public provision and SOEs (figure 3.1, panel b).

Infrastructure SOEs are used as an alternative to direct public provision of infrastructure for multiple reasons. One is the fact that they often operate under private law, giving them more freedom to hire (and fire) labor and to specialize in the operations and maintenance of specific projects. Another is the fact that SOEs are perceived as budget expanding, because they can

**FIGURE 3.1**   **Shares of spending by infrastructure SOEs, 2009–18**

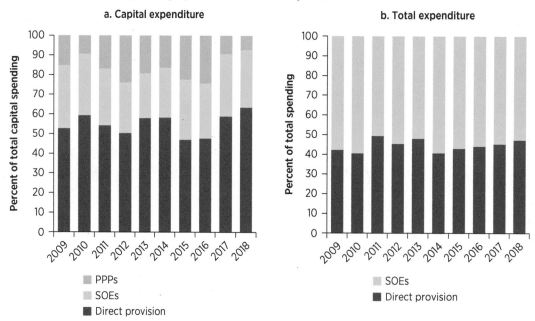

*Source:* Original figure for this publication, based on data from the BOOST, World Bank Infrastructure SOEs, and PPI databases.
*Note:* Capital expenditures in PPPs were distributed over a five-year period beginning the investment year indicated in the PPI Database. Expenditures through direct public provision are for the general government. When spending through direct public provision in the power sector was not available for a country in the BOOST data, total energy spending was used. Data on operating expenditures by PPPs is not available; therefore, PPPs are not included in panel b. Figures are averages over countries. Countries in panel a are Albania, Argentina, Bhutan, Bulgaria, Burundi, Ethiopia, Georgia, Indonesia, Kenya, Kosovo, Peru, Romania, Solomon Islands, South Africa, and Ukraine; countries in panel b are the same as in panel a plus Croatia and Uruguay. PPP = public-private partnership; SOE = state-owned enterprise.

borrow funds using their balance sheet and generate internal funds when they take advantage of their economies of scale. SOEs can also be used as vehicles of patronage and to undertake quasi-fiscal operations (QFOs). They can undertake socially desirable projects for the government (such as connecting remote regions), increase employment (by hiring large numbers of workers), and help politicians subsidize groups of voters or certain economic sectors. SOEs are also often considered vehicles for countercyclical fiscal policy, supposedly helping governments deal with negative shocks.

The creation and expansion of infrastructure SOEs generates significant fiscal risk. Infrastructure projects are intrinsically risky because of infrastructure-specific and exogenous (economic- and disaster-related) risks. The inability of governments to credibly commit not to provide unjustified financial support to the enterprises—that is, soft budget constraints—also increases their risk (figure 3.2). Soft budget constraints are common because SOEs are frequently used to undertake QFOs, they have preferential access to financing, and there are important information asymmetries between the government and SOE managers, as discussed in chapter 1.

The fiscal risks from infrastructure SOEs exist because infrastructure SOEs are larger (relative to GDP), have larger liabilities (relative to GDP), have higher employment costs (relative to revenues), are less efficient, and have lower return on assets than similar private firms. As a result, they require fiscal injections on a regular basis, because small deviations from what is predicted and budgeted in infrastructure SOEs can generate significant losses (cashflow risk). Infrastructure SOEs that write off losses for multiple years end up depleting their equity and requiring major bailouts (bailout risk).

This chapter presents original empirical evidence on the size and incidence of fiscal risks from SOEs, particularly cashflow and bailout risk—its determinants, the fiscal instruments

**FIGURE 3.2** Fiscal risks from infrastructure SOEs

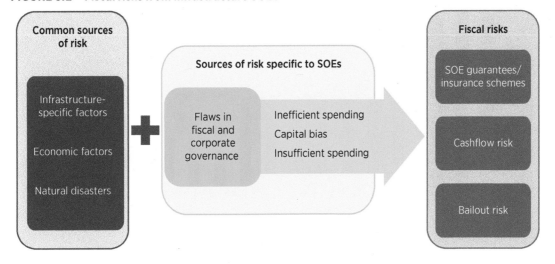

*Source:* Original figure for this publication.
*Note:* SOE = state-owned enterprise.

governments use to support SOEs, and firm-level indicators that can be used to predict the need for fiscal support.

## SIZE, PERFORMANCE, AND COST STRUCTURE AS SOURCES OF FISCAL RISK IN SOEs

The size, financial performance, and cost structure of SOEs can be pieced together with the firm-level data from the new World Bank Infrastructure SOEs Database (see appendix B for details on the database). It includes detailed financials for infrastructure SOEs from 2000 to 2018 that are comparable over time and across countries.[3] The database covers 19 countries, from all regions of the world. It tracks firms controlled by the government, including fully owned SOEs (those with 99 percent or more of state ownership) and SOEs in which ownership is shared with the private sector.

The total operational expenses of infrastructure SOEs as a share of GDP shows how large government-owned firms are in this sector (figure 3.3). Between 2009 and 2018, in the sample of 136 SOEs in 19 countries, SOEs spent 3.2 percent of GDP a year on average. Among the countries with the largest expenses are Bhutan, to a large extent because of the power sector and the airline Drukair; Bulgaria, partly because of its significant expenses in power; the Solomon Islands, because of its expenses in Solomon Airlines and Solomon Power; and South Africa, because of the power company ESKOM.

The ratio of total assets of infrastructure SOEs to GDP reveals a similar picture (figure 3.4). Total assets represent almost 18 percent of GDP on average. This figure seems extremely high

**FIGURE 3.3**    Average operating expenses of infrastructure SOEs in selected countries

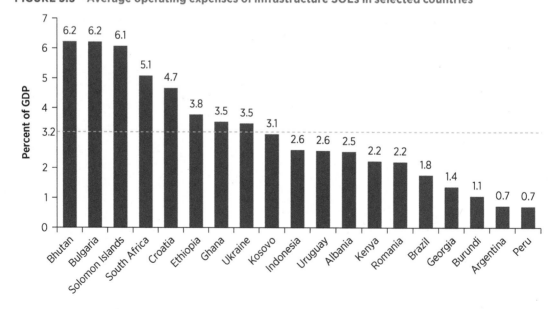

*Source:* World Bank Infrastructure SOEs Database.
*Note:* Figures are averages over 2009–18. Expenses include fuel and energy inputs, employment costs, the cost of leasing assets, maintenance costs, bad debt expense, other taxes and levies, and other expenses. The dotted line represents the average for the sample of countries. GDP = gross domestic product; SOE = state-owned enterprise.

**FIGURE 3.4**   Assets of infrastructure SOEs in selected countries

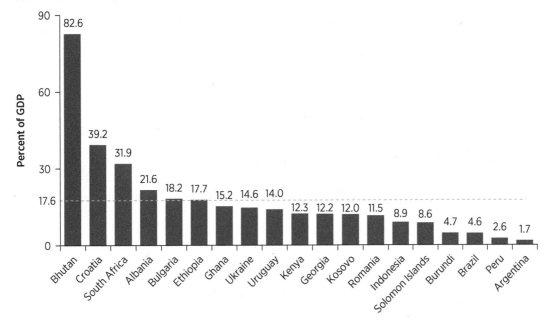

*Source:* World Bank Infrastructure SOEs Database.
*Note:* Figures are averages over 2009–18. The dotted line represents the average for the sample of countries. GDP = gross domestic product; SOE = state-owned enterprise.

given that there is usually only a handful of infrastructure SOEs in each country and countries usually have other SOEs outside infrastructure in their portfolios. The Organisation for Economic Co-operation and Development (OECD 2017) estimates that infrastructure SOEs account for about 60–70 percent of the equity value and employment of all SOEs. These figures range widely across countries, with SOE assets representing 83 percent of GDP in Bhutan and a mere 1.7 percent in Argentina.

## Weak and unpredictable financial performance

A challenge when measuring financial performance in SOEs is disentangling measures of performance from the subsidies and fiscal transfers they receive from the government. Measures of financial performance should be adjusted by netting at least operations subsidies, the budget transfers SOEs receive to pay for QFOs or to cover expected losses.[4]

The difference in financial performance after adjusting for operations subsidies are substantial (figure 3.5). Return on average assets (ROAA) before and after netting out operations subsidies from profits can differ by a few percentage points in the power sector to about 10 percentage points in transport sectors.[5] The average ROAA (of –0.14 percent) suggests that SOEs in infrastructure incur only small losses; once operations subsidies are deducted, the average annual ROAA is –5.1 percent. The power sector is the least subsidized and the best-performing sector, with and without subsidies. It is followed by roads. The railway sector is by far the most heavily subsidized and worst-performing sector, with negative ROAA even after accounting for subsidies, raising concerns about the sustainability and fiscal risk of railway SOEs.

**FIGURE 3.5**     Return on average assets of infrastructure SOEs, with and without adjustment for operations subsidies, by sector

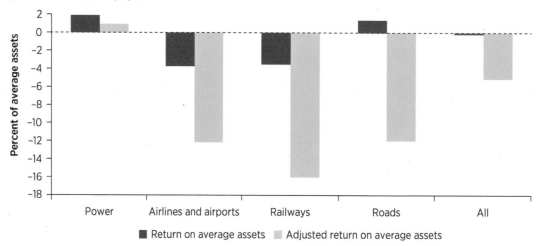

*Source:* Original figure for this publication, based on data from the World Bank Infrastructure SOEs Database.
*Note:* Figures are averages over 2009–18. SOE = state-owned enterprise.

SOEs have frequent losses once their performance is adjusted by operations subsidies (figure 3.6). Losses were pervasive across all sectors except the power sector every year between 2009 and 2018 (figure 3.6, panel a). In the airlines and airports sector (figure 3.6, panel b), 33–57 percent of firms had losses every year. Performance improved toward the end of the sample period. In the railway and road sector (figure 3.6, panels c and d), 66–86 percent of firms failed to turn profits before subsidies every year during the sample period studied, and the share remained relatively constant over time. These figures are high because road and railway SOEs tend to be funded directly by the government to carry out construction and maintenance works. In contrast, less than a third of firms in the power sector suffered losses every year (figure 3.6, panel a). Most countries included in the analysis had reformed their power sectors to improve competition and promote vertical disintegration and cost recovery (Foster and others 2017).

The underperformance of SOEs in infrastructure can be partly linked to their cost structure. Employment costs in transport SOEs are very large as a share of revenues (figure 3.7). In railways, employment costs average 188 percent of revenues. In Argentina, railway SOEs have more than 20,000 employees and did not cover their payroll expenses out of revenues for over a decade. Employment costs are also large at airlines and airports (90 percent) and roads (62 percent) (figure 3.7, panel a). In the power sector, total costs, including dividends to government, represent just over 80 percent of revenue, but the distribution of costs is slightly different: Fuel costs represent 40 percent of revenues, the largest cost item, and employment costs, the government take, and maintenance costs are just 27, 11, and 4 percent of revenues, respectively (figure 3.7).

One of the QFOs SOEs undertake on behalf of governments is generating employment, often paying salaries that are as high as or higher than those of the private sector. The large share of employment expenses relative to revenues in transport SOEs is likely a consequence of the role these SOEs play as employers (figure 3.7, panel a).

**FIGURE 3.6**   **Percent of infrastructure SOEs generating losses before receiving subsidies, by sector, 2009–18**

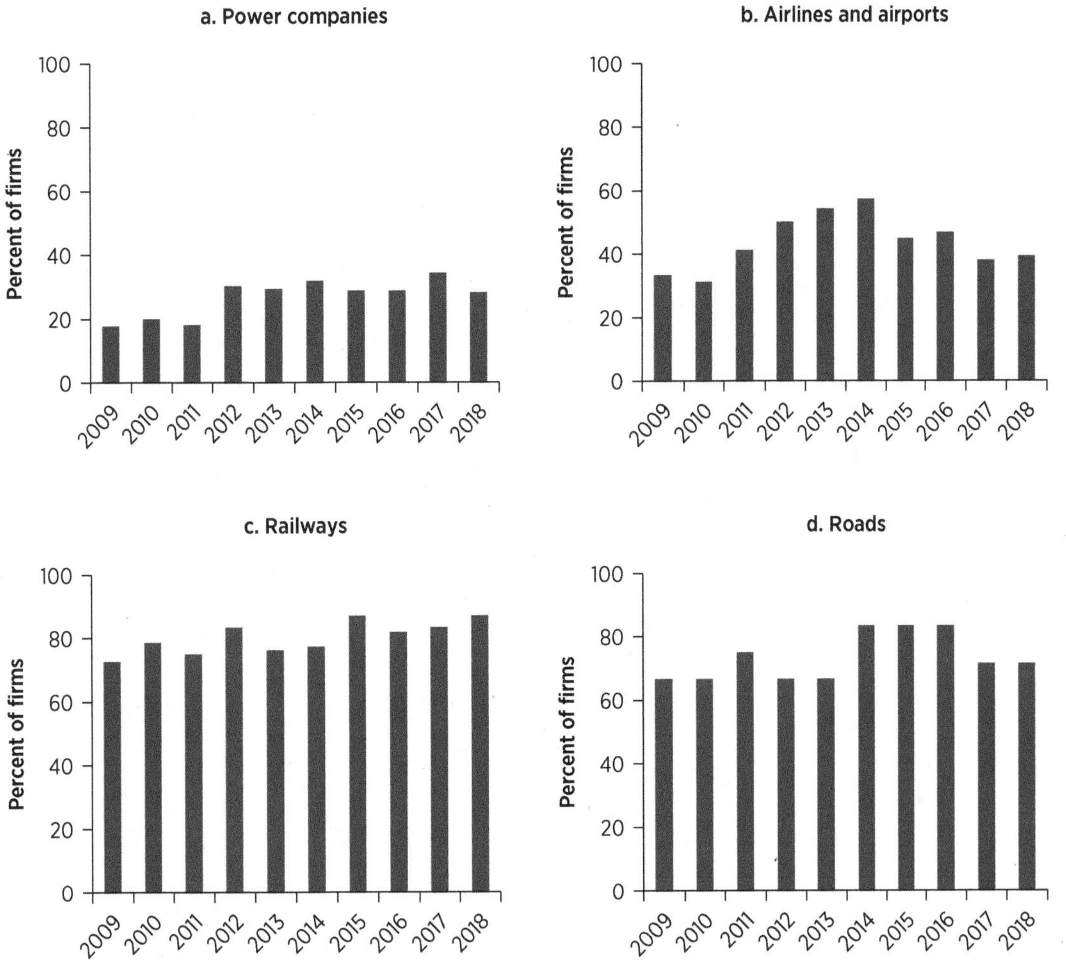

Consistent with this idea, fully owned SOEs have employment costs as a share of revenues that are usually higher than partially privatized companies (figure 3.8). In all sectors, employment costs at partially privatized firms account for less than 22 percent of revenues—about what private firms in infrastructure spend on employees (see the next section). In contrast, fully owned SOEs in the road sector spend 72 percent of revenues (net of government transfers) on employment costs, airlines and airports pay 108 percent, and railways pay 188 percent.

A plausible explanation for the large differences in employment costs among fully owned and partially privatized transport SOEs is that the former are heavily unionized and have less flexibility to reduce their labor force during downturns. Employment costs increase during good times and remain high during bad times. Moreover, politicians sometimes use SOEs as employment vehicles, with governments providing significant subsidies to keep them afloat.

**FIGURE 3.7**    Costs of infrastructure SOEs, by type of cost and sector

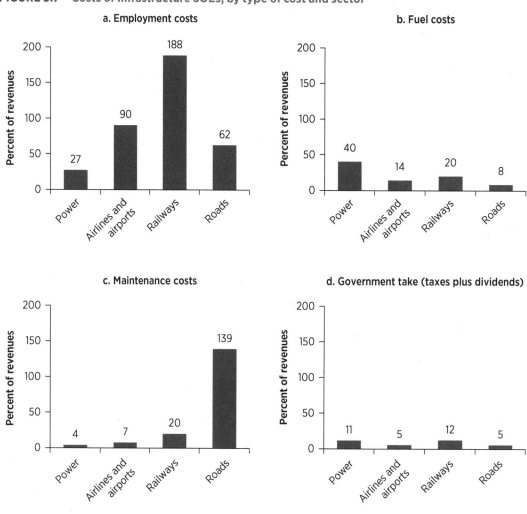

*Source:* Original figure for this publication, based on data from the World Bank Infrastructure SOEs Database.
*Note:* Figures are averages over 2009–18. SOE = state-owned enterprise.

These practices help create extremely large companies with unstable and weak financial performance that require additional fiscal transfers every time there are unexpected deviations from budgeted expenses.

With little financial slack and high ratios of costs to revenues, the financial performance of infrastructure SOEs is volatile and weak, as figure 3.9 shows for the power and railway sectors. The ratios of profits to GDP, adjusted to net out operations subsidies, in the power (panel a) and railway (panel b) sectors shows high volatility over time and unpredictable signs. In some countries, the net income of a power SOE can be 1–2 percent of GDP one year and –1 to –2 percent of GDP the next.

The underperformance and volatility in net income of power SOEs can be explained by variability in fuel costs; exchange rate fluctuations; low and variable revenue collection (during a recession, electricity consumption and revenue collection rates decrease); system

**FIGURE 3.8**    Employment costs as a share of revenues by fully owned and partially privatized infrastructure SOEs, by sector

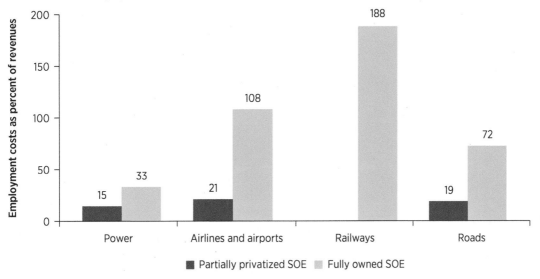

*Source:* Original figure for this publication, based on data from the World Bank Infrastructure SOEs Database.
*Note:* Figures are averages over 2009–18. SOE = state-owned enterprise.

losses; and QFOs that cap tariffs below cost-recovery levels. Fuel costs are high in the power sector. Sudden increases in the price of oil can thus destabilize profitability. Almost 40 percent of power utilities in Africa had collection rates below 90 percent in 2012–18, and collection rates were volatile (Balabanyan and others 2021). In many countries, governments cap tariffs below cost recovery and provide budget transfers to compensate the SOEs for the losses. In Indonesia, the net profit of the power company PT Perusahaan Listrik Negara (PLN) is usually negative because of QFOs that cap electricity tariffs at below cost-recovery levels. Some of the losses are then compensated by the government through operations subsidies.

In railways (see figure 3.9, panel b), volatile financial performance is associated with demand-side risk, unexpected changes in the price of fuel inputs, and the narrow financial slack afforded given the QFOs government charge these companies with. Railways usually have high legacy costs related to current employee costs and pensions and face controls on passenger and cargo tariffs.

Some of the losses of railway SOEs seem predictable. In Bulgaria and Croatia, for example, total subsidies to railways are high and similar year on year. Losses in other countries, such as Argentina, are more volatile and can be extremely high as a percent of GDP. For example, before a major reorganization in 2015, Operadora Ferroviaria Sociedad del Estado received average annual fiscal transfers of 180 percent of assets. Volatility is highest in Ukraine, Ethiopia, and Georgia, where the average difference between a bad year and a good year is equivalent to net income of –0.5 and –1 percent of GDP. If governments have to regularly cover those losses with fiscal transfers, the underperformance of railway SOEs will affect the national budget deficit in significant ways.

The main expense of SOEs in the road sector is maintenance costs, which are highly volatile (the interquartile range is close to 120 percent of revenues). These costs are often tied to weather shocks or deterioration of infrastructure that forces SOEs to undertake urgent repairs.

**FIGURE 3.9**   **Adjusted net income as percent of GDP in the power and railway sectors, by country**

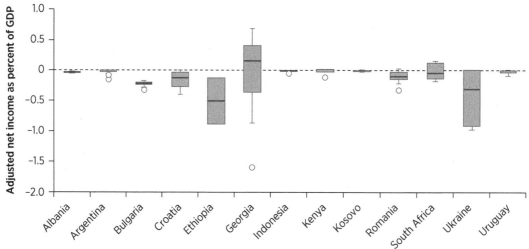

*Source:* Original figure for this publication, based on data from World Bank Infrastructure SOEs Database.
*Note:* Data are for 2009–18. Box plots show the range in adjusted net income, which subtracts operations subsidies from net income for the year. Boxes show the interquartile variation (25–75 percent) in net income to assets. Lines across the boxes show the median. Whiskers show the maximum and minimum of this variable, capped at 1.5 times the interquartile range. Dots represent outliers. GDP = gross domestic product; SOE = state-owned enterprise.

For airlines, average fuel cost represents about 20 percent of revenues. Sudden increases in the price of oil can destabilize profitability and generate a need for further fiscal transfers. Airlines also have large employment expenses, which also increase the volatility of profits.

Sensitivity analysis of net income to changes in fuel costs, foreign exchange, interest rates, and demand for SOEs in Indonesia and Kenya shows that SOEs are highly exposed to

**BOX 3.1** Sensitivity of profitability of infrastructure SOEs in Indonesia and Kenya to changes in fuel costs and demand

Research conducted for this report analyzed how shocks to fuel costs and demand affect the profitability of infrastructure SOEs in Indonesia and Kenya. Airlines are the most sensitive to drastic changes in the cost of fuel (table 3B.1.1): A 5 percent increase in fuel costs is estimated to reduce net income by 46 percent of earnings before interest and taxes (EBIT) in Garuda Indonesia and 195 percent in Kenya Airways.[a] The airport sector is less sensitive to changes in the price of fuel than all of the other infrastructure sectors.

In electricity, sensitivity to changes in the cost of fuel depends on the mix of energy sources. Kenya Electricity Generating Company (KenGen) uses a combination of predominantly hydro and geothermal power to generate electricity. As a result, a 25 percent increase in fuel costs barely reduces its profits. In contrast, Indonesia's Perusahaan Listrik Negara (PLN) generates power largely by burning coal, oil, and natural gas. A 5 percent increase in the price of fuel reduces its earnings before interest and taxes by 27 percent, and a 25 percent increase reduces profits by 136 percent (see box table 3B.1.1). Fuel costs can be as high as 80 percent of revenues at PLN.

The railway sector is also sensitive to the price of fuel, albeit not to the same extent as airlines and power in Indonesia. Fuel does not represent a large proportion of expenses in railways. At Kereta Api (the Indonesian railway SOE), fuel costs were equivalent to 10 percent of revenues in 2019; at Kenyan Railways, they represented 14 percent.

**TABLE 3B.1.1** Sensitivity of net income of infrastructure SOEs to shocks in fuel costs in Kenya and Indonesia (percent of earnings before interest and taxes)

| Sector/SOE | Shock as percent of fuel costs | | | |
|---|---|---|---|---|
| | **−25** | **−5** | **5** | **25** |
| *Airlines* | | | | |
| Garuda Indonesia | 231 | 46 | −46 | −231 |
| Kenya Airways | 973 | 195 | −195 | −973 |
| *Power* | | | | |
| Perusahaan Listrik Negara (PLN) (Indonesia) | 136 | 27 | −27 | −136 |
| Kenya Electricity Transmission Company (KetraCo) | 1 | 0 | 0 | −1 |
| Kenya Electricity Generating Company (KenGen) | 5 | 1 | −1 | −5 |
| Kenya Power and Lighting Company (KPLC) | 277 | 55 | −55 | −277 |
| *Railways* | | | | |
| Kereta Api Indonesia | 14 | 3 | −3 | −14 |
| Kenya Railways Corporation | 3 | 1 | −1 | −3 |
| *Airports* | | | | |
| Angkasa Pura 1 (Indonesia) | 9 | 2 | −2 | −9 |
| Angkasa Pura 2 (Indonesia) | 1 | 0 | 0 | −1 |
| Kenya Airports Authority | 0 | 0 | 0 | 0 |

*Source:* Castalia 2022a, 2022b.
*Note:* Estimates are based on 2019 financial statements. SOE = state-owned enterprise.

*(continued)*

**BOX 3.1** *Continued*

A second set of sensitivity tests examines the effect demand shocks have on the profitability of infrastructure SOEs. As SOEs have large expense-to-revenue ratios, slight changes in demand have large effects on profitability. Airlines seems to have the least slack to buffer shocks in demand: A 5 percent decrease in demand reduces profits by 132 percent of EBIT at Garuda Indonesia and 554 percent of EBIT at Kenya Airways (table 3B.1.2). Although some power companies did not seem to suffer significant declines in profitability, at KPLC a 5 percent decline in demand increased losses by 20 percent.

In the railway sector, Indonesia's Kereta Api appears to be more sensitive to changes in demand than Kenya Railways. At Kenya Railways, the simulated shocks do not affect the size of losses much, because its losses are driven mostly by the huge expense ratios the company already has (expenses were five times revenues in 2019).

Airports show somewhat greater sensitivity to changes in demand than railways and power SOEs. As they depend on fees that are proportional to traffic, shocks to demand directly affect their bottom line.

**TABLE 3B.1.2** **Sensitivity of net income of infrastructure SOEs to shocks in demand in Kenya and Indonesia (percent of earnings before interest and taxes)**

| Sector/SOE | Shock to demand (%) | | | |
|---|---|---|---|---|
| | **−15** | **−5** | **5** | **15** |
| *Airlines* | | | | |
| Garuda Indonesia | −395 | −132 | 132 | 395 |
| Kenya Airways | −1,661 | −554 | 554 | 1,661 |
| *Power* | | | | |
| Perusahaan Listrik Negara (PLN) (Indonesia) | −23 | −8 | 8 | 23 |
| Kenya Electricity Transmission Company (KetraCo) | −1 | 0 | 0 | 1 |
| Kenya Electricity Generating Company (KenGen) | −5 | −1 | 1 | 5 |
| Kenya Power and Lighting Company (KPLC) | −59 | −20 | 20 | 59 |
| *Railways* | | | | |
| Kereta Api Indonesia | −75 | −25 | 25 | 75 |
| Kenya Railways Corporation | −11 | −4 | 4 | 11 |
| *Airports* | | | | |
| Angkasa Pura 1 (Indonesia) | −118 | −39 | 39 | 118 |
| Angkasa Pura 2 (Indonesia) | −73 | −24 | 24 | 73 |
| Kenya Airports Authority | −53 | −18 | 18 | 53 |

*Source:* Castalia 2022a, 2022b.
*Note:* Estimates are based on 2019 financial statements. SOE = state-owned enterprise.

*Note:* SOE = state-owned enterprise.
a. Although the government owns less than 50 percent of Kenya Airways (it is the largest shareholder, with 48.9 percent) and does not have ultimate control over the company—the two criteria used in this report to define an SOE—it is included in the analysis in this box because of the significant fiscal risk estimated.

volatility in these variables (box 3.1). In both countries, airlines are extremely sensitive to changes in the price of fuel; in Kenya, railways are also highly sensitive. The power sector in Indonesia is also extremely sensitive to the movement in fuel prices, because of its reliance on fossil fuels as inputs. Kenya's power companies are less sensitive to changes in the cost of fuel, because most electricity is produced using hydro and geothermal power. When it comes to the sensitivity of SOE performance to changes in demand, airlines are the most sensitive, followed by airports and railways.

Volatility in performance and frequent losses result in annual requests for fiscal support (either expected or unexpected fiscal transfers); they can also rapidly erode the capital base of SOEs and thus create a larger request for fiscal support to recapitalize or bail out the companies in question. As infrastructure SOEs use most of their revenues to cover payroll, maintenance, and fuel expenses, they have little left over that can be directed as retained earnings. With low reserves or retained earnings, firms cannot buffer negative shocks for sustained periods of time.

### Performance of and quasi-fiscal operations by state-owned infrastructure enterprises

The main obstacle to improving the performance of infrastructure SOEs, especially those fully owned by the government, is the fact that they are used to perform QFOs, which are usually not fully compensated (see chapter 1 for a discussion of this topic). Infrastructure SOEs "are directed by their governments to pursue public policy objectives and are not given the resources to do so … the repeated use of such uncompensated quasi-fiscal activities leads to loss accumulation, underinvestment, and/or excess borrowing by the affected SOEs" (Ter-Minassian 2019, 51).

Governments often ask SOEs to perform QFOs, such as providing access to rural communities or low-income households, compensating them by using consumption taxes paid by users. For example, the Rural Electrification Fund and the Fund for Social Inclusion in Peru use fees charged to electricity users to help pay for the expansion of the electricity network. Some of the funds benefit SOEs, and some benefit private firms in the sector.

Governments can compensate QFOs through ex ante agreements that estimate the costs of such operations and budget operations subsidies to cover them. For instance, PLN, the largest SOE in Indonesia, operates most of the country's power generators and the electricity transmission network; it undertakes a variety of QFOs to expand coverage to remote areas. To cover the cost of such QFOs, the government provides it with operations subsidies that are calculated ex ante to cover all the associated costs.

Ex ante budgeting of QFO costs has two problems. First, governments can end up underestimating the actual cost of providing the QFOs. Second, having the government use SOEs to perform QFOs usually opens the door for requests for additional funding from the government in an ad hoc way, either because SOEs can underestimate the cost of the QFOs and then request additional funds to cover losses or because having the opportunity to request funds from the government may allow them to request funding to cover losses from non–QFO activities as well. For example, SOEs like PLN may receive loan guarantees for debt incurred to execute large projects and purchase coal at fixed prices. Despite these subsidies, it often falls short of expected profitability and requires additional funds to cover losses or larger equity injections to recapitalize its balance sheet. Imposing QFOs on SOEs can create an ad hoc fiscal relation with the government that can generate moral hazard and make underperformance and the request for funds harder to prevent.

## PERFORMANCE OF SOEs VERSUS PERFORMANCE OF SIMILAR PRIVATE FIRMS

The research conducted by Herrera Dappe and others (2022a) for this report examines how much of the problems identified with SOEs should be associated with state ownership and how much with characteristics of the infrastructure sector (see appendix C for details of the methodology). Infrastructure SOEs tend to be much larger relative to the size of the economies in which they operate than private firms (by 2 percentage points in Assets to GDP) (figure 3.10). The borrowing behavior of public and private firms also differ, as private firms face more obstacles accessing long-term financing (Dinlersoz and others 2018), something that may explain the larger size and higher leverage of SOEs. They have larger liabilities relative to GDP (by almost 1 percentage point in liabilities to GDP) relative to private firms, suggesting that contingent risks from SOEs may also be larger for their government owners.

The underperformance of infrastructure SOEs is highly correlated with government ownership. The ROAA of infrastructure SOEs is 2.4 percentage points lower and return on assets net of operations subsidies 5.2 percentage points lower than similar private firms (see figure 3.10). The latter difference is very large, considering that the mean of return on assets net of subsidies in the sample is 1.5 percent. The ratio of earnings before interest, taxes, depreciation, and amortization (EBITDA) to revenues is 16.4 percentage points lower and the ratio of EBITDA to assets 4.7 percentage points lower than the average private firm. These magnitudes are also

**FIGURE 3.10**   Comparison of size and performance of infrastructure SOEs and similar private firms using matching techniques

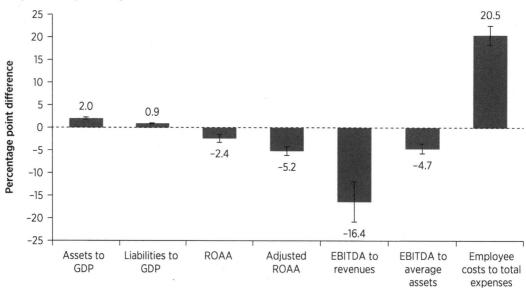

*Source:* Original figure for this publication, based on analysis by Herrera Dappe and others 2022a.
*Note:* ROAA: return on average assets. EBITDA: earnings before interest, taxes, depreciation, and amortization. Bars represent differences in size and performance between SOEs and private firms. Each bar represents the coefficient of a firm-level regression comparing SOEs with similar private firms using coarsened exact matching (see appendix C for details). Each regression includes controls for leverage; size (log of assets); and fixed effects for sector, region, and income level. Whiskers represent confidence intervals. The smaller the whisker, the more statistical accuracy in the estimation of the difference between SOEs and private firms. ROAA is defined as net income over the average of assets the current year and the previous year. Net income is calculated as revenues minus expenses, interests, depreciation and amortization, and taxes. Adjusted ROAA is calculated by subtracting operations subsidies from net income. EBITDA = earnings before interest, taxes, depreciation, and amortization; GDP = gross domestic product; ROAA = return on average assets; SOE = state-owned enterprise.

large considering that the sample average ratio of EBITDA to revenues is 18.8 percent and the average ratio of EBITDA to assets is 6.5 percent. These two differences in operational performance suggest that SOEs suffer from significant operational efficiency differences or that QFOs affect the operational performance of SOEs.

The ratio of employee costs to total expenses is 20.5 percentage points higher for SOEs than private companies. This large difference may explain why SOEs are not profitable and have a hard time paying all of their expenses out of revenues. The larger employee costs of SOEs suggest that governments hire inefficiently or that employment is part of their QFOs.

SOEs tend to be in constant expansion: In good times, they tend to hire, and in bad times they do not lay off workers (party because of higher unionization rates among public sector workers). The financial performance of infrastructure SOEs is expected to deteriorate over time and to suffer from negative shocks as a result of their lack of flexibility to adjust their payroll according to the business cycle.

## SOEs AND FISCAL RISK: SLOW DRIP OR TAIL RISK?

The fiscal risk of SOEs is often thought of as stemming from extreme events (tail risk). The evidence from this report indicates that fiscal risks are actually a series of small to medium-size deviations from budgeted figures requiring annual fiscal injections of 0.04–0.25 percent of GDP. Fiscal risk in SOEs should thus be thought of as "deviations in fiscal variables from what was expected at the time of the budget or other forecast" (Cebotari and others 2009, 4).

Annual fiscal injections to SOEs average 0.25 percent of GDP for power, 0.24 percent for roads, 0.12 for railways, and 0.04 percent for airlines and airports (figure 3.11). These figures include increases in capitalization and/or substitutions of liabilities (that is, net fiscal transfers), all as a percent of assets. This measure goes beyond the accounting of direct subsidies from the government, incorporating also changes in the stock of government equity (recapitalizations) and changes in the loans SOEs receive from financial and nonfinancial SOEs, all net of asset increases or as a percent of GDP. Box 3.2 provides definitions and examples of the different types of fiscal transfers.[6]

Not all fiscal injections are small or isolated sectoral events. Very large recapitalizations are often made in response to large, unexpected shocks (figure 3.12, panel a). The 187 country-year observations for 2009–18 captured in this report included 4 events with total fiscal injections to SOEs of more than 1 percent of GDP at the country level, 38 with fiscal injections of 0.2–1 percent of GDP, and 64 with fiscal injections below 0.2 percent of GDP (figure 3.12, panel b). In 57 percent of the country-years studied, fiscal injections (net of assets increases) were provided to infrastructure SOEs (see appendix D for all the country-year events in the sample). This incidence is greater than that found by Bova and others (2019).

The extent to which countries use fiscal injections to support their infrastructure SOEs and the type of fiscal injections they use varies (figure 3.13). During 2009–18, Bulgaria provided the most support, with average annual fiscal injections to its airport, railway, and power SOEs of 0.8 percent of GDP; Bhutan, Croatia, and Kosovo followed, with average fiscal injections of about 0.4–0.5 percent of GDP. In Bulgaria, Indonesia, Romania, and Uruguay, operations subsidies were the main instrument used to support infrastructure SOEs. In Albania, government support was channeled mainly through government loans. In Croatia and Kosovo, governments used both operations subsidies and government loans. Loans from SOEs were important in Bhutan and Bulgaria. Equity injections were important in Argentina, Bhutan, and Ghana.

**FIGURE 3.11**    **Average fiscal injections to infrastructure SOEs, by sector**

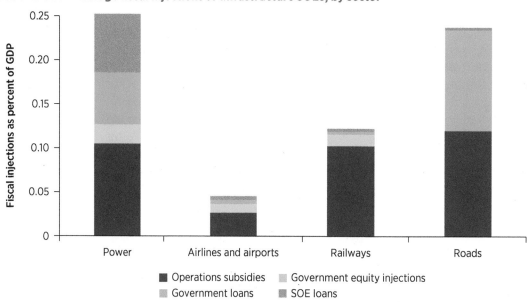

*Source:* Original figure for this publication, based on data from the World Bank Infrastructure SOEs Database.
*Note:* Averages are over positive fiscal injection events in 2009–18. Government loans and SOE loans capture annual positive increases in long-term debt or loans. This figure was constructed by adding operations subsidies, government equity injections, and increases in government loans and SOE loans and subtracting changes in assets from the previous year by SOE for each year to determine whether there was a fiscal injection (that is, a positive difference). Fiscal injections were then added in by sector in each country for each year and the resulting figure was divided by GDP. All country-year observations of positive fiscal injection events were then averaged by sector. GDP = gross domestic product; SOE = state-owned enterprise.

**FIGURE 3.12**    **Fiscal injections to infrastructure SOEs, at the sectoral and country level**

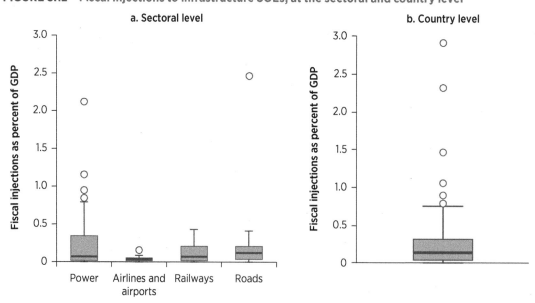

*Source:* Original figure for this publication, based on data from the World Bank Infrastructure SOEs Database.
*Note:* Data are for 2009–18. Boxes show interquartile variation (25–75 percent) of fiscal injections to GDP. Lines across the boxes show the median per year. Whiskers show the maximum and minimum of this variable per year, capped at 1.5 times the interquartile range. Dots represent the outliers. Distributions are over positive fiscal injection events. GDP = gross domestic product.

**BOX 3.2     A taxonomy of fiscal injections to SOEs**

Governments support SOEs in a variety of ways, including providing direct fiscal transfers to fund operations and/or capital expenditures and providing credit from the government or from other SOEs or state-owned banks.

**Operations subsidies:** Operations subsidies are annual fiscal transfers provided to SOEs to cover shortfalls and, often, to compensate them for specific quasi-fiscal operations (QFOs). These subsidies can amount to a large percent of assets, especially when they are used to cover equity shortfalls (that is, to recapitalize an SOE). In some countries, these subsidies are recurrent, especially when governments compensate SOEs ex ante for specific QFOs and mandates. Operations subsidies also include extraordinary transfers to cover unexpected losses and shortfalls in capital investments, among others.

**Government injections of equity:** Governments can bail out and recapitalize SOEs by injecting equity. These equity injections may increase the equity owned by the government. They can be either direct (by a domestic government entity, such as a ministry or a government agency) or indirect (by a domestic government entity through shareholding in another company, such as another SOE or any other enterprise with government participation).

**Government loans:** This variable is created by adding up long-term debt or loans from the government or other government affiliated creditors except SOEs and state-owned banks. This credit usually has a direct impact on the budget and on the support governments report for its SOEs. It includes loans from international financial institutions to the government that are then on-lent to SOEs.

**SOE loans:** State-owned banks or SOEs often extend credit or roll over existing loans to an underperforming SOE. This form of credit may or may not have an impact on the government budget directly the year the transaction happens, depending on whether the bank or lending SOE has cash reserves or sufficient capital buffers to take on the loan on its balance sheet. These loans usually create significant fiscal costs, as they may reduce dividends or taxes for the government when the credit is extended. These inter–SOE transfers have two advantages for governments, which make them an appealing transaction for SOE managers and government officials. First, this form of support can be kept off budget for the government and may not manifest itself as fiscal risk unless either the SOE does not pay the loan or the lending party has less profitability because of the transaction and therefore pays less in dividends and taxes to the government. Second, these transactions may hide the underperforming results of an SOE for a few years, until one of the parties has to ultimately face the losses. If politicians have short discounting horizons, they may support these kinds of transactions, hoping things will pick up in the future or that they can defer the pain of an SOE bailout.

*Source:* Herrera Dappe and others 2022b.
*Note:* SOE = state-owned enterprise.

**FIGURE 3.13**   **Average fiscal injections to infrastructure SOEs in 2009–18, by country and type of support**

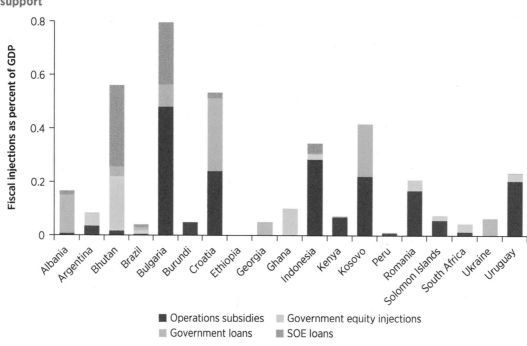

*Source:* Original figure for this publication, based on data from the World Bank Infrastructure SOEs Database.
*Note:* Government loans and SOE loans capture annual positive increases in long-term debt or loans. The figure was constructed by adding operations subsidies, government equity injections, government loans, and SOE loans and subtracting changes in assets from the previous year by SOE for each year to determine whether there was a fiscal injection (that is, a positive difference). Fiscal injections were then added by country for each year and the resulting figure was divided by GDP. All country-year observations of positive fiscal injection events were then averaged by country. GDP = gross domestic product; SOE = state-owned enterprise.

In Kenya, the government consistently provided operating and capital subsidies for its SOEs that represented around 0.26 percent of GDP; it also provided equity injections that represented 1.6–4.0 percent of the government budget. The largest recipient of operating and capital subsidies in Kenya was the Kenya Power and Lighting Company (KPLC), the sole electricity distributor in the country and the largest player in the distribution sector. These fiscal injections were used partly to cover projects for rural electrification, particularly to pay for "last-mile" connection costs, which are heavily subsidized by the company. Kenya Railways Corporation (KRC) received subsidies to expand the commuter rail network. The government also supported SOEs by facilitating their access to financing with direct loans, on-lending, and debt guarantees. The largest beneficiaries of the loans were KPLC and KRC. Kenya Airways and the Kenya Electricity Generating Company (KenGen) were the largest beneficiaries of debt guarantees (Castalia 2022b).

Fiscal transfers to support infrastructure SOEs are large relative to the assets of the receiving firms. Figure 3.14 shows how much each form of fiscal support is used by sector. The average fiscal injections to total assets are usually bailouts large enough to be considered full recapitalizations—more than 8–10 percent of assets, the capital to asset ratios SOEs usually have when they are fully capitalized.

There are also sectoral differences in terms of how governments support their SOEs. In the power sector, governments use a combination of equity injections, SOE loans, and (to a lesser

**FIGURE 3.14** **Average fiscal injections to infrastructure SOEs in 2009–18, by sector**

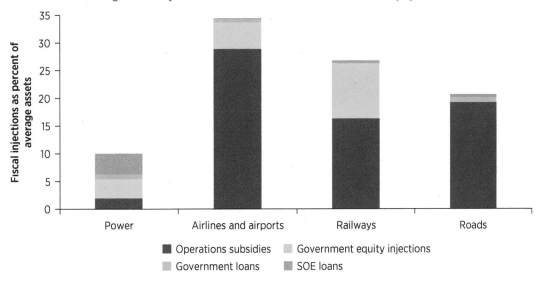

*Source:* Original figure for this publication, based on data from the World Bank Infrastructure SOEs Database.
*Note:* Government loans and SOE loans capture the annual positive increases in long-term debt or loans. The figure was constructed by adding operations subsidies, government equity injections, increases in government loans and SOE loans, and subtracting the change in assets from the previous year by SOE for each year to determine whether there was a fiscal injection (that is, a positive difference). Fiscal injections were then added in by SOE for each year and the figure divided by total assets of the SOE. All SOE-year observations of positive fiscal injection events were then averaged by sector to create the bars. SOE = state-owned enterprise.

degree) operations subsidies and government loans. In airlines and airports, the shares of subsidies and equity injections are larger, in part because more fully owned SOEs receive equity injections. Roads are more dependent on the government budget. The main form of fiscal injection they receive is operations subsidies, usually transfers to fund their annual operations (mostly construction and maintenance of roads). Subsidies represent the largest budgetary transfers the sector received in Uruguay and some other countries. Railways also rely heavily on operations subsidies, as well as equity injections.

## PREDICTING FISCAL RISKS

Fiscal risk can be tracked and prevented by using forward-looking indicators that come from the literature on insolvency. The methodology can be used to monitor SOE performance and predict the need for fiscal injections (Herrera Dappe and others 2022b).

Mitigating fiscal risk has focused on improving the way governments account for contingent liabilities and hidden deficits. For instance, Kharas and Mishra (2001, 3) propose setting aside every year an amount "equal to its long-run average hidden deficit, so that the country can meet future contingent claims." Lewis and Mody (1998, 2–4) also recommend building reserves for unexpected costs "based on government aversion to making frequent funding requests" from Congress. They argue that part of the problem is the cash budget accounting system used by most governments and recommend keeping a good account of assets and liabilities, including contingent liabilities, to be able to calculate "the expected loss exposure of each of its contingent liabilities independently," taking into account the "aggregate loss distribution of the government's portfolio of risks, using value-at-risk" methodologies. Except for the latter, these methodologies are not forward looking and have been hard to apply to SOEs.

A forward-looking indicator would make a useful addition to the tools used to assess fiscal risks from SOEs. Altman (2000, 2018) proposes a methodology for studying the determinants of bailout events. By comparing the financials of private (not publicly traded) firms that were insolvent or bankrupt with those of similar firms that were not facing distress, Altman identified four financial ratios—working capital to assets, retained earnings to total assets, earnings before interest and taxes (EBIT) to assets, and book value to total liabilities, all normalized by assets or liabilities to facilitate comparison of firms of different sizes—which he used to create an index (a $Z''$ score) for forecasting financial distress of private firms:

- Working capital to assets (current assets minus current liabilities divided by total assets) is a good measure of the working capital or liquidity available in the balance sheet of a firm or SOE in a specific year. It measures the liquidity buffer SOEs have to deal with shocks.
- Retained earnings to total assets captures the amount of "reinvested earnings and/or losses of a firm over its entire life" (Altman 2000). For SOEs, the higher this retained earnings ratio is, the less the SOE will have to request financial support from the government, because it will have reserves from which to write off losses.
- EBIT to total assets is a proxy for the operational efficiency of the firm's assets, "independent of any tax or leverage factors" (Altman 2013). For SOEs, this factor captures whether there is cost recovery in the tariffs it charges or the firm faces losses due to inefficiency. It is the factor that usually has the highest correlation with insolvency.[7]
- Book value of equity to total liabilities indirectly captures the leverage of the firm and the extent to which the capital base can sustain its liabilities. It is a key measure for SOEs, which usually operate undercapitalized, because governments commonly let them erode their capital base before they recapitalize them.

The $Z''$ score is calculated using the following parameters, which Altman (2018) estimated as

$$Z'' = 3.25 + 6.56 \frac{\text{Current assets} - \text{Current liabilities}}{\text{Total assets}} + 3.26 \frac{\text{Retained earnings}}{\text{Total assets}}$$

$$+ 6.72 \frac{\text{EBIT}}{\text{Total assets}} + 1.05 \frac{\text{Book value of equity}}{\text{Total liabilities}},$$

where the $Z''$ is a numerical score estimated to range from 0 to 8.8 (Altman 2018), where 0 is equated with bankruptcy. Higher Altman $Z''$ scores are usually correlated with higher credit ratings, even though credit rating agencies use a variety of qualitative scores beyond financials to estimate the risk of default of a company.

The median infrastructure SOE in the World Bank Infrastructure Database has financials that look like those of a firm that can issue bonds of speculative grade but not high risk. The estimated $Z''$ score for infrastructure SOEs has a median value of 5.29, just above the median value of private firms with a credit rating of BB– (table 3.1). The 75th percentile of the sample has a $Z''$ score at levels that are just above the median for firms rated AAA and AA+, the highest credit ratings for firms that issue debt. A quarter of the infrastructure SOEs in the World Bank Database are thus financially strong.

The estimates of the $Z''$ score can then be used as a forward-looking indicator to signal the need for fiscal injections in SOEs and their likely magnitude. Using the approach presented in

**TABLE 3.1**   Average $Z''$ score and predicted fiscal injections for infrastructure SOEs, by credit rating

| Rating | Average $Z''$ across samples | Predicted fiscal injection (percent of total assets) |
|---|---|---|
| AAA/AA+ | 8.15 | 5.34 |
| AA/AA− | 7.78 | 5.54 |
| A+ | 7.61 | 5.63 |
| A | 7.04 | 5.94 |
| A− | 6.54 | 6.21 |
| BBB+ | 6.17 | 6.41 |
| BBB | 6.00 | 6.50 |
| BBB− | 5.90 | 6.55 |
| BB+ | 5.72 | 6.65 |
| BB | 5.55 | 6.74 |
| BB− | 5.16 | 6.95 |
| B+ | 4.79 | 7.15 |
| B | 4.16 | 7.49 |
| B− | 3.72 | 7.72 |
| CCC+ | 3.01 | 8.11 |
| CCC | 2.42 | 8.42 |
| CCC− | 1.70 | 8.81 |
| CC/D | 0.30 | 9.56 |

*Source:* Average $Z''$ scores across samples are from Altman 2018. Predicted fiscal injections were calculated for this table using the equation in box 3.3.
*Note:* SOE = state-owned enterprise.

box 3.3, Herrera Dappe and others (2022b) show that the $Z''$ score of an SOE in a given year is a good predictor of the fiscal injections to that SOE the following year.

The $Z''$ score of an SOE can be calculated based on the financials of the current year and compared with the $Z''$ scores in table 3.1 or the quintiles in figure 3.15 to assess the fiscal injections the SOE would need the following year. An SOE with a $Z''$ score of 8.43 (the 75th percentile) would require fiscal injections of 5.2 percent of assets the following year (figure 3.15). An SOE with the median $Z''$, of 5.47, would require fiscal injections of about 6.78 percent of assets the year after. SOEs with $Z''$ scores below 3.17 (the 25th percentile) would require fiscal injections of 8.0–9.6 percent of assets, equivalent to a full recapitalization of the firm (assuming normal capital ratios of 8–10 percent of assets).

SOEs with more volatile costs tend to have higher $Z''$ scores, indicating the need for preventive measures to avoid the need for larger fiscal injections in the future. Governments can thus use $Z''$ tracking to monitor fiscal risk and require financial buffers (for example, larger retained earnings) for SOEs with volatile financials or lower $Z''$ scores.

Creating forward-looking measures of fiscal risk is feasible when systematic and timely financial information has been compiled for all infrastructure SOEs. Efforts to improve the

**BOX 3.3**     **Predicting fiscal injections to SOEs**

The analysis uses the measures of fiscal injections presented in box 3.2 as dependent variables and checks whether the lagged $Z''$ score can help predict such injections. The estimated regression is

$$Fiscal\ injection_{it} = 9.73 - 0.54\ Z''_{SOEit-1},$$

where $Fiscal\ injection_{it}$ measures the total fiscal injection to firm $i$ in year $t$. Total fiscal injection includes direct subsidies from the government, changes in the stock of government equity, and changes in the loans SOEs receive from the government and from financial and nonfinancial SOEs, all net of asset increases. For the SOEs in the World Bank Infrastructure SOEs Database, the regression lags the $Z''$ one year and includes no additional controls or clustering of errors, in order to let the financials of the firms, and not variation that affects firms, define the fiscal events. The estimated coefficients are significant at the 0.001 significance level.

*Note:* SOE = state-owned enterprise.

**FIGURE 3.15**     **Predicted fiscal injections to infrastructure SOEs based on estimated $Z''$ scores**

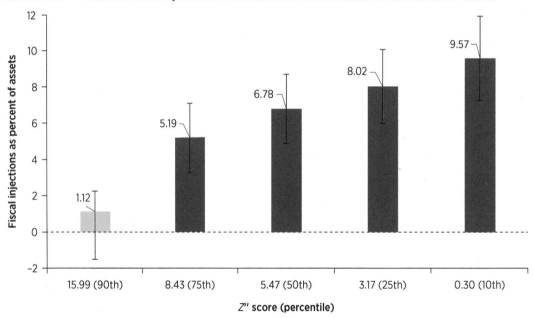

*Source:* Original figure for this publication, based on data from the World Bank Infrastructure SOEs Database.
*Note:* Whiskers indicate 95 percent confidence intervals. The yellow bar indicates that the coefficient is not statistically significant at the 5 percent level. SOE = state-owned enterprise.

compilation and reporting standards of SOEs have usually been accompanied by government reforms to centralize the monitoring of SOEs. Kenya has tried to improve the reporting standards of SOEs, but most of the data currently provided by SOEs "are in hard copy and follow different reporting standards and formats.... In addition, there are significant discrepancies in financial data on individual companies between different reports" (Fiebelkorn, Owuor, and Nzioki 2021, 29). In contrast, Peru has centralized the reporting of a very thorough and standardized set of financials for SOEs under the holding company Fonafe (Centeno Zavala 2021;

Musacchio and Pineda Ayerbe 2019). Efforts to reduce fiscal risk go hand in hand with governance reforms of the monitoring of SOEs (OECD 2015).

## CAPACITY OF SOEs TO DEAL WITH SHOCKS

To what extent can SOEs act as countercyclical spending vehicles during a crisis or a severe negative shock? Do SOEs have buffers to allow them to act as countercyclical policy vehicles, or do their structural characteristics and lack of flexibility end up reinforcing shocks and turning them into burdens for the ministry of finance when coping with shocks?

These questions are particularly important because of the effects of the COVID-19 pandemic and the negative demand shock it caused for many infrastructure services, especially those related to travel. Garuda, Indonesia's state-owned airline, did not receive significant subsidies before COVID-19; as a result of the negative shock of the pandemic, the government had to bail it out. Although it did not systematically lose money, Garuda did not have stable performance before the pandemic, leaving it with declining buffers to pay for current liabilities (current assets could cover only 30 percent of current liabilities). It increased its leverage before 2019, giving it less room to borrow during the pandemic to buffer the shock (Castalia 2022a).

In Kenya, the pandemic significantly altered the fiscal results of SOEs. Kenyan infrastructure SOEs lost money, after many years of positive performance (Fiebelkorn, Owuor and Nzioki 2021). The pandemic exposed the large expense ratios of many of these enterprises (see examples of the sensitivity of Kenyan SOEs to shocks in box 3.1).

A significant negative shock forces SOEs to ask for sizable fiscal injections and in some cases to reduce their capital expenditure (figure 3.16). Research conducted for this report compares how SOEs that were and were not affected by negative shocks performed by studying the effect of a drastic decline in the price of oil in 2014 on SOEs in countries that were net exporters of oil or gas and had significant reserves (countries that suffered a negative macroeconomic shock) with comparable SOEs in non-energy-rich countries (countries that did not face a negative macroeconomic shock) (Herrera Dappe and others 2022c).[8]

SOEs in countries that experienced a negative macroeconomic shock received an increase in total fiscal injections immediately after it of 3.5 percentage points of assets. This injection was economically significant, given that the mean fiscal injection for the sample was 1.1 percent of average assets (figure 3.16, panel a). The increase in fiscal injections was large, given that SOEs in infrastructure operate with capital ratios of 8–10 percent of assets. After two and three years, the total fiscal injections that the affected SOEs received increased, but they were not statistically different from those of the comparable SOEs that did not face the shock.

However, one, two, and three years after the shock, SOEs that faced a negative macroeconomic shock received larger loans from government and financial SOEs than SOEs that did not face the shock (see figure 3.16, panel b). Loan injections were 3.5, 2.4, and 1.2 percentage points of average assets higher one, two, and three years after the shock, respectively. When the fiscal space decreased, governments resorted to loans to keep the SOEs afloat. The result was an increase in the government's direct and indirect (through state-owned financial institutions) exposure to infrastructure SOE risk, as the ratio of government and financial SOE loans to total assets increased by 5.6 percentage points the first year after the shock and by 4.0 percent the second year (see figure 3.16, panel c).

Capital expenditures in fully owned infrastructure SOEs decreased by 3.5 percentage points of average assets the year after the negative shock (see figure 3.16, panel d). This decrease was

**FIGURE 3.16** Impact of a negative macroeconomic shock on infrastructure SOEs

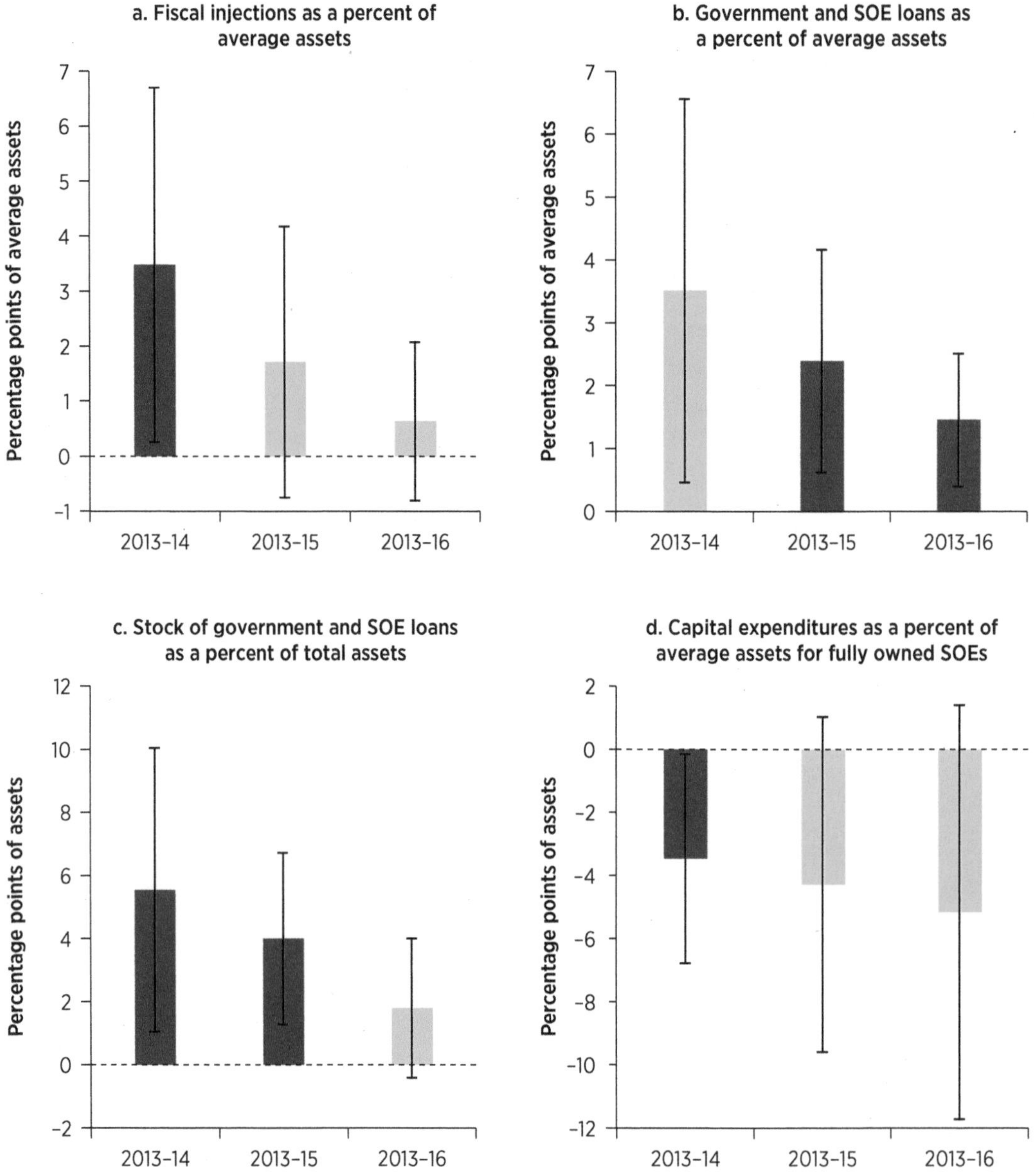

a. Fiscal injections as a percent of average assets

b. Government and SOE loans as a percent of average assets

c. Stock of government and SOE loans as a percent of total assets

d. Capital expenditures as a percent of average assets for fully owned SOEs

*Source:* Original figure for this publication, based on data from the World Bank Infrastructure SOEs Database.
*Note:* Coefficients are from firm-level fixed effects regressions. Observations are matched on sector (power and air transport), country income group, average fuel expenditure as a percent of total expenditures for the period 2011–13, and average total assets as a percent of GDP for the same period. All regressions include SOE fixed effects. In panel a, fiscal injections are defined as increases in operations subsidies, government equity injections, and increases in government loans and SOE loans minus the change in average assets. Whiskers indicate 95 percent confidence intervals. Government and SOE loans in panel b capture annual positive increases in long-term debt or loans. Yellow bars indicate that the coefficient is not statistically significant at the 5 percent level. GDP = gross domestic product; SOE = state-owned enterprise.

equivalent to about 40 percent of the average capital expenditure in the sample for that period. The finding suggests that even after receiving sizable fiscal injections, fully owned SOEs found it hard to keep up with their capital expenditure schedules. The finding also implies that there are other medium-term effects that are not measured here, as a reduction in capital expenditures of fully owned SOEs in affected countries likely leads to a decrease in productivity and operational performance in the years after the shock.

This evidence suggests that SOEs can amplify negative macroeconomic shocks and increase fiscal risk, because SOEs need fiscal injections precisely when governments are under pressure from the fall in total tax revenues. In times of crisis, when governments want to use countercyclical fiscal policy to stimulate the economy, infrastructure SOEs do not help the government by using their buffer reserves to withstand the shock, they become a drag on the budget, requiring injections of fiscal resources to survive.

## IN SUM

Infrastructure SOEs represent larger and more frequent drains on public finances than regularly assumed. They require average annual fiscal injections of 0.25 percent of GDP to remain afloat, with fiscal injections reaching as high as 3 percent of GDP in some countries. They need these injections because they are large, inefficient, and often forced to perform QFOs.

Financial performance—and therefore the incidence and magnitude of fiscal risks—varies by sector. On average, power SOEs perform better financially than the average infrastructure SOE. The transport sector is more likely to receive fiscal injections than the power sector. On average, power sector SOEs absorb the most fiscal resources, with average annual fiscal injections of 0.25 percent of GDP. They are followed by the roads, rail, and airline and airport sectors, with average annual fiscal injections of 0.24, 0.12, and 0.04 percent of GDP, respectively. The transport sector also receives a significant implicit subsidy, with the average ROAA of rail, road, and aviation SOEs ranging between −16 and −12 percent when operations subsidies are not considered and between −4.0 and 1.4 percent when operations subsidies are included.

Fiscal risks from SOEs are exacerbated during major downturns: Rather than acting as tools of expansionary fiscal policy during recessions, infrastructure SOEs turn into a drag on the budget. SOEs that face a negative macroeconomic shock received an increase in total fiscal injections that was equivalent to a significant recapitalization of the SOEs. Fully owned SOEs reduced capital expenses right after a negative macroeconomic shock, which can have longer-term implications on the performance of the SOE and the economy, as capital investments needed to support long-term economic growth get postponed or cancelled.

In some cases, QFOs are compensated through commensurate fiscal transfers; in many cases, however, the transfers are inadequate, creating losses in SOEs even after accounting for operations subsidies. When compensation for QFOs is not properly calculated, it creates the incentive for SOEs to operate inefficiently and request ad hoc fiscal transfers. For regulated SOEs in the power sector that have to set tariffs at below cost-recovery levels because of QFOs, coordination between the ministry of finance and the regulator, which is best placed to determine the compensation, can help mitigate fiscal risks from SOEs.

Mitigating fiscal risks from SOEs requires understanding the full extent of the fiscal dependency and its cause and being prepared to deal with fiscal surprises. One reason why the full extent of the fiscal dependency is not always clearly understood is that governments use a wide range of fiscal instruments to support infrastructure SOEs. The $Z''$ score developed by Altman (2018, 2000) can be used to monitor SOE performance and predict the need for fiscal injections.

## NOTES

1. The countries are Albania, Argentina, Bhutan, Brazil, Bulgaria, Burundi, Croatia, Ethiopia, Georgia, Ghana, Indonesia, Kenya, Kosovo, Peru, Romania, Solomon Islands, South Africa, Ukraine, and Uruguay.
2. This figure is an underestimation of expenditures in electricity and transport, because it excludes SOEs in the waterways, port, and public transport sectors.
3. Comparability was ensured by using a standardized template and identifying each item as defined by the template using the notes to the financial statements rather than relying on the way such items are presented in the main financial tables.
4. Operations subsidies are all of the subsidies an SOE receives for operational expenses. They include both extraordinary and recurrent subsidies to cover overall losses or QFOs, as disclosed by the SOE, including those reported as revenue. Operations subsidies are different from capital subsidies, which are the amortized amount of deferred income due to capital assets granted to the SOE by the government. If not reported as a separate item in the income statement, the figures were inferred from the deferred income notes.
5. ROAA is defined as net income over the average of assets of the current year and the previous year. Net income is calculated as revenue minus expenses, interest, depreciation and amortization, and taxes. Adjusted ROAA is calculated by subtracting operations subsidies from net income. Data were inspected for disproportionate changes in asset valuations; no important variations were found. Averaging total asset values over two consecutive years mitigates the effect of minor changes in asset revaluations.
6. The idea behind this measurement of fiscal injections is to capture fiscal transfers that increase government involvement in the financing of the operation of the SOE only and not transfers to fund investments. SOEs can account for financial support from the government in other ways as well. For instance, there could also be support in the form of increases in trade payables to another SOE. As not all trade payables can be identified as government support, the methodology errs on the side of caution, underestimating fiscal injections ratios by leaving out trade payables from the calculations. There can also be cases in which the government steps in and makes payments to PPPs on behalf of an SOE. Such fiscal support is not captured here, unless the payments show up in the SOE's financial statements.
7. To avoid distorting EBIT for SOEs, all estimations should use EBIT before subsidies.
8. See appendix E for details of the methodology the authors used.

## REFERENCES

Altman, Edward I. 2000. "Predicting Financial Distress of Companies: Revisiting the Z-Score and Zeta Models." *Journal of Finance* 43: 1427–59.

Altman, Edward I. 2013. "Predicting Financial Distress of Companies: Revisiting the Z-Score and ZETA® Models." In *Handbook of Research Methods and Applications in Empirical Finance*, edited by Adrian R. Bell, Chris Brooks, and Marcel Prokopczuk, 428–56. Northampton, MA: Edward Elgar.

Altman, Edward I. 2018. "Applications of Distress Prediction Models: What Have We Learned after 50 Years From The Z-Score Models?" *International Journal of Financial Studies* 6 (3): 70.

Balabanyan, Ani, Yadviga Semikolenova, Arun Singh, and Min A. Lee. 2021. *Utility Performance and Behavior in Africa Today (UPBEAT): Summary Report*. ESMAP Paper, World Bank, Washington, DC.

Bova, Elva, Marta Ruiz-Arranz, Frederik Giancarlo Toscani, and Hatice Elif Ture. 2019. "The Impact of Contingent Liability Realizations on Public Finances." *International Tax and Public Finance* 26 (2): 381–417.

Castalia. 2022a. "Indonesia Country Case Study: Fiscal Costs and Risks." Background paper prepared for this report. World Bank, Washington, DC.

Castalia. 2022b. "Kenya Country Case Study: Fiscal Costs and Risks." Background paper prepared for this report. World Bank, Washington, DC.

Cebotari, Aliona, Jeffrey Davis, Lusine Lusinyan, Amine Mati, Paolo Mauro, Murray Petrie, and Ricardo Velloso. 2009. "Fiscal Risks: Sources, Disclosure, and Management." *Departmental Papers* 2009 (001).

Centeno Zavala, Carlos. 2021. "A Case Study to Analyze Fiscal Costs and Risks of Power State-Owned Enterprises (SOEs) in Peru." Background paper prepared for this report. World Bank, Washington, DC.

Dinlersoz, Emin, Sebnem Kalemli-Ozcan, Henry Hyatt, and Veronika Penciakova. 2018. "Leverage over the Life Cycle and Implications for Firm Growth and Shock Responsiveness." NBER Working Paper 25226, National Bureau of Economic Research, Cambridge, MA.

Fiebelkorn, Andreas, Christine Owuor, and Diana Nzioki. 2021. *Kenya State Corporations Review: Corporate Governance and Fiscal Risks of State Corporations.* Washington, DC: Word Bank.

Foster, Vivien, Samantha Witte, Sudeshna Ghosh Banerjee, and Alejandro Moreno. 2017. *Charting the Diffusion of Power Sector Reforms across the Developing World.* Washington, DC: World Bank.

Herrera Dappe, Matías, Aldo Musacchio, Carolina Pan, Yadviga Semikolenova, Burak Turkgulu, and Jonathan Barboza. 2022a. "Infrastructure State-Owned Enterprises: A Tale of Inefficiency and Fiscal Dependence." Policy Research Working Paper 9969, World Bank, Washington, DC.

Herrera Dappe, Matías, Aldo Musacchio, Carolina Pan, Yadviga Semikolenova, Burak Turkgulu, and Jonathan Barboza. 2022b. "Smoke and Mirrors: Infrastructure State-Owned Enterprises and Fiscal Risks." Policy Research Working Paper 9970, World Bank, Washington, DC.

Herrera Dappe, Matías, Aldo Musacchio, Carolina Pan, Yadviga Semikolenova, Burak Turkgulu, and Jonathan Barboza, 2022c. "State-Owned Enterprises as Countercyclical Instruments: Experimental Evidence from the Infrastructure Sector." Policy Research Working Paper 9971, World Bank, Washington, DC.

Kharas, Homi, and Deepak Mishra. 2001. "Fiscal Policy, Hidden Deficits, and Currency Crises." World Bank Economists' Forum, Washington, DC.

Lewis, Christopher M., and Ashoka Mody. 1998. "Contingent Liabilities for Infrastructure Projects: Implementing a Risk Management Framework for Governments." *Viewpoint*, World Bank, Washington, DC.

Musacchio, Aldo, and Emilio Pineda Ayerbe, eds. 2019. *Fixing State-Owned Enterprises: New Policy Solutions to Old Problems.* Washington, DC: Inter-American Development Bank.

OECD (Organisation for Economic Co-operation and Development). 2015. *OECD Guidelines on Corporate Governance of State-Owned Enterprises.* Paris: OECD Publishing.

OECD (Organisation for Economic Co-operation and Development). 2017. *The Size and Sectoral Distribution of State-Owned Enterprises.* Paris: OECD Publishing.

Ter-Minassian, Teresa. 2019. "Identifying and Mitigating Fiscal Risks from State-Owned Enterprises (SOEs)." In *Fixing State-Owned Enterprises: New Policy Solutions to Old Problems*, edited by Aldo Musacchio and Emilio Pineda, 49–72. Washington, DC: Inter-American Development Bank.

# Fiscal Risks and Costs of Public-Private Partnerships

4

## MAIN MESSAGES

1. A large share of public-private partnership (PPP) contracts are renegotiated, leading to a small but frequent drain of fiscal resources. The annual fiscal cost of renegotiation averages about 0.2 percent of gross domestic product (GDP) in the countries studied, which can be seen as a lower bound because these countries are among the best in the world in terms of PPP governance. The fiscal risks from demand guarantees tend to be smaller, particularly if projects are properly structured.

2. For electricity and transport PPPs, early termination is less frequent than renegotiation, with only about 3 percent of PPPs in developing countries having been terminated early. This share is small, but terminations can be costly, because multiple terminations often occur at the same time. The predicted fiscal risks from early termination in a sample of developing countries are 0.1–2.8 percent of 2020 GDP. These risks are highly procyclical. A negative macroeconomic shock can increase the fiscal risk from early terminations in the immediate aftermath of the shock by a factor of 12–19. Given this risk, developing countries need to set aside significant resources to mitigate the fiscal implications of early termination of PPPs.

3. The power sector has attracted more private capital through PPPs than the transport sector. However, transport PPPs have a higher rate of renegotiation, are renegotiated sooner, and are more likely to result in direct fiscal transfers than power PPPs. Airport, rail, and road PPPs are about five times more likely to be terminated early than electricity PPPs. Together with the fact that transport PPPs are larger than electricity PPPs on average, this increased risk of early termination leads to higher fiscal risks of transport PPPs than electricity PPPs. The average fiscal risks as a share of the portfolios' size is 6–14 percent in the transport sector and 2–4 percent in the power sector, depending on the scenario considered.

## INTRODUCTION

Investments in infrastructure through PPPs have grown rapidly in the developing world since the early 1990s (figure 4.1, panel a). Total investments as a percent of the developing world's

**FIGURE 4.1    Total investment in PPPs in the developing world, 1990–2021**

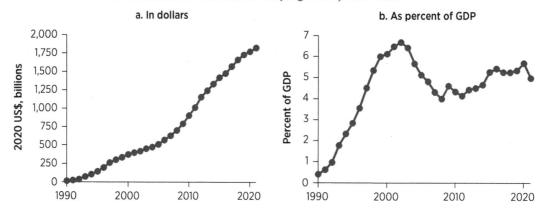

*Source:* Original figure for this publication, based on data from the PPI Database and World Development Indicators.
*Note:* GDP = gross domestic product; PPP = public-private partnership.

GDP grew rapidly during the 1990s, decreased between 1999 and 2008, and started growing again after 2008 (figure 4.1, panel b). At the end of 2021, cumulative investment in PPP projects was about $1.83 trillion,[1] according to the World Bank Private Participation in Infrastructure (PPI) Project Database.[2] Ninety-three percent of the investment ($1.71 trillion) was in PPPs that were still active at the end of 2021.

Seventy-nine percent of all PPP projects in the developing world were in the energy and transport sectors (3,396 out of 6,691 in energy and 1,893 out of 6,691 in transport). The remaining projects were in the water and sewerage (973 projects), natural gas (306 projects), and information and communications technology (123 projects) sectors. More than half of all PPP investment was in the power sector ($927 billion), followed by transport ($703 billion). The average transport PPP ($384 million) was significantly larger than the average power PPP ($288 million).

New evidence based on detailed data from 15 developing countries shows the importance of PPPs relative to direct public provision and SOEs. Capital spending through PPPs accounted for 3–13 percent of total capital spending in infrastructure on average between 2009 and 2018 (figure 4.2).

Well-structured PPPs can increase efficiency, but PPPs create liabilities for governments, including contingent ones. The uncertainty around the construction and operation of infrastructure, and the long-term contractual nature of PPPs, can create substantial fiscal risks that would not exist or would be of a different magnitude than under public provision (figure 4.3).[3] If PPPs are not properly planned, designed, and managed and fiscal treatment of PPPs is inadequate, fiscal surprises can be great.

The analysis of PPPs in Chile by Engel and others (2022) conducted for this report shows how risky infrastructure projects, particularly PPPs, are. The internal rates of return (IRRs) of PPPs in Chile ranged widely, from –23 percent to 25 percent, with 7 out of 50 PPPs analyzed having negative IRRs. The mean IRR was 6.8 percent and the standard deviation 9.4 percent. The returns for highway PPPs (mean of 9.1 percent) were considerably higher than for airport PPPs (mean of 2.9 percent), and the standard deviation was smaller (5.8 percent versus 12.5 percent). These findings suggest that private participation entails significant risk-shifting from the budget to concessionaires and their financiers, which explains the pressure for contract renegotiation and early termination.

**FIGURE 4.2** Share of capital spending through PPPs, 2009–18

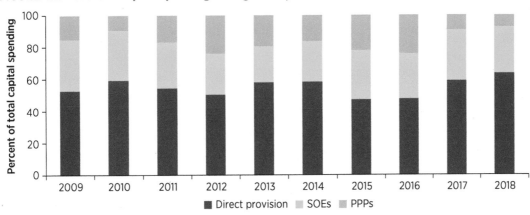

*Source:* Original table for this publication, based on data from the BOOST, World Bank Infrastructure SOEs, and PPI databases.
*Note:* Figures show averages over all countries in the sample. Capital expenditures in PPPs were distributed over a five-year period beginning the investment year indicated in the PPI Database. Expenditures through direct public provision are for the general government. When data on spending through direct public provision in the power sector were not available for a country in the BOOST Database, total energy spending was used. Countries include Albania, Argentina, Bhutan, Bulgaria, Burundi, Ethiopia, Georgia, Indonesia, Kenya, Kosovo, Peru, Romania, Solomon Islands, South Africa, and Ukraine. PPP = public-private partnership; SOE = state-owned enterprise.

**FIGURE 4.3** Fiscal risks from PPPs

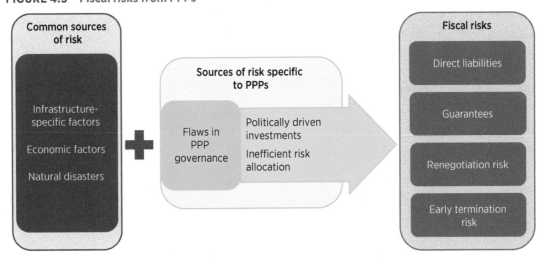

*Source:* Original figure for this publication.
*Note:* PPP = public-private partnership.

This chapter presents empirical evidence on the magnitude, incidence, and determinants of fiscal risks from guarantees, renegotiations, and early terminations of energy and transport PPPs and on the frameworks to manage fiscal risks from PPPs across the world.

## GUARANTEES

Governments often provide guarantees to ensure the commercial feasibility and bankability of PPPs. Lenders may require that the government provide a minimum revenue guarantee to ensure that the project generates sufficient revenues to meet all or at least a substantial part of the debt service. Guarantees shift risk from the private partners to the government as part of the risk-sharing arrangement. Typical PPP guarantees include minimum revenue or demand guarantees, exchange rate guarantees, interest rate guarantees, and debt guarantees.

Guarantees are contingent liabilities that can lead to fiscal surprises. The occurrence, timing, and magnitude of the payment commitments under a guarantee depend on some uncertain future event, outside the control of the government. The government therefore needs to carefully design the risk-sharing arrangement to ensure that it can afford the potential fiscal costs without jeopardizing its fiscal position. It also needs to avoid providing excessive guarantees, which can increase fiscal risks and reduce the value for money from PPPs by weakening the incentive of financers to undertake the due diligence to assess the reliability of the assumptions underlying the business case and monitor the progress of the project.

Most international reporting and statistical standards indicate that contingent liabilities from PPPs should be disclosed in notes to the accounts and reports. The IMF's *Manual on Fiscal Transparency* (IMF 2007) states that budget documentation should include a statement indicating the purpose of each contingent liability, its duration, and intended beneficiaries and that major contingencies should be quantified where possible.

Few countries track and report the contingent liabilities related to PPP guarantees. The type of contingent liabilities disclosed varies across countries. The most common practice is to disclose only explicit loan guarantees. Some countries—including Australia, Chile, Peru, the Philippines, and Türkiye—also disclose other types of contingent liabilities (World Bank 2022).

In Chile, the fiscal costs of minimum revenue guarantees have been negligible. The Ministry of Finance issued guarantees for 70–80 percent of expected traffic demand on fixed-term toll road PPPs, corresponding to the desired leverage in PPPs. The guarantees reduced the risk to long-term institutional lenders; the remaining risk was left to the PPP equity holder, giving it skin in the game (Engel and others 2022). The expected net contingent risk from these guarantees never surpassed 0.25 percent of GDP in 2003–21; the realized costs (annual outlays) represented at most 0.04 percent of GDP (figure 4.4). The largest payment was made in

**FIGURE 4.4**   **Actual and expected payments for minimum revenue guarantees in Chile, as percent of GDP, 2003–21**

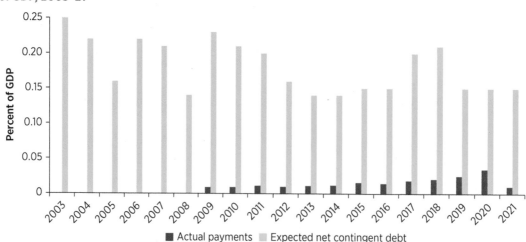

*Source:* Engel and others 2022.
*Note:* GDP = gross domestic product.

2020, during the COVID-19 pandemic. In other years, the annual fiscal costs of guarantees were less than 0.02 percent of GDP.

The fiscal costs from minimum revenue guarantees have also been negligible in Peru, which granted guarantees to six toll road and two port projects for a specific number of years. Only once was a guarantee paid—in 2007, because of the Pisco earthquake, at a fiscal cost of only $2.6 million. Another PPP almost triggered the guarantee in 2017 because of El Niño but ultimately did not. Even with the 50-day emergency declaration in 2020 because of the pandemic, when no tolls were collected, the revenue of toll road PPPs was above the minimum revenue guaranteed (Marchesi 2022). Government estimates of the maximum expected fiscal costs from minimum revenue guarantees with 99 percent confidence until 2037 are less than 0.02 percent of 2020 GDP (Marchesi 2022).

The fiscal costs of guarantees in Chile and Peru were low for several reasons. Chile started its PPP program on a small scale. It improved its project selection and structuring process based on experience. Both Chile and Peru have been conservative in providing guarantees to attract private investments. Although there was some uncertainty on traffic demand in the projects with guarantees, the projects were sensible. All were initiated during periods of strong economic growth in both countries, and traffic volumes grew rapidly in most projects. As these projects aged, the number of years in which guarantees might be paid declined, and the need for new guarantees decreased, because of the strong track records of both PPP programs. In Chile, beginning around 2007, most PPPs were variable-term present-value-of-revenue contracts that did not require guarantees.

Experience from South Africa also shows that the cost of guarantees can be manageable, even during a pandemic. The decrease in traffic in 2022 triggered two PPP guarantees in the transport sector: the minimum revenue guarantee of the Gautrain rail project and the debt guarantee of the Chapman's Peak toll road. According to the National Treasury (National Treasury 2021), provincial governments paid out less than $30 million to their private partners in 2020. The fiscal cost of the guarantees was low because the government had granted only two guarantees to transport PPPs. All other toll roads in South Africa are insured against low demand.

The experience of Türkiye and the Republic of Korea shows that fiscal costs from guarantees can be sizable. Türkiye initiated an ambitious program of highway and bridge PPPs in the late 2000s and early 2010s. The projects, which were to be fully funded by user fees, were granted generous minimum revenue guarantees in hard currency as well as debt guarantees to attract private sector participation. Three of the projects became partially operational during the second half of 2016; by the end of 2021, seven highway and bridge projects had become fully operational. The fiscal cost of the minimum revenue guarantees was only 0.04 percent of GDP in 2017, but it reached 0.12 percent in 2019 and 0.21 in 2020 and 2021 (figure 4.5).

In the 1990s, the Korean government guaranteed 80 percent of a 20-year forecast of revenue for the Incheon International Airport Expressway PPP. When the road opened, in 2000, traffic revenue was less than half the forecast; it remained at least 53 percent below projections until the end of 2007 (Kim and others 2011). As a result, between 2001 and 2014, the government paid the concessionaire W1,414 billion, 71 percent of the original cost of the expressway.[4]

If governments pursue infrastructure expansion in a short-sighted manner, based on optimistic expectations, the fiscal costs of guarantees can be sizable. It may be tempting for governments to grant generous guarantees to make PPPs attractive to private investors, as

**FIGURE 4.5** Fiscal costs of minimum revenue guarantees of road PPPs as percent of GDP in Türkiye, 2017–21

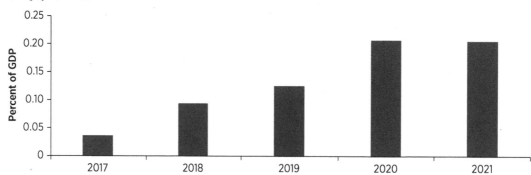

*Source:* Original figure for this publication, based on data from KGM (2018, 2019, 2020, 2021, 2022); Sayıştay (2020 and 2021); UAB (2019, 2020, 2021, 2022); and World Development Indicators.
*Note:* GDP = gross domestic product; PPP = public-private partnership.

contingent liabilities materialize only after they are no longer in power. Optimism bias is a serious problem in infrastructure projects that leads to unrealistic demand forecasts, which can lead government officials to believe guarantees will never or rarely be called (Flyvbjerg 2007; World Bank 2017).

## RENEGOTIATION OF PPPs

PPP contracts are inherently incomplete, because it is not possible to contract for all contingencies over the lifetime of a typical PPP. Unforeseen project-specific, economic, and environmental circumstances may lead one party to challenge the contract. Even when the occurrence of an event can be predicted, its operational and financial impacts on a PPP cannot be predicted at the contracting stage.

Renegotiations may therefore be needed. They provide the flexibility necessary to adapt to extraordinary conditions. However, PPP contracts are renegotiated too frequently and too early, costing the public too much to be justified as an efficient outcome (Guasch 2004).

Renegotiations are ubiquitous in infrastructure projects. They are more common in the transport sector than in the electricity sector. Most of the systematic evidence on renegotiations comes from Latin America. By the end of 2013, 68 percent of the infrastructure PPPs in Latin America had been renegotiated at least once (78 percent in the transport sector and 41 percent in the electricity sector) (table 4.1). Data from all PPPs in Brazil, Chile, and Portugal and from 22 of the 33 transport PPPs in Peru (representing 93 percent of total initial investments commitments) yield similar results, with the renegotiation rate ranging from 56 percent to 91 percent. A global sample of 146 PPPs shows a renegotiation rate of 33 percent (58 percent for the Latin American PPPs), with transport PPPs renegotiated more frequently than electricity sector PPPs (GIH 2018). Within the transport sector, road PPPs appear to be renegotiated more often than other PPPs. All 13 highways in Peru and all 13 roads in Portugal were renegotiated, and 21 of 25 highway PPPs in Colombia were renegotiated.

Most renegotiations occur shortly after the awarding of the contract. They can be viewed as resetting the terms of the partnership. The average time to first renegotiation in Latin America was 1.0 year among the PPPs renegotiated by 2013; the global average was 3.6 years. Transport projects seem to be renegotiated sooner than energy projects, and the average time to

**TABLE 4.1**   Renegotiation rate and average years to first renegotiation, globally and in selected countries in Latin America, by period and sector

| Country or region | Period | Sector | Renegotiation rate (percent) | Average years to first renegotiation | Source |
|---|---|---|---|---|---|
| Brazil | 2006–16 | All | 64 | n.a. | Neto, Cruz, and Sarmento (2017) |
| | | Transport | 58 | 2.4 | |
| Chile | 1997–2020 | All | 56 | 4.3 | Engel and others (2022) |
| Colombia | 1993–2010 | Roads | 84 | 1.0 | Bitran, Nieto-Parra, and Robledo (2013) |
| Peru | 2001–20 | Transport | 91 | n.a. | Based on data from Marchesi (2022) |
| | | Roads | 100 | n.a. | |
| | | Airports | 75[a] | n.a. | |
| | | Ports | 66[a] | n.a. | |
| | | Urban rail | 100[a] | n.a. | |
| Portugal | 1984–2008 | All | 67 | 6.3 | Cruz and Marques (2013) |
| | | Transport | 51 | 3.3 | |
| | | Roads | 100 | 2.4 | |
| | | Railways | 100[a] | 3.7[a] | |
| | | Ports | 14 | 7.0[a] | |
| | | Energy | 19 | 15.0[a] | |
| Latin America | 1990–2013 | All | 68 | 1.0 | Guasch and others (2014) |
| | | Transport | 78 | 0.9 | |
| | | Electricity | 41 | 1.7 | |
| Global | 2005–15 | All | 33 | 3.6 | Global Infrastructure Hub (2018) |
| | | Transport | 42 | n.a. | |
| | | Electricity | 24 | n.a. | |

*Source:* Original table for this publication.
*Note:* "All" includes all sectors covered by the study indicated. Definition of infrastructure may differ from that used in this report.
n.a. = Not available.
a. Calculated using fewer than four projects.

renegotiate road sector PPPs appears to be the shortest. In Portugal it took 2.4 years to renegotiate a road PPP contract on average; a longer period elapsed before PPPs in the railway, port, energy, and other infrastructure sectors were renegotiated.

Frequent and early renegotiations may be a symptom of poor project planning and preparation. Project-specific factors—such as insufficient assessment of design and construction risks or problems encountered in securing right-of-way—may lead to early renegotiation of contracts to accommodate the realized risks. Excess risk allocation to the concessionaire may result in bankability problems, which may prohibit the concessionaire from achieving financial closure; the government may step in to assume some of the risk, so that financing can be secured. It can do so by raising tariffs or fiscal transfers, making capital subsidies available for the concessionaire during construction, or increasing availability payments.

## The fiscal risks and costs of renegotiations

PPP contract renegotiations usually favor the concessionaire and pose a fiscal risk for the government. In many countries, the concessionaire can negotiate with the government bilaterally, without competition. For example, before the 2010 reform (described below), renegotiation outcomes in Chile were often the outcome of bilateral agreements between the private partner and the Ministry of Public Works. Renegotiations usually ended with government payments, increases in revenues from user fees, and contract extensions. In the energy sector, renegotiations usually ended with tariff increases. In the transport sector, the most common outcome was additional government payments for changes in the scale and scope of the project (Guasch 2004; Cruz and Sarmento 2021; GIH 2018).

Renegotiations pose a significant fiscal risk, as suggested by data from Chile. Figure 4.6 shows the cost of additional works agreed through renegotiations of PPPs in Chile between 1997 and 2020 (the year refers to the year of the renegotiation). These numbers should be interpreted as lower bounds of the fiscal costs from renegotiations, as no concessionaire would agree to additional works unless it is compensated for the additional cost; it is possible that the government ended up overcompensating the concessionaire, given the concessionaire's stronger bargaining power, particularly before the changes implemented by the 2010 reform. Compensation took the form of additional payments by the Ministry of Public Works,[5] additional revenues from user fees (through an extension of the PPP or change in the revenue sharing rule), reductions in payments to the Ministry of Public Works, or a combination of the three.

The costs of renegotiations were much higher than those of guarantees. Between 1997 and 2020, 55 of the 98 PPP contracts in Chile were renegotiated (189 times in total). Thirty-two PPP contracts were renegotiated a total of 70 times by the end of their construction (Engel and others 2022). Between 1997 and 2020, the annual cost of renegotiations was 0.2–0.5 percent of GDP in three years and exceeded 0.5 percent in two years, with an average over the period of 0.14 percent of GDP. In all but three years, the costs of renegotiations were 2–54 times the costs of minimum revenue guarantees. The cumulative cost of renegotiations at the end of 2020 amounted to 2.1 percent of 2020 GDP. In contrast, the cumulative cost of guarantees amounted to just 0.18 percent of 2020 GDP.

**FIGURE 4.6**    Costs of renegotiation of PPPs in Chile, 1997–2020

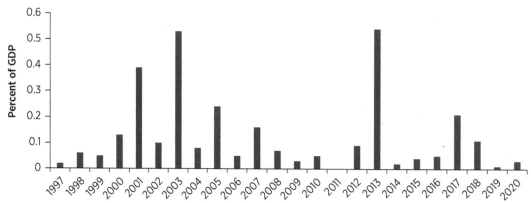

*Source:* Engel and others 2022.
*Note:* Renegotiation costs were 0 in 2011. GDP = gross domestic product; PPP = public-private partnership.

**FIGURE 4.7**    Annual fiscal costs of renegotiation of PPPs in Peru, 2006–20

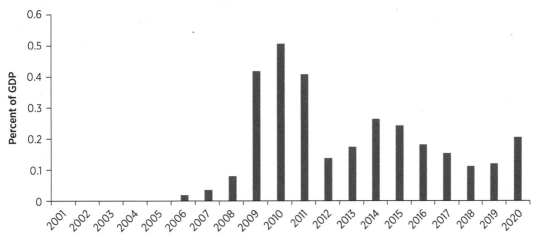

*Source:* Original figure for this publication, based on data from Marchesi 2022.
*Note:* Peru incurred no renegotiation costs between 2001 and 2005, although there were PPPs. GDP = gross domestic product; PPP = public-private partnership.

The fiscal costs of renegotiations were high and persistent in Peru, as evidenced by data collected for this study. Figure 4.7 presents actual government payments, including payments to concessionaires and payments for land acquisition, because of changes in the scale and scope of PPP projects. Between 2009 and 2011, the fiscal cost of renegotiations exceeded 0.4 percent of GDP; it remained above 0.1 percent of GDP every year between 2012 and 2020. Between 2006 and 2020—the period over which Peru's transport PPP portfolio matured—the average fiscal cost was 0.2 percent of GDP. The resulting cumulative costs related to additional payments amounted to 2.9 percent of 2020 GDP. The fiscal risks from renegotiations were significantly higher than the risks from guarantees.

In Peru, PPP contracts are amended through renegotiations between the line ministry and the concessionaire but require the approval of the sector regulator and the Ministry of Finance (Marchesi 2022). According to OSITRAN, the transport regulator, the main reasons for amending contracts have been changes in technical details, loss of funding, loss of concession assets, budget difficulties, the need for additional payments to the operator, the granting of contract extensions, land expropriation, arbitrage disputes, tariff setting, and revenue sharing (Aguirre 2015).

Although formal dispute-resolution processes did not create any fiscal costs in Peru until the end of 2020, there is a significant litigation risk from active disputes related to transport and electricity PPPs. As of 2022, there were nine active International Centre for Settlement of Investment Disputes (ICSID) cases related to 13 transport and electricity PPPs against the government of Peru. In these cases, concessionaires' claims totaled more than $1.2 billion. Four additional hydroelectric power plants (Alli, Ayanunga, Karpa, and Kusa) are in domestic arbitration under the jurisdiction of Lima's Chamber of Commerce. The claims in three of the ICSID cases are not available, and the data on the domestic litigations processes are not publicly available; the actual risk may therefore be significantly higher. One of the projects involved, Chinchero Airport–Cusco, has already been terminated; the dispute over it poses an additional early termination risk of $284 million. For the active projects, the ICSID claims

**TABLE 4.2**   Fiscal cost of renegotiations in Chile, Colombia, Peru, and Portugal

| Country | Period | Sector | Fiscal cost as percent of GDP in latest year in period | Fiscal cost as percent of planned cost |
|---------|--------|--------|--------------------------------------------------------|----------------------------------------|
| Chile | 1997–2020 | All | 2.1 | 31 |
| Colombia | 1993–2010 | Roads | 2.4 | 85 |
| Peru | 2001–20 | Transport | 2.9 | 36 |
| Portugal | 1984–2008 | Roads and railways | 1.8 | 25 |

*Source:* Original table for this publication, based on data from Engel and others 2022; Marchesi 2022; Bitran, Nieto-Parra, and Robledo 2013; and Cruz and Marques 2013.
*Note:* GDP = gross domestic product.

amount to at least $931 million, including $572 million in the first arbitration case concerning Lima Metro Line 2, where ICSID has already found the government liable for damages but is yet to rule on compensation (Marchesi 2022).

Fiscal costs incurred by Chile and Peru are not unique; renegotiations have resulted in comparable or higher fiscal costs as a percent of GDP in other countries (table 4.2). In Colombia, the total fiscal cost of PPP road sector renegotiations between 1993 and 2010 was 2.4 percent of annual GDP (Bitran, Nieto-Parra, and Robledo 2013). In Portugal, renegotiations of road and rail PPPs granted between 1984 and 2008 cost the government about 1.8 percent of GDP (Cruz and Marques 2013). The additional fiscal costs from renegotiations are significant compared with the original scale of the projects (see table 4.2).

### Evidence on the determinants of renegotiations

Transport PPPs are more likely to be renegotiated than energy PPPs, and the renegotiations are more likely to result in direct fiscal transfers. One of the reasons for this difference is that the level of competition is higher in the energy sector (Guasch 2004). Governments may be able to find an alternative electricity provider when an independent power producer fails. In contrast, the services a road provides can rarely be replaced by another existing road. This higher level of asset specificity gives more bargaining power to transport concessionaires.

Another reason for the difference is that electricity tariffs paid by final consumers are regulated and can be readily adjusted to ensure the profitability of electricity PPPs, even of transmission and generation PPPs. In Peru, for example, even though transmission projects are awarded on the basis of required payments for investment and maintenance of the infrastructure, concessionaires are compensated through electricity tariffs that are routinely adjusted to make the concessionaire whole. In contrast, the revenues of transport PPPs come from direct users or government payments, and it is usually politically difficult to increase tolls or railway fares. For this reason, transportation projects in Peru have been renegotiated frequently, leading to substantial direct fiscal payments (Marchesi 2022).

Energy sector renegotiations can also impose a fiscal cost on governments, especially in times of macroeconomic distress. In the face of financial crises in developing economies in the late 1990s and early 2000s, some governments renegotiated their energy tariffs, which spiked to unaffordable levels, because they were indexed to hard currencies. In most of Asia, renegotiations ended with partial nationalizations and subsidies to concessionaires. In Latin America, most governments froze tariffs without compensation, but many of these cases ended up being adjudicated in international arbitration, where they were effectively renegotiated through the dispute-resolution process, if not cancelled (Reside and Mendoza 2010).

Contractual factors, such as investment requirements, also increase the incidence of PPP contract renegotiations. PPP contracts often include investment requirements in monetary terms in addition to or instead of performance requirements. These requirements sometimes become contentious and lead to renegotiations when the desired performance is not achieved, and the concessionaire and the contracting authority cannot agree on the monetary value of a physical investment (Guasch 2004). When investment requirements are significant, the return of a PPP becomes more sensitive to market-related shocks, which impose an unavoidable cost (Guasch, Laffont, and Straub 2008). Rigidity in the contract creates a reason (or a pretext) for renegotiations.

Electoral cycles affect renegotiations by increasing the incentives for politicians and concessionaires to act opportunistically, both before and after elections. Evidence shows that incumbents are more willing to renegotiate PPP contracts during election cycles (Aguirre 2015), as more infrastructure investment may appeal to voters. An incumbent is willing to pay a premium to the concessionaire for the political benefit, especially as most of the additional burden falls on future administrations (Engel, Fischer, and Galetovic 2019). In Chile, for example, more than 60 percent of the costs of renegotiations fall on future administrations (Engel and others 2022). There is also evidence that renegotiations increase after the election year, as newly elected governments implement their policy priorities through PPPs (Guasch 2004).

Better regulatory institutions reduce the incidence and cost of renegotiations. In countries with better bureaucratic quality and an independent PPP regulatory body, PPP contracts tend to be renegotiated less frequently (Guasch, Laffont, and Straub 2008). Better regulatory quality and institutions and an independent PPP regulatory body allow more resources to be allocated to prepare new contracts and monitor ongoing projects, improving the effectiveness of contract management. There is also evidence that such institutions may provide stronger bargaining power to the contracting authority and allow it to make more credible commitments, reducing opportunistic behavior. Better regulatory institutions reduce both concessionaire- and government-led renegotiations (Guasch and Straub 2009).

Corruption is associated with a higher incidence of renegotiations led by concessionaires and a lower incidence of renegotiations led by the government. When the concessionaire needs a term in a contract changed after the awarding of the contract, it can do so through bribes and other corrupt dealings. The more corrupt the environment, the easier it is for governments and private parties to strike ex ante deals that favor the concessionaire (Guasch and Straub 2009).

Higher corruption is associated with higher fiscal costs from renegotiated contracts. Evidence from the Odebrecht case in Brazil shows that in projects in which the company paid bribes, project costs rose almost 71 percent, at the expense of government finances (Campos and others 2021).[6] In many countries struggling with corruption, only a few companies obtain a majority of the contracts from the government, signaling returns to scale to investing in bargaining power with the government.

### Evidence on governance reforms to reduce fiscal risks from renegotiations

Strengthening the legal, regulatory, and contractual approaches can help governments reduce fiscal risks from renegotiations, as experiences in Chile, Colombia, and Peru show. All three countries experienced significant fiscal risks from renegotiations, and all of them implemented reforms to their PPP governance frameworks in the 2010s to reduce those risks. Thanks to their efforts in improving their governance frameworks, the three countries occupy the top three places in Latin America in the 2019 Infrascope ranking of the environment for PPPs (EIU 2019). According to the World Bank's 2020 *Benchmarking Infrastructure Development Report*, Chile ranked 3rd, Peru 8th, and Colombia 18th in PPP contract management in the world (World Bank 2020a).

In all three countries, early PPP projects were contracted under general procurement laws that enabled private provision of public infrastructure services. The first law that allowed PPPs in Chile was passed in 1982, but no PPPs were contracted until the law was amended in the 1990s. The amended law shifted more risk to the government while creating an institutional infrastructure to manage PPP contracts by creating a PPP unit under the Ministry of Public Works (Engel and others 2022). Early PPP projects in Colombia were contracted using the general government procurement law of 1993; the government started implementing PPPs soon after the law's enactment (CAF 2018). The first few concessions in Peru were initiated in 1994, under the general regulatory framework, which promoted private investments in the country. The first law specific to private investment in infrastructure services was passed in 1996, but it was only after the establishment of a centralized agency in 2002, which facilitated the development of investment projects, that a significant number of PPPs started to be developed, especially in the transport sector (CGR 2015).

The PPP portfolios in Chile, Colombia, and Peru grew rapidly; the inadequacy of the initial frameworks made renegotiations pervasive and a serious source of fiscal risk. In Chile, the Ministry of Finance struggled to restrain the bilateral renegotiations between the concessionaire and the Ministry of Public Works. Concessionaires could use a supervening event as a reason for renegotiating contracts; the law allowed for contract renegotiations to be initiated immediately after contract signing. Renegotiations usually involved some of the following in exchange for new investments: direct fiscal transfers from the budget to the concessionaire, spread across multiple years; reduction in some investments; term extensions; early participation of the private party in toll revenues from public projects; and reductions in contracted payments to the Ministry of Public Works (Engel and others 2022).

The 1993 law in Colombia ordered the state to preserve the financial equilibrium of the original contract, which effectively assigned all construction risk (such as geological, land acquisition, and environmental risks) to the government and allowed unlimited fiscal transfers to be made to the concessionaire. The law limited total transfers to 50 percent of the original investment amount, but it could not be enforced. The 2007 amendment of the law lifted the fiscal transfer cap, instead limiting term extensions. Combined with poor project planning resulting from a lack of a coherent institutional structure and the government's willingness to modify or expand existing works for political reasons, PPP contracts were renegotiated frequently and early, costing the government a large share of the cost of infrastructure delivery (Bitran and others 2013; CAF 2018; Larrahondo C. 2017).

In Peru, the first law dedicated to PPPs was enacted in 2008. The high incidence of early renegotiations led to high fiscal costs, as acknowledged by Peru's comptroller general in 2015. The comptroller identified changes in the scope and scale of works, problems with financial closure, and land acquisition problems as the top three recurring issues leading to renegotiations. Although the 2008 law restricted renegotiations during the first three years after award of the contract, early renegotiations were still common, as legal exceptions were executed (CGR 2015). Right after enactment of the 2008 law, the global crisis erupted. To facilitate implementation of several priority projects—initially 12, later expanded to more than 52—various additional exemptions were granted to modify the contracts (World Bank 2022).

All three countries implemented reforms to their PPP governance frameworks in the 2010s. Chile amended its public works procurement law in 2010, in response to the endemic renegotiation of PPPs. Colombia passed a PPP law in 2012, after various institutional reforms in 2011 to facilitate the expansion of its PPP program while avoiding the problems faced by the earlier PPPs. Peru started to reform its PPP regime with a new PPP law in 2015. That law was modified in 2016 and the changes consolidated in 2018 in a third law.

The 2010 reform in Chile reduced the bargaining power of the concessionaire and the incentives to renegotiate. It reduced the concessionaire's bargaining power by eliminating the occurrence of a supervening event as grounds for renegotiation and requiring all risk not expressly allocated to the government to be assumed by the concessionaire, except for unforeseeable acts of government that were specific to the PPP sector and significantly reduced the profitability of the project. The amendment also reduced the incentives of both the concessionaire and the government to renegotiate by requiring any additional work to be procured in a competitive auction. The upper bound for bids is based on the unit prices from the original contract. The concessionaire is allowed to make a lower offer for the additional works after bids are opened, which can be contested by a lower offer from the lowest bidder in the auction. This procedure reduced both the expected gains of the concessionaire from triggering a renegotiation and the government's temptation to use renegotiations as an easy way to expand infrastructure investment (Engel and others 2022).

The PPP reform in Chile created an independent expert panel to mediate any contractual conflict and issue a recommendation. If the parties do not accept the recommendation, they can still appeal to the Arbitration Commission for PPPs. The panel is also tasked with reviewing any renegotiations that exceed 25 percent of the original investment value, which acts as another check on renegotiations with high fiscal costs (Engel and others 2022).

With the 2010 PPP reform, variable-term present-value-of-revenue (PVR) contracts became a standard option in Chile rather than a scheme to be used in exceptional cases. In a PVR procurement auction, the contracting authority sets the tariff schedule and the discount rate, and firms bid on the lowest PVR (Engel, Fischer and Galetovic 2020). The resulting contract has a variable term: the concessionaire is guaranteed to receive its present discounted value bid over the period that sufficient demand materializes, reducing the market-related risk of the concessionaire and the renegotiation risk from the PPP.

The reforms in Colombia aimed at increasing project planning capacity, limiting the expansion of projects' scope and scale, and clarifying the distribution of risks. The institutional reforms created a PPP agency responsible for transport PPPs, an environmental licensing authority, an infrastructure coordination commission, and a national development bank to improve project development. The National Planning Department was tasked with performing value-for-money analysis to rationalize the use of PPPs over public procurement. To tackle the fiscal risks from renegotiations directly, the new law lowered the cap on fiscal contributions from any public source for additional works—including implicit contributions resulting from project extensions—to 20 percent of the contracted value of the project.

The Colombian government shifted some of the construction risks to the concessionaire, reducing the government's liability from such risks and the concessionaire's incentives for renegotiation. For example, contracts for new road concessions stipulate that if the additional costs for land acquisition, environmental licenses, and related expenses are no more than

20 percent of the estimated costs, the concessionaire has to cover them in full. If the additional costs exceed 20 percent of the estimated costs of these items, the concessionaire and the government will bear them jointly, with the concessionaire paying no more than 44 percent of the estimated additional costs. A similar risk allocation scheme, with different cutoffs, is stipulated for geological risks (CAF 2018; DNP 2021).

In Peru, the new PPP laws made the project preparation process more rigorous. The new laws introduced extensive evaluation and reporting requirements in the project preparation phase, including more stringent land acquisition requirements: 100 percent of the land needed to be available for single-site projects and at least 30 percent for linear settings such as road, railway, and transmission PPPs (World Bank 2020b, 2022). These changes were aimed at avoiding past mistakes in project preparation that led to costly renegotiations for the government in the form of payments for additional works and land expropriation and changes to the funding schemes.

The new laws in Peru increased the authority of the Ministry of Finance over approval of contracts and renegotiations. The laws tasked the Ministry with approving the project plans at every stage of the PPP project cycle, including inclusion of the project in the pipeline, first and final drafts of the contract, and any modification of the contract after its awarding if the modification could have any fiscal consequences. Before the new law, the Ministry had been responsible only for approving the final version of the contract (World Bank 2020b). The new laws ensure that the Ministry of Finance shares its views about project affordability from the start and approves any modifications resulting from renegotiations.

Empirical evidence from Chile suggests that the 2010 PPP reform reduced the costs and incidence of renegotiations. Figure 4.8 shows the renegotiation costs as a percent of total costs and the number of renegotiated PPP contracts as a percent of the total number of projects for renegotiations during construction, by type of project before and after the 2010 reform. The reason for focusing on renegotiations during construction is to avoid

**FIGURE 4.8**   **Number of renegotiated fixed- and variable-term contracts in Chile during construction and costs of renegotiations, before and after the 2010 reform**

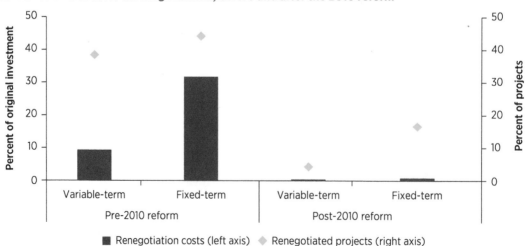

*Source:* Engel and others 2022.

overstating the renegotiation costs before the 2010 reform, as the average project initiated before 2010 is well into operation while the average project initiated after 2010 has only recently started operations. Furthermore, focusing on renegotiations during construction is a good test of whether the more problematic early renegotiations can be avoided under the new law.

Even after controlling for the change in the composition of project types, the 2010 reform in Chile dramatically reduced renegotiations and the costs associated with them during construction. Before the 2010 reform, renegotiation costs made up about 32 percent of total project costs for fixed-term contracts; after the reform, they accounted for only 0.87 percent of the total costs of fixed-term contracts. A similar effect can be seen in variable-term contracts. Renegotiation costs represented only 0.44 percent of the total costs after the reform, down from 9.4 percent before. The frequency of renegotiations declined for both types of projects as well, from about 38.0 percent to 4.3 percent for variable-term contracts and from 44.0 percent to 16.7 percent for fixed-term contracts. Variable-term contracts were less frequently renegotiated than fixed-term contracts, and their renegotiated costs were much lower, both before and after the reform.

The effect of the 2010 reform in Chile does not seem to be confined to the early years of construction. Figure 4.9 shows renegotiated costs during the first six years after construction as a percent of original investment requirements before and after the reform. For highway, transport, and all PPPs, renegotiation costs during the first six years of operations decreased to 0.9–1.2 percent, an order of magnitude lower than the 14.0–16.5 percent before the 2010 reform. These results imply that the 2010 reform appears to have had long-term effects.

The new legal and regulatory framework enabled a new generation of road PPPs in Colombia. Forty-six projects were contracted between 2014 and 2017, up from 23 before the reform, worth almost four times the value of the earlier projects (CAF 2018). Although most of these projects were in the construction phase, nine of the new contracts were modified by 2018, six of them as a result of disputes (Rodríguez Porcel and others 2018). Although the new system

**FIGURE 4.9**   **Renegotiation costs in Chile during first six years of operation, before and after the 2010 reform, by sector**

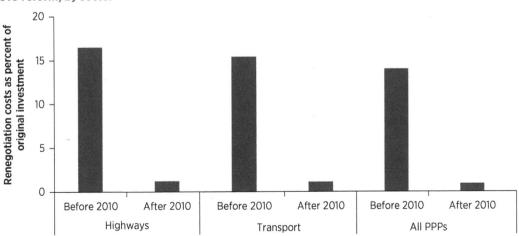

*Source:* Engel and others 2022.
*Note:* PPP = public-private partnership.

is not renegotiation proof, the early renegotiations seem to be less frequent than they had been in earlier periods, when renegotiations occurred for almost all projects, on average within just a year of contract award.

In Peru, the new PPP reform led to better project development and oversight at the expense of slower project development. Additions to the PPP portfolio dropped significantly after 2016, although the country still has a full pipeline (World Bank 2022). Since 2016, 13 electricity PPPs and 2 transport PPPs have been implemented nationally (Marchesi 2022).

More data are needed to evaluate the causal effects of the reforms, but the evidence indicates that Peru is taking a more cautious approach to its project preparation although there are indications that the Ministry of Finance will not shy away from using its new powers. Based on the authority given to it by the 2018 law, it rejected the contract modification resulting from a renegotiation of a municipal road project, on the grounds that the municipality did not have the budgetary capacity to shoulder the resulting costs, there was a lack of clarity that could cause arbitration, and the new anti-corruption clause was not strict enough.[7]

## EARLY TERMINATION OF PPPs

When renegotiations fail, PPPs are terminated early, often leading to sizable fiscal costs. Almost 3 percent of power and transport PPPs in developing countries (151 PPPs) were terminated early between 1990 and 2020.[8] This share is small, but terminations can be costly, because they tend not to be isolated events. Only 26 percent of the cancelled power and transport PPPs were isolated events: 25 power and transport PPPs were cancelled in India in 2012–14, 15 in Mexico in 1996–97, 9 in China in 2002–04, 6 in Brazil in 2004–06, 5 in Malaysia in 2001–02, and 5 in China in 1999–2001 (figure 4.10).

**FIGURE 4.10**   **Number of early terminations of PPPs in developing countries, 1990–2020**

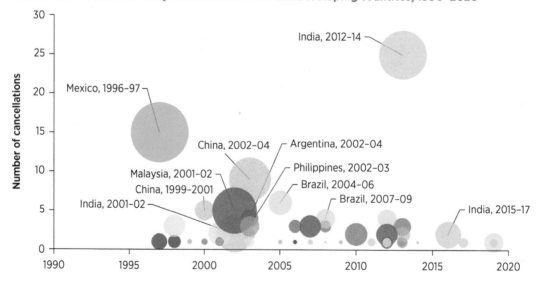

*Source:* Original figure for this publication, based on data from the PPI Database.
*Note:* The size of the bubbles represents total investment in the cancelled PPPs, and each color represents a country. The bubbles that cover several years are centered at the middle of the period (the second year if only two years are covered). Only the largest bubbles have been labeled. PPP = public-private partnership.

There are three main reasons for early termination of PPPs: the government's default or voluntary termination of the project, the private partner's default or breach of contract, and force majeure. Governments are generally exposed to obligations from the debt and equity financing of an infrastructure project when the PPP is terminated early; as the ultimate guarantor of the public infrastructure service, the government steps in to resolve the matter. The rationale for such involvement is that without explicit or implicit guarantees, private finance cannot be mobilized, especially in emerging markets and developing economies.

The government's exposure depends on the causes of termination. When the government defaults or a project is voluntarily terminated, the practice is to compensate the private party for the outstanding debt plus the equity return it had forecasted for the remainder of the contract (World Bank 2019). When the private partner defaults or is in breach of contract, the practice is to provide some compensation, on the grounds that without it, the government might be seen as enjoying windfall gains and would have a hard time attracting lenders and investors for PPP projects in general (EPEC 2013; World Bank 2019). Even in the case of its own default, the private partner may legally allege government responsibility, so the government becomes liable to compensate the private party or incur additional legal costs (World Bank 2019). In the case of force majeure, because the distress event is outside both parties' control, both parties should share the risk. The government is liable for less than full compensation and has the right to take over the relevant asset; the private partner loses any return on its invested equity and possibly some of the equity it invested (EPEC 2013; World Bank 2019).

A good practice for managing fiscal risks from early termination is to identify and set out in the contract the grounds for termination and their consequences. In the majority of the 140 economies surveyed in the World Bank's *Benchmarking Infrastructure Development 2020* report, the grounds for terminating the PPP contract and its consequences were well defined. In some countries, termination clauses favor the private party, creating significant fiscal costs (box 4.1).

In some cases, the contract establishes that the government needs to re-tender the PPP and use the proceeds to compensate the private party in the cancelled PPP. Such is the case in transmission PPP contracts in Peru. The government has 18 months to conduct up to two tendering processes in the case of early termination and use the proceeds to compensate the private party. Where it decides to re-tender the PPP even if it is not a requirement in the contract, the government faces a liability until the tendering is completed or fails, which could have a significant impact on the fiscal situation of the country.

### Features and drivers of early terminations

Analysis of all infrastructure PPP projects in low- and middle-income countries reveals that PPP projects are more likely to be cancelled early in the contract period. The risk of cancellation for a project increases rapidly until about 20 percent of the contract period elapses. It plateaus at this level before declining slightly until it reaches 50 percent. During the second half of the contract period, the risk of early termination decreases until the project approaches the end of the contract period, except for a small increase at about the 80 percent mark.

Airport, rail, and road PPPs were about five times more likely to be terminated early than electricity and port PPPs (figure 4.11). Road PPPs had high rates of early termination because of grossly overestimated demand coupled with difficulties in adapting contracts to changing macroeconomic conditions, and bidding processes that led to unrealistic financial conditions, as the experience in Brazil, India, and Mexico shows. In the case of rail PPPs, optimism bias also

**BOX 4.1    Termination clauses of PPPs favorable to the private party**

Compensation practices for contract termination vary across countries and sectors. In an airport project in Albania, if the project company defaults, the government takes on its liabilities. In road PPPs in Argentina, even if the company defaults, the government has to compensate the private party for the total accumulated unamortized project cost net of penalties charged to the private sponsor for failing to fulfill the contract. In India, road concession agreements do not foresee any compensation on equity in the case of default by the project company, but they stipulate that the National Highway Authority of India will pay 90 percent of the project company's debt due less insurance claims to the project company as termination payment. In road PPPs in Kenya, if the project company defaults, the government is liable for the debt due.

In the case of early termination of the contract by the government, many countries stipulate full compensation for the total accumulated investment and some measure of return on the invested equity. In Bulgaria, this type of compensation is written into the PPP law. In Albania and Kosovo, the private party is entitled to compensation on its debt, a share of the capital, and additional accumulated equity. In Kenya, the private party is due the net present value of the equity it invested in the project. In Peru, the concessionaire is entitled to the nonamortized value of the concession in the transport sector; in the case of electricity power purchase agreements (PPAs), it is entitled to the remaining value of the PPA. In road PPPs in Argentina, on top of the unamortized investments, the private sponsor receives a termination payment determined as the expected loss of the company as a result of loss of the concession contract. In India, in the case of default by the public authority, road concession agreements entitle the private sponsor to 150 percent of its equity, which is gradually adjusted downward as the project nears the end of its lifetime to reflect the decline in the expected total return on the equity initially invested.

In the case of force majeure, the contracts of road PPPs in Argentina mandate that the government compensate the private party for the entire accumulated investment amount without penalties. In Peru, the concessionaire is entitled to the nonamortized value of the concession. In India, in the case of a force majeure event indirectly caused by a political event, the private sponsor of a road PPP is entitled to 110 percent of the equity it invested in the project.

*Note:* PPP = public-private partnership.

led to early termination. Governments unrealistically assume that the private sector can earn enough on a low-traffic railway to pay for rehabilitation and maintenance of the infrastructure, and the private sector, when bidding, thinks it is going to increase the traffic more than it can.

The probability of early termination of brownfield projects is not statistically different from that of greenfield projects. Private sponsors tend to express a preference for brownfield projects because the returns of greenfield projects are uncertain. The results show that ex ante uncertainty about the return of projects is not necessarily associated with higher risk of early termination.

Larger projects are associated with a higher probability of early termination than smaller projects, except for the largest projects. The level of committed investment in physical assets is associated with a higher probability of early termination, as long as the investment is less than $3.4 billion. For investments in physical assets above $3.4 billion (about the 99th percentile of the project size distribution in the sample), the higher the investment, the lower the probability of early termination.

Contract design features can affect the probability of early termination. Government support that decreases financing risk is most effective in preventing early termination. Direct government

**FIGURE 4.11** **Impact of sector, type, and size of project on probability of early termination of PPPs**

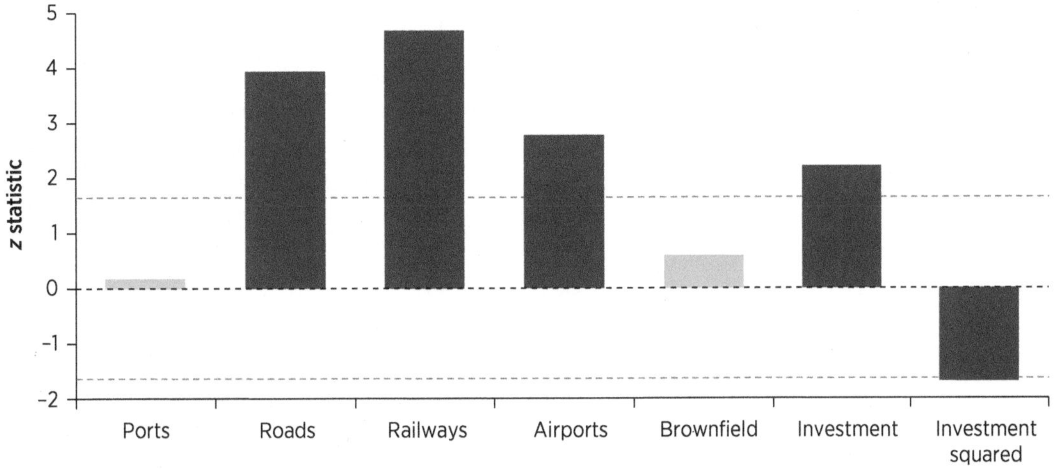

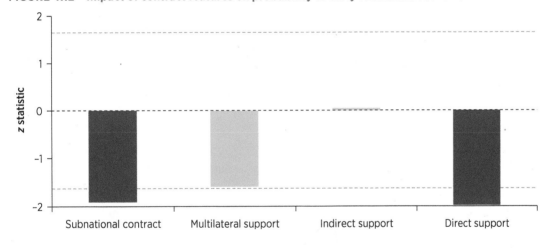

*Source:* Original figure for this publication, based on data from PPI Database, the Polity IV Project, World Development Indicators Database, and Laeven and Valencia 2020.
*Note:* Ports, roads, railways, and airports sector estimates are relative to electricity sector. Bars show the *z* statistic of the estimated parameter from the hazard regression (see appendix F). Blue bars indicate statistically significant impact; yellow bars indicate statistically insignificant impact. The dashed lines show the significance thresholds at 90 percent. PPP = public-private partnership.

**FIGURE 4.12** **Impact of contract features on probability of early termination of PPPs**

*Source:* Original figure for this publication, based on data from PPI Database, the Polity IV Project, World Development Indicators Database, and Laeven and Valencia 2020.
*Note:* Bars show the *z* statistic of the estimated parameter from the hazard regression (see appendix F). Blue bars indicate statistically significant impact; yellow bars indicate statistically insignificant impact. The dashed lines show the significance thresholds at 90 percent. PPPs = public-private partnerships.

support, including capital and revenue subsidies and in-kind transfers, is associated with a lower probability of early termination (figure 4.12). Indirect government support, which includes various guarantees to the sponsors, has no discernible effect on the probability of early termination. Support from multilateral organizations seem to reduce the probability of early termination, but the coefficient is not statistically different from zero at standard levels.

PPPs with subnational governments, such as states and provinces, are less likely to face early termination than PPPs with central governments. This finding may reflect better project selection at the subnational level, as local authorities may understand local problems better or oversee projects better because of their proximity. It may also be the case that national governments tend to engage in risky projects because they can better bear the termination risk from an individual PPP project, thanks to a more diversified PPP portfolio and fiscal resources. In India, for example, all of the highway projects that were cancelled between 2012 and 2015 were PPPs with the central government. State governments continued to enter into successful PPPs for road construction and operation.

Country-level characteristics and shocks can affect the probability of early termination. Greater constraints on the executive branch are associated with lower probability of early termination (figure 4.13). When the government can exercise authority without adequate checks and balances, it leaves PPPs vulnerable to expropriation by the government through a change in policy or political takeover, leaving the project susceptible to policy and political risks (Irwin 2007; Grimsey and Lewis 2017). When the constraints on the executive are not stringent enough, the contract loses its value in mediating the relationship between the government and the private party, leaving the project more susceptible to cancellation.

Deviation of the annual depreciation rate from its long-run average—a surprise local currency depreciation—is associated with a higher risk of cancellation. Irwin (2007) notes that exchange rate risk affects infrastructure investment in two ways. First, many infrastructure PPPs, such as those in power generation, use inputs priced in foreign currency. Second, given insufficient local savings and underdeveloped local currency markets in most low- and

**FIGURE 4.13**   **Impact of country-level characteristics and shocks on probability of early termination of PPPs**

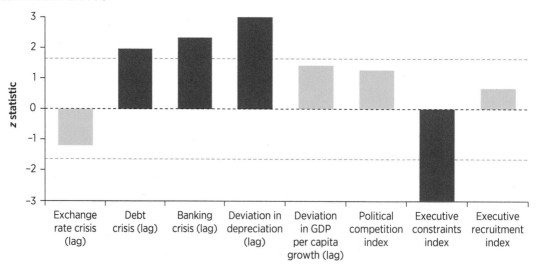

*Source:* Original figure for this publication, based on data from PPI Database, the Polity IV Project, World Development Indicators Database, and Laeven and Valencia 2020.
*Note:* Bars show the *z* statistic of the estimated parameter from the hazard regression (see appendix F). Blue bars indicate statistically significant impact; yellow bars indicate statistically insignificant impact. Lag indicates previous year's value. The dashed lines show the significance thresholds at 90 percent. GDP = gross domestic product; PPP = public-private partnership.

middle-income countries, financing of long-term infrastructure projects usually relies on debt denominated in foreign currency and revenues in local currency. The currency mismatch between revenues and costs can push the project company to insolvency very quickly if the local currency sharply depreciates.

The occurrence of systematic banking and debt crises is associated with higher rates of early termination. A systematic banking crisis undermines the ability of financial institutions to provide the financing needed to sustain long-term infrastructure projects. A debt crisis can limit the government's ability to fund PPP projects according to the terms of the contracts. It may hinder the ability of a local private party to secure debt financing through the market and increase the cost of its outstanding debt, leading to early termination of PPP projects. Because of the long-term nature of PPPs and the high transactions costs of preparing, procuring, and awarding them, both parties try to negotiate changes to the contract or some kind of compensation in response to negative macro-financial shocks. Early termination occurs only if the parties cannot reach an agreement, hence the lag in the impact of macro-financial shocks.

### Fiscal costs and risks from early termination

Early terminations are less frequent than renegotiations, but their fiscal costs tend to be larger. In Mexico, cancellations of toll roads created a significant cost for the Treasury, including a 1.6 percent of GDP debt assumption in 1997 (Bova and others 2019). The government of India paid $2.4 billion for the cancelled Dabhol Power Project in 2001 (Pratap and Chakrabarti 2017). Analysis undertaken for this report using the value-at-risk approach estimates the maximum expected loss from early termination of PPP portfolios with 99 percent confidence (that is, the 99 percent value-at-risk).[9] It estimates that fiscal risks from early termination of the current portfolios of electricity and transport PPPs in a sample of 17 low- and middle-income countries (box 4.2) were as high as 2.8 percent of 2020 GDP (9 percent of 2020 government revenues), under stable macroeconomic conditions.

The analysis looks at low, medium, and high scenarios. In the low scenario, the government covers 79.3 percent of the PPP's debt in the event of early termination, the average ultimate recovery rate of debt to PPPs estimated by Moody's Investor Service (2019). The government does not cover the loss of private equity, losing only its own equity in the PPP. In the medium scenario, the government covers the entire debt and private equity, thereby guaranteeing the total financing of the project. This outcome is equivalent to compensating the project company for the accumulated investment amount in the PPP. In the high scenario, on top of the debt, the government compensates the private party for 150 percent of the equity it invested in the project, in line with the contract terms used in some countries, such as India.

Among the sample countries, the fiscal risks from early termination of active PPPs as a share of 2020 GDP are highest in Brazil, Peru, and Albania (figure 4.14). Over the lifetime of the PPP portfolio, the fiscal risks are 0.87–2.78 percent of GDP in Brazil, 0.44–1.19 percent in Peru, and 0.44–1.17 percent in Albania. Indonesia (0.37–0.64 percent), Ghana (0.26–0.52 percent), and Kosovo (0.20–0.49 percent) follow. Although the size of the PPP portfolio amounts to more than 15 percent of GDP in the Solomon Islands, the fiscal risk associated with its portfolios is just 0.24–0.33 percent of GDP. These figures represent the amount, as a percent of 2020 GDP, each government needs to put aside today in a contingency fund to cover the maximum expected loss over the entire contract period with 99 percent confidence.

**BOX 4.2   Countries included in the analysis**

The analysis in this section examines public-private partnerships (PPPs) in electricity, airports, railways, roads, and ports in 17 of the 19 low- and middle-income countries studied in chapter 3. Figure B4.2.1 presents the size of the PPP portfolio as a percent of gross domestic product (GDP) as of December 2021, in these countries. Brazil, with its large PPP portfolio (698 projects), and Albania rank at the top, with active PPP portfolios representing 22.7 percent and 19.3 percent of their GDP, respectively. Peru's PPP portfolio amounts to 15.6 percent of GDP, and the Solomon Islands' single active PPP represents about 15.2 percent of its GDP. Bhutan, Ghana, South Africa, Argentina, Kosovo, Georgia, and Indonesia follow, with active portfolios reaching at least 5 percent of their GDP. The PPP portfolios of Ethiopia and Burundi represent less than 1 percent of their GDP.

**FIGURE B4.2.1**   Size of PPP portfolios as a percent of GDP in selected developing countries, as of the end of 2021

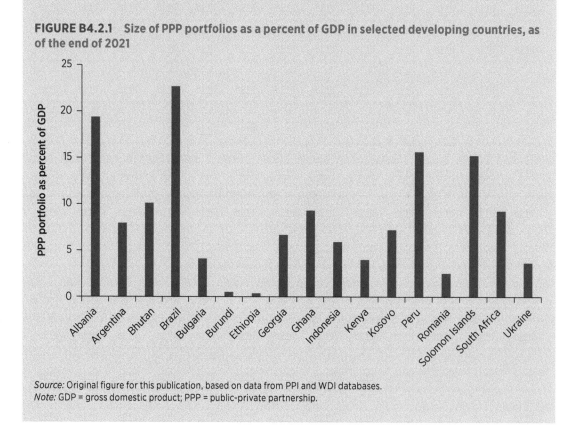

*Source:* Original figure for this publication, based on data from PPI and WDI databases.
*Note:* GDP = gross domestic product; PPP = public-private partnership.

The amount in the contingency fund needs to be adjusted every year, because projects age, changing the probability of early termination; some PPPs reach the end of their contract; and new PPPs are awarded.

Although there is an apparent relationship between the size of the PPP portfolio (figure B4.2.1) and the fiscal risk from early termination of PPPs in a country (see figure 4.14), the relationship is significantly influenced by the determinants of early termination discussed in the previous section. Fiscal risks under the high scenario range from 2.2 to 12.2 percent of the size of the PPP portfolio for the countries in the sample. The highest incidence ratio is for

**FIGURE 4.14** Fiscal risks from early termination of PPPs as a percent of GDP in selected countries

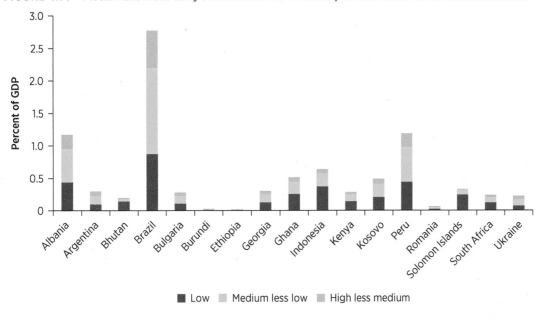

■ Low ■ Medium less low ■ High less medium

*Source:* Original figure for this publication, based on analysis of data from PPI Database, the Polity IV Project, World Development Indicators Database, and Laeven and Valencia 2020.

*Note:* Fiscal risks are the maximum expected loss over the entire contract period with 99 percent confidence, expressed as a percent of GDP of a single year. The low scenario assumes that 79.3 percent of a PPP's debt (the average ultimate recovery rate of debt to PPPs estimated by Moody's Investor Service [2019]) is covered by the government in the event of early termination and no private equity is covered. The medium scenario assumes that the government covers all debt and private equity. The high scenario assumes that on top of the debt, the government compensates the private party for 150 percent of the equity it invested in the project. The estimations for Ukraine do not consider the impact of the Russian invasion. GDP = gross domestic product; PPP = public-private partnership.

Brazil; Indonesia—where the fiscal risk from early termination of PPPs amount to 10.8 percent of the size of the portfolio under the high scenario—is a close second.

The greater likelihood of early termination and the larger size of transport PPPs leads to higher fiscal risks from early termination of transport PPPs than electricity PPPs. The average fiscal risks of the portfolios' size is 6–14 percent of GDP in the transport sector and 2–4 percent of GDP in the power sector, depending on the scenario. In all countries where there are transport and electricity PPPs except South Africa, the fiscal risks from early termination as a percent of total investments are larger for transport PPPs than for electricity PPPs.

Figure 4.15 presents the fiscal risks for different periods, all starting at the end of 2020, as a percent of 2020 GDP. The largest fiscal risk is in Brazil, followed by Peru and Albania or Ghana, depending on the scenario. The fiscal risk in Brazil is about 1.2 percent of 2020 GDP in 2022–26, 43 percent of the fiscal risks over the lifetime of the portfolio. The maturity of the portfolios drives the share of total fiscal risks that are specific to 2022–26. For countries with more mature portfolios, such as Brazil, Ghana, Kenya, Kosovo, South Africa, and Ukraine, 37–53 percent of the fiscal risks are concentrated in 2022–26. In Argentina, which implemented 95-year electricity distribution projects in the 1990s, only 23–33 percent (depending on the scenario) of the fiscal risks are concentrated in 2022–26.

Expressing the fiscal risks as a percent of annual government revenues gives an idea of the fiscal challenge each country could face. Brazil's fiscal risks are 2.74–8.71 percent of annual

**FIGURE 4.15 Cumulative low, medium, and high fiscal risks from early termination of PPP portfolio as a percent of GDP in selected countries, 2022–26**

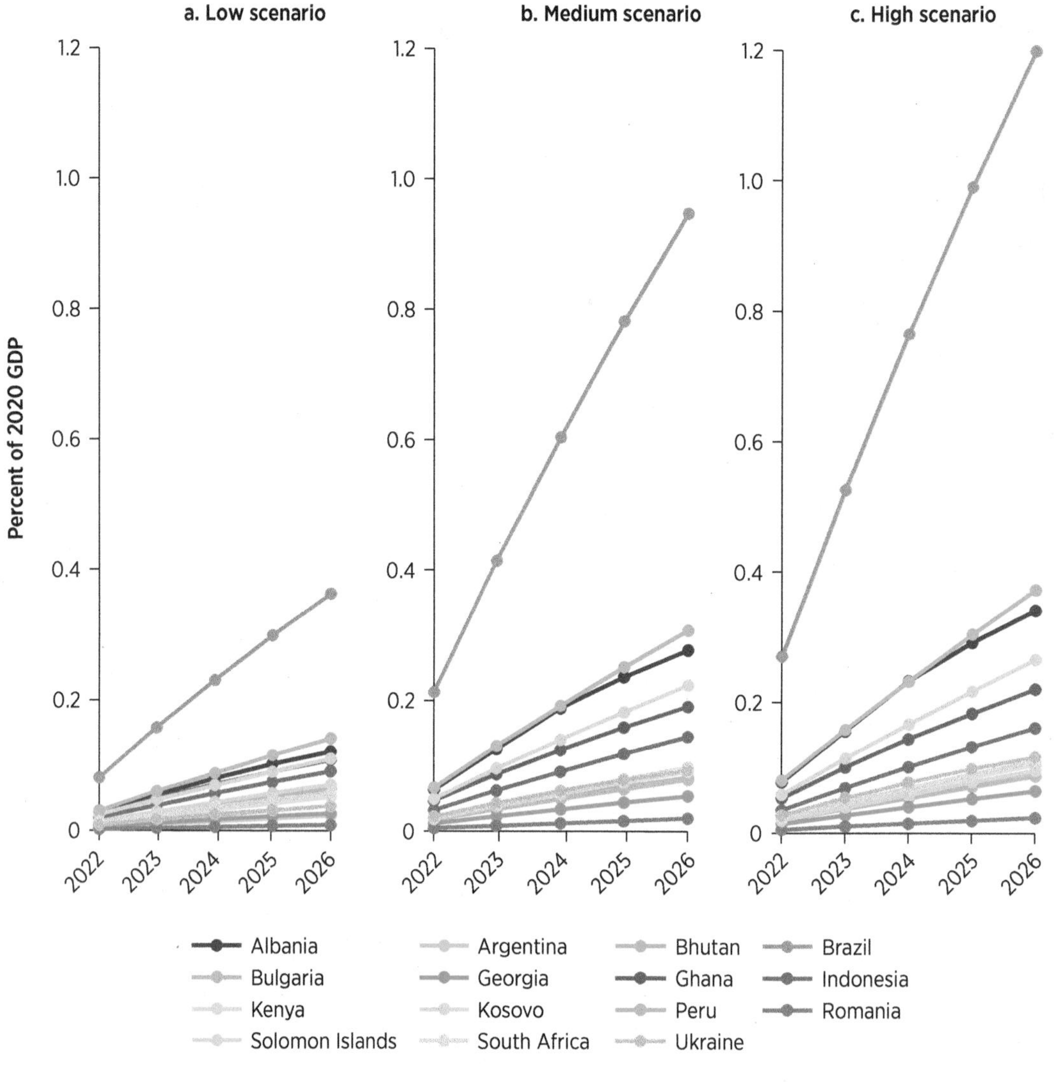
a. Low scenario
b. Medium scenario
c. High scenario
Percent of 2020 GDP
1.2
1.0
0.8
0.6
0.4
0.2
0
2022
2023
2024
2025
2026
Albania
Argentina
Bhutan
Brazil
Bulgaria
Georgia
Ghana
Indonesia
Kenya
Kosovo
Peru
Romania
Solomon Islands
South Africa
Ukraine

*Source:* Original figure for this publication, based on analysis of data from PPI Database, the Polity IV Project, World Development Indicators Database, and Laeven and Valencia 2020.
*Note:* Each data point represents the maximum expected loss from early termination of the PPP portfolio with 99 percent confidence over the period starting at the end of 2021 and ending at the end of the corresponding year, as a percent of 2020 GDP. Figure excludes Burundi and Ethiopia, for which the highest fiscal risk estimates did not reach 0.01 percent of GDP. The low scenario assumes that 79.3 percent of the PPP's debt (the average ultimate recovery rate of debt to PPPs estimated by Moody's Investor Service [2019]) is covered by the government in the event of early termination and no private equity is covered. The medium scenario assumes that the government covers all debt and private equity. The high scenario assumes that on top of the debt, the government compensates the private party for 150 percent of the equity it invested in the project. The estimations for Ukraine did not take into account the impact of the Russian invasion. GDP = gross domestic product; PPP = public-private partnership.

government revenues, depending on the scenario (figure 4.16). The fiscal risks as a percent of government revenues in Peru are much closer to those of Brazil when expressed as a percent of GDP. When expressed as a percent of annual government revenues, the fiscal risks from early termination of PPPs in Ghana and Indonesia become more prominent; in Indonesia,

**FIGURE 4.16**    **Fiscal risks from early termination of PPP portfolio as a percent of government revenue in selected countries**

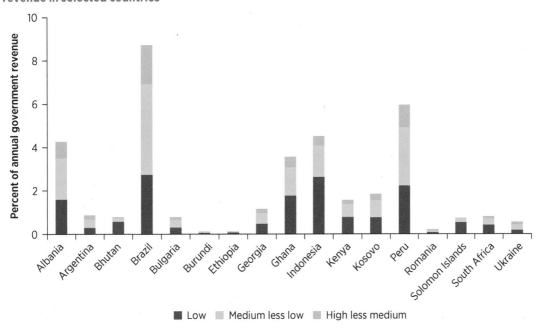

*Source:* Original figure for this publication, based on analysis of data from PPI Database, the Polity IV Project, World Development Indicators Database, and Laeven and Valencia 2020.
*Note:* Fiscal risks are the maximum expected loss over the entire contract period with 99 percent confidence, expressed as a percent of annual government revenue. The low scenario assumes that 79.3 percent of a PPP's debt (the average ultimate recovery rate of debt to PPPs estimated by Moody's Investor Service [2019]) is covered by the government in the event of early termination and no private equity is covered. The medium scenario assumes that the government covers all debt and private equity. The high scenario assumes that on top of the debt, the government compensates the private party for 150 percent of the equity it invested in the project. The estimations for Ukraine do not take into account the impact of the Russian invasion. PPP = public-private partnership.

they surpass the fiscal risks in Albania. These risks are as high as 3.56 percent of GDP in Ghana and 4.51 percent of GDP in Indonesia.

### Fiscal risks under macro-financial shocks

Early terminations are procyclical, as negative macro-financial shocks increase the probability of early termination of PPPs, which increases fiscal risks. Analysis conducted for this report simulates the impact of a negative macro-financial shock. The simulation assumes a 48.3 percentage point depreciation shock and the occurrence of both a banking and a debt crisis in year 0. Such a profound macroeconomic crisis is similar to some crises in emerging markets and developing economies that led to early termination of many PPPs.[10] The PPP portfolio of each country is assumed to be that at the end of 2021.

A profound macroeconomic crisis in year 0 would significantly increase the fiscal risks from early termination of PPPs, particularly the first year after the shock. The year after the shock, the fiscal risks would be 11.7–19.2 times the fiscal risks without a shock (figure 4.17), with an average ratio of 15.9. Relative to the case without a shock, South Africa would experience the largest increase in fiscal risks and Brazil would experience the smallest increase. Given the size of Brazil's portfolio and the magnitude of its fiscal risks without a macroeconomic shock, its fiscal risks could be as high as 6.1 percent of 2020 GDP in the immediate aftermath of the shock.

**FIGURE 4.17**  Increase in fiscal risks from early termination of PPP portfolio associated with a profound macro-financial shock

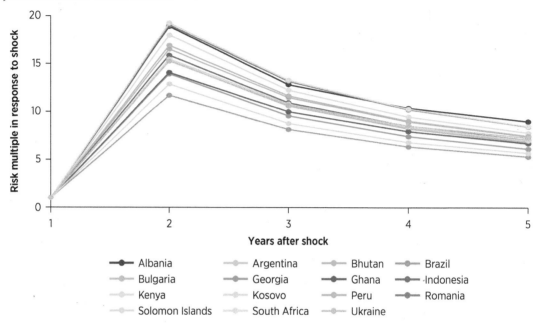

*Source:* Original figure for this publication, based on analysis of data from PPI Database, the Polity IV Project, World Development Indicators Database, and Laeven and Valencia 2020.
*Note:* Each data point represents the ratio of the maximum expected losses from early termination of the PPP portfolio with 99 percent confidence level over the period starting in year 0 and ending in the corresponding year with a severe adverse shock to that without a shock under the high scenario. The estimations for Ukraine do not take into account the impact of the Russian invasion. PPP = public-private partnership.

## FRAMEWORKS FOR MANAGING FISCAL RISKS FROM PPPs

Clear, robust, and firmly enforced project governance and decision-making procedures can help mitigate fiscal risks from PPPs.[11] However, most countries do not follow best practices in the preparation, procurement, and management of PPP contracts, as the World Bank's *Benchmarking Infrastructure Development 2020* shows. Relative to the benchmark of 100, the global average scores for preparation, procurement, and contract management for PPP projects among 140 countries are 44, 63, and 63, respectively (World Bank 2020a).

Globally, most countries do not have systems to plan and account for the fiscal liabilities originating from PPPs. Only 37 percent of governments have systems in place to budget for the liabilities from PPPs, and only 26 percent have systems to report such liabilities (figure 4.18). Adoption of national accounting conventions specific to liabilities from PPPs is also low, at 36 percent. Most countries with an accounting system in place are members of the European Union and must adhere to the European System of Accounts. It requires governments to account for PPP–related liabilities if the public sector retains substantial risk in the project. Only 9 of the 140 countries have adopted the more stringent International Public Sector Accounting Standards, which requires a PPP to be consolidated in the public sector's balance sheet if the public retains control over the service or has a residual interest in the project (World Bank 2020a).

**FIGURE 4.18**    **Percent of countries with systems for budgeting, reporting, and accounting for PPP liabilities**

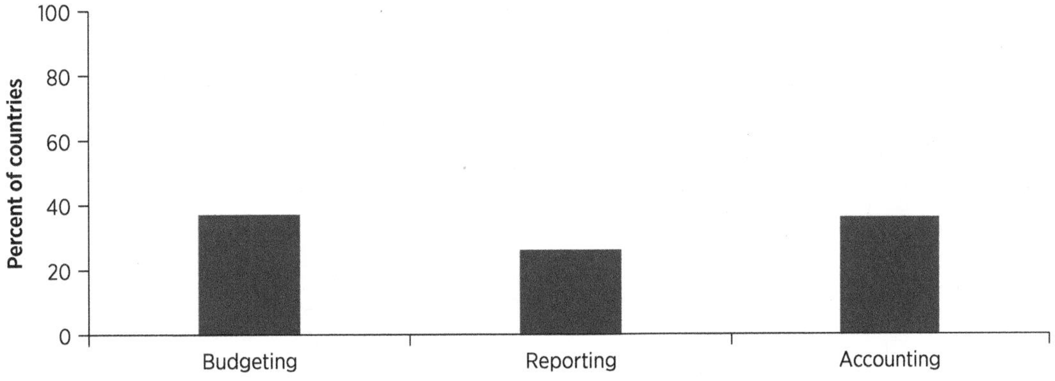

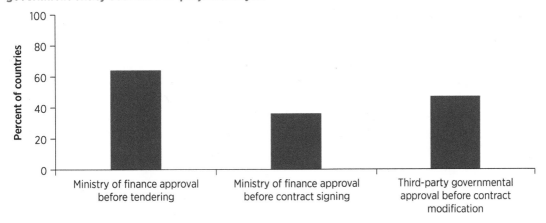

*Source:* World Bank 2020a.
*Note:* PPP = public-private partnership.

**FIGURE 4.19**    **Percent of countries requiring approval by ministry of finance or other third-party government entity over the PPP project lifecycle**

*Source:* World Bank 2020a.
*Note:* PPP = public-private partnership.

The oversight authority of the ministry of finance or other third-party government entity responsible for the fiscal risks from PPPs over the project lifecycle is limited in most countries. In 64 percent of countries, a project requires approval from the ministry to be included in the pipeline; only 36 percent of countries require ministry approval of the final version of the contract before signing (figure 4.19), and only 16 percent need approval from the ministry for renegotiations. In many countries, governments thus set the terms of the partnership and later modify them without the knowledge or say of the fiscal authorities.

Most countries assess multiple dimensions of a PPP during the planning phase, but these requirements are generally not based on established methodologies, which would systematize the process and make it less error prone. For example, 81 percent of countries require a fiscal affordability assessment before implementing a PPP, but only 58 percent have a standardized methodology for doing so (figure 4.20). Only 24 percent of countries require assessment of the procurement strategy.

**FIGURE 4.20** Percent of countries requiring assessment of selected aspect of PPP projects during planning and using established methodology for assessment

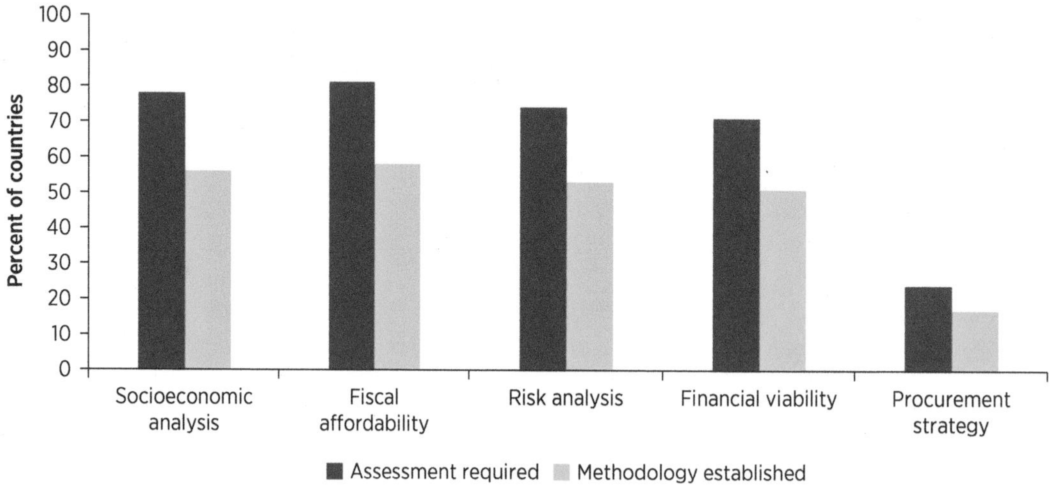

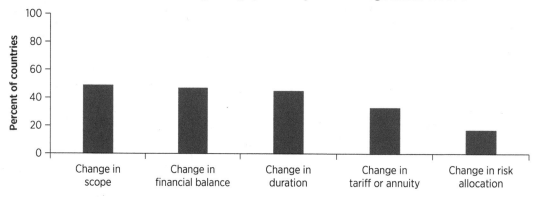

■ Assessment required ■ Methodology established

*Source:* World Bank 2020a.
*Note:* PPP = public-private partnership.

**FIGURE 4.21** Percent of countries regulating specific aspects of renegotiation of PPPs

*Source:* World Bank 2020a.
*Note:* PPP = public-private partnership.

Most countries do not regulate specific effects of PPP contract renegotiations, although 90 percent regulate contract renegotiations (World Bank 2020a). Less than half of countries regulate changes in PPPs' scope, risk allocation, financial balance, duration, and revenues (figure 4.21). Only 39 percent set a threshold for increases in scope that need to be tendered separately (World Bank 2020a).

Some legal and regulatory frameworks fail to capture various events that pose fiscal risks. For example, 25 percent of the countries studied do not regulate force majeure events, and 29 percent do not specify the consequences of early termination of a PPP contract (figure 4.22). Only 55 percent of the sample countries regulate lender step-in rights, which have the potential to help governments avoid fiscal risks from early terminations

**FIGURE 4.22**    **Percent of countries regulating important events potentially affecting PPPs**

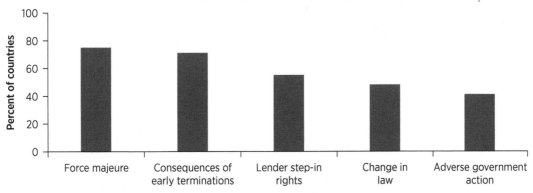

*Source:* World Bank 2020a.
*Note:* PPP = public-private partnership.

by letting creditors take over the concession when a project company defaults. Even fewer countries regulate the effects of government actions such as material adverse government actions and changes in law.

## IN SUM

Shifting risks and responsibilities to the private sector through infrastructure PPPs does not insulate the fiscal accounts from financing pressures related to that infrastructure. On the contrary, the off-budget nature of PPPs and the accounting challenges presented by the contingent nature of the liabilities can lead to significant fiscal surprises. It is therefore important that governments identify and manage fiscal risks from infrastructure PPPs to avoid unpleasant surprises.

The evidence on fiscal risks from demand guarantees, renegotiations, and early terminations points to some stylized facts on their relative likelihoods and magnitudes that can inform risk management decisions by governments.[12] Renegotiations tend to be small, repeated drains of fiscal resources. Annual fiscal costs amounted to less than 0.6 percent of GDP in the countries studied. These figures are lower bounds, however, because the countries studied are among the best in the world in terms of PPP governance. Demand guarantees do not usually represent significant fiscal risks, particularly if projects are properly structured.

Early terminations are less frequent than renegotiations, but the fiscal risks from them can be substantial—0.1–2.8 percent of 2020 GDP in most countries studied—partly because they are usually not isolated events. The fiscal risks from early termination are highly procyclical. A negative macroeconomic shock can increase the fiscal risk from early terminations in the immediate aftermath of the shock by a factor of 12–19.

Transport PPPs are more likely to be renegotiated and terminated early than electricity PPPs. Some contract characteristics, such as direct government support, can reduce the probability of early termination. Robust project selection and demand forecasting and flexible term contracts can reduce the cost of demand guarantees. Demand guarantees can also reduce the fiscal risks from renegotiation and early termination, by allocating demand risk to the government. Strong and independent regulatory institutions that limit political interference in planning, design, procurement, and contract management and strong anti-corruption measures can reduce the fiscal risks from PPPs. Robust macroeconomic management is key for overall management of fiscal risks from PPPs.

PPPs can help emerging markets and developing economies expand their infrastructure stock, build required infrastructure more efficiently, and maintain it more effectively over the long run. These benefits need to be weighed against the fiscal costs of PPPs to assess the net benefits of PPPs. Fiscal costs that need to be included in such analysis, in addition to those included in this chapter, are the costs of direct liabilities, such as availability payments, and the transactions costs of PPPs. The fact that renegotiations and early terminations are important sources of fiscal risks shows that transactions costs over the life of a PPP are high and need to be considered (data on such costs are very hard to obtain, however).

## NOTES

1. Dollar figures are expressed in 2020 US dollars, inflated using the US Consumer Price Index (CPI) series.
2. See https://ppi.worldbank.org/en/ppidata.
3. A study by the IMF and World Bank Group (IMF and WBG 2019) identifies 11 risk categories and 48 subcategories.
4. All figures are in 2014 billion won. See Kim and others (2011) for project details and payments between 2001 and 2007. Data on minimum revenue guarantee data for 2008–14 were collected from reports of the PPP's parent company, the Macquarie Korea Investment Fund, as reported by the Regulatory News Service of the London Stock Exchange until the fund's delisting in 2016.
5. Before the 2010 reform, 56 percent of the renegotiated amounts were compensated through payments by the Ministry of Public Works (Engel and others 2022).
6. The cost data on Odebrecht includes both PPPs and direct procurement contracts.
7. The private party in the project is a consortium that included Odebrecht (World Bank 2022).
8. The share increases to 3.5 percent and 242 projects if water, information and communications technology, and natural gas are included.
9. For a brief discussion of the methodology see appendix F. For a more detailed discussion, see Herrera Dappe, Melecky, and Turkgulu (2022).
10. The systematic banking crises dataset of Laeven and Valencia (2020) identifies 104 banking crisis episodes among the countries included in the PPI Database, 13 of which also involved sovereign debt and currency crises. During these 13 episodes, the maximum annual deviation in the depreciation rate from its long-run average ranged from 15.1 to 116.0 percentage points, with an average of 48.3 percentage points.
11. This section is based on World Bank (2020a).
12. These findings should be taken as stylized facts that vary across countries based on the characteristics of the PPP contracts, portfolios, and governance.

## REFERENCES

Aguirre, Julio C. 2015. "Electoral Cycles and Renegotiation of Transport Infrastructure Concession Contracts." In *The Economics of Infrastructure Provisioning: The Changing Role of the State*, edited by Arnold Picot, Massimo Florio, Nico Grove, and Johann Kranz, 315–37. Cambridge, MA: MIT Press.

Bitran, Eduardo, Sebastián Nieto-Parra, and Juan Sebastián Robledo. 2013. "Opening the Black Box of Contract Renegotiations: An Analysis of Road Concessions in Chile, Colombia and Peru." Working Paper 317, OECD Development Centre, Organisation for Economic Co-operation and Development, Paris.

Bova, Elva, Marta Ruiz-Arranz, Frederik Giancarlo Toscani, and Hatice Elif Ture. 2019. "The Impact of Contingent Liability Realizations on Public Finances." *International Tax and Public Finance* 26 (2): 381–417.

CAF (Development Bank of Latin America). 2018. *Public-Private Partnership in Latin America. Facing the Challenge of Connecting and Improving Cities.* Bogota.

Campos, Nicolás, Eduardo Engel, Ronald D. Fischer, and Alexander Galetovic. 2021. "The Ways of Corruption in Infrastructure: Lessons from the Odebrecht Case." *Journal of Economic Perspectives* 35 (2): 171–90.

CGR (Contraloría General de la República). 2015. *Causas y efectos de las renegociaciones contractuales de las asociaciones público-privadas en el Perú.* Lima.

Cruz, Carlos Oliveira, and Rui Cunha Marques. 2013. "Exogenous Determinants for Renegotiating Public Infrastructure Concessions: Evidence from Portugal." *Journal of Construction Engineering and Management* 139 (9): 1082–90.

Cruz, Carlos Oliveira, and Joaquim Mirando Sarmento. 2021. *The Renegotiations of Public Private Partnerships in Transportation: Theory and Practice.* Cham, Switzerland: Springer.

DNP (Departamento Nacional de Planeación). 2021. *Public Private Associations–APP–in Infrastructure in Colombia.* Bogota. https://colaboracion.dnp.gov.co/CDT/Participacin%20privada%20en%20 proyectos%20de%20infraestructu/Official%20March%202021.pdf.

Engel, Eduardo, Martín Ferrari, Ronald Fischer, and Alexander Galetovic. 2022. "Managing Fiscal Risks Wrought by PPPs: A Simple Framework and Some Lessons from Chile." Policy Research Working Paper 10056, World Bank, Washington, DC.

Engel, Eduardo, Ronald Fischer, and Alexander Galetovic. 2019. "Soft Budgets and Endogenous Renegotiations in Transport PPPs: An Equilibrium Analysis." *Economics of Transportation* 17: 40–50.

Engel, Eduardo, Ronald Fischer, and Alexander Galetovic. 2020. "When and How to Use Public-Private Partnerships in Infrastructure: Lessons from International Experience." NBER Working Paper 26766, National Bureau of Economic Research, Cambridge, MA.

EIU (Economist Intelligence Unit). 2019. *The 2019 Infrascope: Evaluating the Environment for Public-Private Partnerships in Latin America and the Caribbean.* London.

EPEC (European PPP Expertise Centre). 2013. *Termination and Force Majeure Provisions in PPP Contracts: Review of Current European Practice and Guidance.* Luxembourg.

Flyvbjerg, Bent. 2007. "Policy and Planning for Large-Infrastructure Projects: Problems, Causes, Cures." *Environment and Planning B: Planning and Design* 34 (4): 578–97.

GIH (Global Infrastructure Hub). 2018. *Managing PPP Contracts after Financial Close: Practical Guidance for Governments Managing PPP Contracts, Informed by Real-Life Project Data.* Sydney.

Grimsey, Darrin, and Mervyn K. Lewis. 2017. *Global Developments in Public Infrastructure Procurement: Evaluating Public-Private Partnerships and Other Procurement Options.* Cheltenham, United Kingdom: Edward Elgar.

Guasch, J. Luis. 2004. *Granting and Renegotiating Infrastructure Concessions: Doing It Right.* WBI Development Studies, World Bank Institute, Washington, DC.

Guasch, J. Luis, Jean-Jaques Laffont, and Stéphane Straub. 2008. "Renegotiation of Concession Contracts in Latin America: Evidence from the Water and Transport Sectors." *International Journal of Industrial Organization* 26 (2): 421–42.

Guasch, J. Luis, and Stéphane Straub. 2009. "Corruption and Concession Renegotiations. Evidence from the Water and Transport Sectors in Latin America." *Utilities Policy* 17 (2): 158–90.

Guasch, José Luis, Daniel Benitez, Irene Portabales, and Lincoln Flor. 2014. "The Renegotiation of PPP Contracts: An Overview of Its Recent Evolution in Latin America." Discussion Paper 2014-18, International Transport Forum, Organization for Economic Co-operation and Development, Paris.

Herrera Dappe, Matías, Martin Melecky, and Burak Turkgulu. 2022. "Fiscal Risks from Early Termination of Public-Private Partnerships in Infrastructure." Policy Research Working Paper 9972, World Bank, Washington, DC.

IMF (International Monetary Fund). 2007. *Manual on Fiscal Transparency.* Washington DC: International Monetary Fund.

IMF (International Monetary Fund), and WBG (World Bank Group). 2019. *PPP Fiscal Risks Assessment Model: PFRAM 2.0.* Washington DC: International Monetary Fund.

Irwin, Timothy C. 2007. *Government Guarantees: Allocating and Valuing Risk in Privately Financed Infrastructure Projects.* Directions in Development: Infrastructure. Washington, DC: World Bank.

KGM (T.C. Karayolları Genel Müdürlüğü). 2018. *2017 Faaliyet Raporu.* T.C. Ulaştırma, Denizcilik ve Haberleşme Bakanlığı. Ankara, Türkiye.

KGM (T.C. Karayolları Genel Müdürlüğü). 2019. *2018 Faaliyet Raporu*. T.C. Ulaştırma ve Altyapı Bakanlığı. Ankara, Türkiye.

KGM (T.C. Karayolları Genel Müdürlüğü). 2020. *2019 Faaliyet Raporu*. T.C. Ulaştırma ve Altyapı Bakanlığı. Ankara, Türkiye.

KGM (T.C. Karayolları Genel Müdürlüğü). 2021. *2020 Faaliyet Raporu*. T.C. Ulaştırma ve Altyapı Bakanlığı. Ankara, Türkiye.

KGM (T.C. Karayolları Genel Müdürlüğü). 2022. *2021 Faaliyet Raporu*. T.C. Ulaştırma ve Altyapı Bakanlığı. Ankara, Türkiye.

Kim, Jay-Hyung, Jungwook Kim, Sunghwan Shin, and Seung-yeon Lee. 2011. *Public-Private Partnership Infrastructure Projects: Case Studies from the Republic of Korea, vol. 1: Institutional Arrangements and Performance*. Manila: Asian Development Bank.

Laeven, Luc, and Fabian Valencia. 2020. "Systematic Banking Crises Database II." *IMF Economic Review* 68: 307–61.

Larrahondo C., Paola A. 2017. "The Fourth Generation of Road Concessions in Colombia and the New PPP Legal Model: What Have We Learnt from Over-Renegotiation and Over-Litigation Trends?" *Revista de Derecho Público* 38.

Marchesi, Giancarlo. 2022. "Fiscal Cost and Risks of Electricity and Transport PPPs: The Case of Peru." Background paper prepared for this report. World Bank, Washington, DC.

Moody's Investor Service. 2019. *Default and Recovery Rates for Project Finance Bank Loans, 1983–2017*.

National Treasury. 2021. *Budget Review 2021*. Pretoria. http://www.treasury.gov.za/documents/national%20budget/2021/review/FullBR.pdf.

Neto, Dimas de Castro e Silva, Carlos Oliveira Cruz, and Joaquim Mirando Sarmento. 2017. "Understanding the Patterns of PPP Renegotiations for Infrastructure Projects in Latin America: The Case of Brazil." *Competition and Regulation in Network Industries* 18 (3–4): 271–96.

Pratap, Kumar V., and Rajesh Chakrabarti. 2017. Public-Private Partnerships in Infrastructure: Managing the Challenges. Singapore: Springer

Reside, Renato E., and Amado M. Mendoza. 2010. "Determinants of Outcomes of Public-Private Partnerships (PPP) in Infrastructure in Asia." Discussion Paper 2010-03, University of Philippines, School of Economics. Quezon.

Rodríguez Porcel, Manuel, Ana María Pinto Ayala, Natalia Ariza, Ginette Lozano, Julián Márquez, Paula Castillo, and Ricardo de Vecchi. 2018. *Participación privada en infraestructura: Su evolución en Colombia y el apoyo del grupo BID*. Banco Interamericano de Desarrollo.

Sayıştay (T.C. Sayıştay Başkanlığı). 2020. *Karayolları Genel Müdürlüğü 2019 Yılı Sayıştay Denetim Raporu*. Ankara, Türkiye.

Sayıştay (T.C. Sayıştay Başkanlığı). 2021. *Karayolları Genel Müdürlüğü 2020 Yılı Sayıştay Denetim Raporu*. Ankara, Türkiye.

UAB (T.C. Ulaştırma ve Altyapı Bakanlığı). 2019. *Ulaştırma ve Altyapı Bakanlığı 2018 Yılı Faaliyet Raporu*. Ankara, Türkiye.

UAB (T.C. Ulaştırma ve Altyapı Bakanlığı). 2020. *Ulaştırma ve Altyapı Bakanlığı 2019 Yılı Faaliyet Raporu*. Ankara, Türkiye.

UAB (T.C. Ulaştırma ve Altyapı Bakanlığı). 2021. *2020 Yılı Ulaştırma ve Altyapı Bakanlığı Faaliyet Raporu*. Ankara, Türkiye.

UAB (T.C. Ulaştırma ve Altyapı Bakanlığı). 2022. *2021 Yılı Ulaştırma ve Altyapı Bakanlığı Faaliyet Raporu*. Ankara, Türkiye.

World Bank. 2017. *Public-Private Partnerships: Reference Guide Version 3*. Washington, DC: World Bank.

World Bank. 2019. *Guidance on PPP Contractual Provisions*. Washington, DC: World Bank.

World Bank. 2020a. *Benchmarking Infrastructure Development 2020: Assessing Regulatory Quality to Prepare, Procure, and Manage PPPs and Traditional Public Investment in Infrastructure Projects*. Washington, DC: World Bank.

World Bank. 2020b. *Policy Note on Attracting Private Investment to Infrastructure in Peru: Achievements, Challenges and a Way Forward*. Washington, DC: World Bank.

World Bank. 2022. *Managing the Fiscal Implications of Public Private Partnerships in a Sustainable and Resilient Manner*. Washington, DC: World Bank.

# A Reform Agenda to Create Sustainable Fiscal Space for Infrastructure

# 5

## MAIN MESSAGES

1. To close the infrastructure gap, governments need to create sustainable fiscal space for infrastructure, by mitigating the fiscal risks from infrastructure, in order to get more out of their spending envelopes. Doing so requires fixing the flaws in infrastructure governance that create perverse incentives and building adequate capacity in government to mitigate the risks that cannot be eliminated or that the government is best placed to deal with.

2. A reform agenda to mitigate fiscal risks from infrastructure should follow a four-pronged approach that implements robust integrated public investment management, establishes an effective fiscal and corporate governance of state-owned enterprises (SOEs), implements a robust public-private partnership (PPP) framework, and undertakes integrated fiscal risk management. Building capacity and ensuring transparency and accountability should be central in each of these areas. The actions under each component need to be tailored to the sources of risk and the institutional and socio-political characteristics of each country, as well as to government capacity.

## INTRODUCTION

Closing the infrastructure gap requires getting more out of spending envelops for infrastructure by mitigating fiscal risks from infrastructure. In some countries, doing so may also entail raising additional budget revenues. This report and the reform agenda put forward in this chapter focus on risk mitigation.

The fiscal risks of infrastructure come from a combination of vulnerability to exogenous shocks and the prevalence of perverse incentives faced by government officials, SOE managers, and private partners, which lead to moral hazard and principal–agent problems. Any reform agenda to mitigate the fiscal risks from infrastructure should therefore aim to remove the flaws in infrastructure governance giving rise to the perverse incentives and strengthen the capacity to mitigate the risks that cannot be eliminated or that the government is best placed to deal with. Creating adequate incentives requires transparency to observe and control the actions of all agents and accountability of all stakeholders.

**FIGURE 5.1    Building blocks of a reform agenda to mitigate fiscal risks from infrastructure**

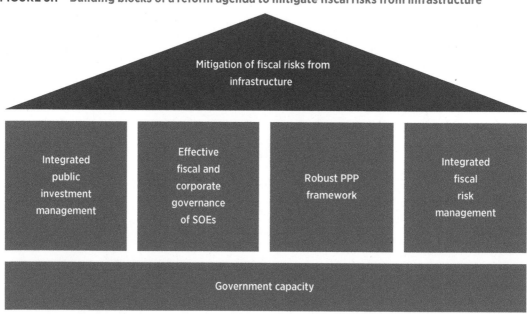

*Source:* Original figure for this publication.
*Note:* SOE = state-owned enterprise; PPP = public-private partnership.

Any reform agenda to mitigate fiscal risks from infrastructure should include the four building blocks shown in figure 5.1 and be grounded in an effort to build government capacity.

The proposed reform agenda includes both macro-fiscal and infrastructure-specific reforms, with some reforms specific to a particular provision modality and others covering all modalities. Most reforms are broadly applicable to both the electricity and transport sectors, with reforms specific to a provision modality more relevant to sectors that rely more heavily on that modality.

## INTEGRATED MANAGEMENT OF FISCAL RESOURCES AND RISKS

Creating sustainable fiscal space for infrastructure requires managing fiscal resources and risks efficiently. Fiscal resources and risks should be managed in an integrated manner—that is, across government, sectors, and provision modalities—for several reasons. First, there is one pool of fiscal resources for the entire government. Decisions by one government authority—such as a transport authority awarding PPPs—have fiscal implications that the ministry of finance will have to deal with and that may affect the fiscal resources available to other sectors and provision modalities. Second, lack of a unified framework can lead to incoherent decisions regarding investment selection across sectors and government authorities, undermining efficiency in the use of fiscal resources. Third, there are potential interactions across risks and portfolio effects. For example, macroeconomic shocks lead to cuts in infrastructure spending, particularly capital spending; turn SOEs into a drag on the budget; and significantly increase the risks from renegotiation and early termination of PPPs. As a result, when fiscal space is limited, SOEs and PPPs can put more stress on a country's fiscal position.

This section describes possible policy and institutional reforms to mitigate fiscal risks through integrated management of fiscal resources and risks from infrastructure.

### Integrated public investment management

Integrated public investment management (PIM) is key to the integrated management of fiscal resources and risks. Investments through direct public provision and PPPs are often managed through different systems and institutions. Both should fall within the scope of the PIM system, because both use public financial resources, even if only on a contingent basis.

In the case of investments by SOEs, the government's interest, as a shareholder, in ensuring good governance and sound financial performance of its commercial SOEs may be better exercised separately from PIM, reflecting the distinct legal status of SOEs and the shareholder–management relationship implied by their corporatized status. However, SOE investments may be included in PIM in certain cases. If a government is financing SOE investments to achieve public policy objectives (that is, a compensated quasi-fiscal operation), such investments should fall within the scope of the PIM system. In countries in which SOE governance is still in the early stages of development, there may be a case for extending the scope of PIM to SOEs (Kim, Fallov, and Groom 2020).

Integration requires cohesive decision-making, a standard methodology to examine the need for government intervention to address a given situation, and a single appraisal manual for all investments. Under an integrated PIM system, infrastructure investments need to be identified and appraised based on their alignment with the country's development goals and the investment's net economic benefits, independently of the provision modality that ends up being used. Once investments are appraised, the best provision modality for each investment should be selected, based on fiscal affordability and value for money.

International experiences in infrastructure planning vary, with some countries adopting more decentralized decision-making models and others more centralized ones (Allen and others 2020). Some have gone back and forth between the two models. Line ministries are generally in charge of preparing infrastructure investment proposals for their sectors; their review and consolidation into national plans is typically the responsibility of a central agency, which may be the ministry of finance, a separate ministry of planning, or a unit in the office of the prime minister or president. Although there is no clear evidence in favor of one approach or another, strong involvement of the ministry of finance in the process is essential to ensure that the plans are consistent with funding and financing availabilities.

Weaknesses in the project appraisal and selection phases of the infrastructure investment process need to be addressed. Clear, technically sound, and consistently applied methodologies to vet proposed infrastructure projects are key to ensuring good value for money and reducing the risk of wasting scarce budgetary resources on white elephants. The limited availability of relevant data and technical capacities significantly constrains the use of full-fledged cost–benefit analysis of project proposals, however, especially in low- and middle-income countries. Simpler methods—such as focusing only on cost comparisons for alternative proposed projects or weighing alternatives on the basis of multiple qualitative or quantitative indicators of projected impacts—are often used, despite being technically inferior and providing more scope for discretion.[1] Whatever method is used, it is important that it be clearly specified and made publicly available to promote accountability in its use. Over time, investing in the development of the required databases and staff capacities can yield significant returns in terms of improved appraisal and selection of investment projects.

Sound appraisals need to be supported by selection processes that give weight to the appraisal's findings. Although these processes cannot be fully insulated from socio-political influences, which may lead to the selection of lower-ranked projects or a suboptimal modality, it is important that they at least respect minimum acceptability thresholds set out in the appraisal methodology. Independent review of project proposals is important in this respect, with the ministry of finance playing a gatekeeping role in the PIM system.

An integrated PIM system should include an overall fiscal management framework covering all public investments. It should assess the fiscal affordability of all investments and control the aggregate amount of fiscal commitments allocated to direct provision, PPPs, and SOE investments, if covered by the PIM. The framework should include accounting and reporting standards that ensure that the impact of PPPs on the main fiscal aggregates is the same as that of purely publicly financed projects, such as International Public Sector Accounting Standards (IPSAS) (the penultimate section in this chapter presents recommendations for including PPPs in the fiscal management framework).

Most countries, including many advanced economies, can benefit from better integration of investment planning and budgeting. A key step in this direction is the adoption of sufficiently disaggregated rolling medium-term fiscal frameworks (MTFFs) and medium-term expenditure frameworks (MTEFs) to guide the annual budget process.[2] MTEFs should incorporate the information contained in sectoral and national plans regarding policy priorities for infrastructure investments. Doing so is easier when the plans are of a rolling nature. MTFFs and MTEFs should include PPPs, to ensure proper integrated planning.

Integrated project implementation and evaluation are key parts of an integrated PIM system. All investment projects should be subject to the same procurement rules and conditions. Governments should conduct ex post reviews of all projects, to assess how well project preparation and implementation have gone and to determine whether any part of the PIM needs adjustment.

The legal and institutional framework should facilitate integration. PIM units should be given the powers to deal only with matters specific to project implementation; they should not be given mandates to promote any specific implementation modality. Newly created PPP units should not be given roles that duplicate or supersede those of existing PIM institutions (Kim, Fallov, and Groom 2020). There is a need for clear guidance on practices, procedures, and roles and responsibilities of the main stakeholders to create an integrated PIM framework covering projects delivered through direct public provision, PPPs, and SOEs, if included.

### Integrated fiscal risk management

A well-functioning fiscal risk management system should provide the right information to the right people at the right time. To do so, it needs to identify, analyze, and disclose the fiscal risks; incorporate them in the budget; mitigate them; and monitor and review them. Most of these tasks are best handled in a centralized manner, by either the ministry of finance or a high-level interagency committee chaired by it. A weakness in many countries is the absence of a systematic and centralized approach to identifying, analyzing, and monitoring fiscal risks (Budina and Petrie 2013).

Identification of fiscal risk exposures needs to be centralized within the government to account for potential interactions and portfolio effects. Responsibilities for identifying fiscal risks need to be clearly allocated. Line ministries and agencies should be required to regularly and routinely submit information on risks to the ministry of finance, which should centralize the information needed to identify fiscal risks. Line ministries could be required to submit information on fiscal risks to the ministry of finance in their annual budgets. Countries with weak capacity could instead prepare a fiscal matrix as proposed by Brixi and Mody (2002).

The ministry of finance needs the capacity to analyze, in an integrated manner, the fiscal risks of infrastructure, in order to incorporate them into its overall fiscal analysis. It can use several approaches to do so. One is to analyze the fiscal risks from the perspective of asset-liability management and government net worth. This approach allows for the analysis of fiscal risks arising from direct and contingent liabilities from SOEs and PPPs by considering their impact in an extended government balance sheet that includes future revenues as well as assets, long-term obligations, and direct and contingent liabilities.

Qualitative and quantitative approaches and tools can be used as part of an integrated analysis, depending on data availability and government capacity. Examples include the $Z''$ score, used in this report to analyze contingent liabilities from SOEs (chapter 3); value at risk, used to analyze the contingent liabilities from early termination of PPPs (chapter 4), which can also be used for other contingent liabilities; and the PPP Fiscal Risk Assessment Model (PFRAM), discussed later in this chapter.

Lack of data may make it difficult to quantify the cost and likelihood of contingent liabilities. In such cases, a simple classification of the probability and magnitude of contingent liabilities into high, medium, and low, based on available information or educated guesses, can be used.

To assess overall fiscal risk exposure, the ministry of finance should consolidate the stock of contingent liabilities from SOEs, PPPs, and other sources; public debt; and other public liabilities. Using this consolidated portfolio, it should identify correlations and assess the sensitivity to macroeconomic and policy scenarios to capture potential interactions and portfolio effects.

Transparency allows civil society to keep the government accountable. It is a tenet of good fiscal management. Transparency on public spending, public debt, SOE operations and liabilities, and PPP fiscal commitments and contingent liabilities can create stronger incentives to ensure that all risks are identified, quantified, and managed.

Many countries have increased transparency in recent years, but much work remains to be done to improve debt transparency, including by publishing core public and publicly guaranteed debt statistics annually and limiting and defining the scope of confidentiality clauses in fiscal commitments, as discussed in World Bank (2021). Governments also need to disclose comprehensive information on contingent liabilities from SOEs, PPPs, and other sources.

As part of a centralized, systematic, and transparent approach to managing fiscal risks, disclosure of fiscal risks can be done through a single statement presented with the budget (IMF 2007). These statements should present macroeconomic risks and details of specific risks, such as public debt, contingent liabilities, and risks arising from PPPs, SOEs, and subnational governments, as relevant.

Mitigating fiscal risks entails reducing potential risks before they are taken on or materialize and reducing the cost once a risk materializes. Mitigating fiscal risks from infrastructure starts with sound macroeconomic and debt management to reduce a country's vulnerability to crisis and the need to support SOEs and cover explicit and implicit contingent liabilities from PPPs. Integrated public investment management reduces fiscal risks before they are taken on.

Setting limits on debt, PPP fiscal commitments, and SOE guarantees in an integrated manner also reduces potential fiscal risks.

To mitigate the impact of fiscal surprises, governments can create a contingency line in the budget from which unexpected payments can be made to cover specific contingent liabilities. The budget line should be under the control of the ministry of finance, with stringent conditions for the use of the resources and appropriate auditing of actual disbursements. If there is a proliferation of guarantees for PPPs and SOEs, the government can charge the sponsoring ministries, agencies, and SOEs a fee for guarantees to limit their use.

Natural disasters, particularly those related to extreme weather events, can affect infrastructure and non-infrastructure assets, requiring integrated approaches to mitigate them. Various actions can reduce potential risks before they materialize. They include identifying assets at greatest risk and relocating them if possible or strengthening their design specifications. Some climate risk can be insured against, either through explicit insurance policies for physical infrastructure or through national disaster funds, such as the Mexican Disaster Relief Fund (de Janvry, del Valle, and Sadoulet 2016). International institutions have designed insurance facilities to manage risks from natural disasters, such as the Caribbean Catastrophe Risk Insurance Facility (World Bank 2008). Because of the increased variability in weather patterns and the severity of extreme events, some insurance mechanisms may be insufficient to cover unexpected costs, especially in countries with no disaster relief endowments. Therefore, fiscal planning should incorporate tools such as the Infrastructure Planning Support System, which estimates the fiscal impact of climate change in roads (Schweikert and others 2014), to mitigate the fiscal impact of extreme weather events.

Effective integrated risk management requires a legal and administrative framework that clearly allocates roles and responsibilities between the central government and other public sector entities and between the ministry of finance and line ministries. Risk mitigation costs may be lower if actions are centralized.

The degree of centralization in risk management depends on country characteristics. Countries with strong capacity tend to assign line ministries responsibilities for monitoring SOEs, autonomous agencies, and PPPs. If line ministries are allowed to take on risks, they should have clearly specified responsibilities for managing the fiscal risks from their activities and be required to have in place both a risk management strategy and monitoring and reporting arrangements. Even in this case, the ministry of finance should have the authority to control risk-taking by line ministries if their actions can impose costs on others.

In an integrated fiscal risk management system, the central government, particularly the ministry of finance, should also monitor the risks retained by the government and the actions taken to mitigate them. Clear requirements for reporting by line ministries and agencies should be in place. Internal audit institutions should have a mandate to review all areas of fiscal risk and initiate audits of high-risk areas.

### Reforms to ensure the availability of adequate fiscal resources for infrastructure spending

In some countries, creating fiscal space for infrastructure may also entail raising additional budget revenues for it. Rationalizing budgetary spending can help ensure that there are sufficient fiscal resources for infrastructure. Efforts can include reforms to facilitate sustained budgetary reallocations from current to capital spending, such as reforms of the pension system, government employment and wage policies, and subsidies.[3]

Well-structured, comprehensive spending reviews can help identify opportunities for such reallocations (Robinson 2013).

Reforms of existing numerical fiscal rules that unduly constrain governments' access to sustainable financing can help ensure adequate resources for public investments. Significant empirical evidence shows that rigid numerical rules are associated with lower and more volatile levels of public investments, especially in emerging economies (Ardanaz and others 2021; Basdevant and others 2020). Inclusion of escape clauses; periodic review clauses; and, in countries with adequate capacity, the use of cyclically adjusted bases for the rules can help moderate such volatility (Schaechter and others 2012).

Some countries exclude capital expenditures from the bases of the rules (so-called golden rules). Such blanket exclusions do not ensure debt sustainability; can favor inappropriate public investments (white elephants) over more efficient social spending; and can incentivize the use of inappropriate accounting practices to classify current expenditures as capital ones. An alternative to protecting public investments is to combine a debt-based rule with a rule limiting the growth of current spending. This approach safeguards public debt sustainability.

### Summary

Table 5.1 (on the next page) summarizes the main recommendations on integrated management of fiscal resources and risks from infrastructure.

## EFFICIENT DIRECT PUBLIC PROVISION OF INFRASTRUCTURE

A range of reforms can sustainably increase the fiscal space for the direct public provision of infrastructure. These reforms improve the efficiency of spending, largely by strengthening PIM.

In most countries, reforms are needed to strengthen various aspects of the project implementation process, including procurement, the monitoring of the physical and financial execution of projects, and reductions in delays and cost overruns. Well-publicized open tenders, based on transparent and clear selection criteria, are essential to reduce corruption risks and promote the selection of the most cost-effective bids.[4] Timely monitoring, accounting, and auditing of projects are key to avoid cost overruns, reduce avoidable delays, and ward off favoritism in payments. Public investment management assessments and other diagnostic tools identify weaknesses in these areas and propose specific suggestions to address them.

Several steps can be taken to improve the management of public infrastructure, thereby lengthening their useful life and improving the quality of the services they provide. Careful analysis and quantification of future maintenance requirements of a new investment should be an integral part of the cost–benefit analysis of the project. Governments should establish guidelines, preferably by sector, for such analysis. Projected costs of the maintenance of ongoing and approved new investment projects should be incorporated in the country's expenditure framework. Line ministries and other relevant agencies should establish and put into consistent practice systems to monitor the state of infrastructure, such as road asset management systems, to ensure that maintenance needs are met on a timely basis and according to prespecified standards. In most countries, establishing asset management systems is likely to require significant investment in relevant technologies and databases.

**TABLE 5.1  Recommendations for strengthening integrated management of fiscal resources and risks from infrastructure**

| High-level actions | Detailed actions |
|---|---|
| Implement integrated public investment management | • Identify, appraise, and select all public infrastructure investment projects together, in accordance with integrated infrastructure plans and strategies and based on robust appraisal methodologies:<br>　○ Implement clear and robust project appraisal and selection methodologies for all public investment projects.<br>　○ Invest in the development of the required databases and staff capacities.<br>• Select the best provision modality for each project based on value for money and fiscal affordability.<br>• Grant a gatekeeping role to the ministry of finance in the selection of projects and provision modalities.<br>• Apply International Public Sector Accounting Standards as the accrual accounting framework for all financial reporting.<br>• Apply the same procurement and evaluation rules to all public investment projects.<br>• Adopt rolling MTFFs that include PPPs. |
| Implement integrated fiscal risk management | • Create a central institutional structure, within the ministry of finance or chaired by the ministry, in charge of managing all fiscal risks, including risks from infrastructure:<br>　○ Assign line ministries and agencies responsibility for providing the required fiscal information to the ministry of finance.<br>• Improve debt transparency, including by publishing core public and publicly guaranteed debt statistics annually and limiting and defining the scope of confidentiality clauses in fiscal commitments.<br>• Disclose comprehensive information on fiscal risks, through a single statement presented with the budget, for example.<br>• Create a contingency line in the budget to cover specific contingent liabilities.<br>• Undertake sound macroeconomic and debt management.<br>• Limit government debt, fiscal commitments from PPPs, and guarantees to SOEs.<br>• Take measures to mitigate the fiscal impact of climate risk:<br>　○ Relocate and strengthen assets most at risk.<br>　○ Insure against climate risk through explicit insurance policies for physical infrastructure or national disaster funds. |
| Ensure the availability of adequate fiscal resources for infrastructure spending | • Rationalize budgetary spending based on well-structured, comprehensive spending reviews that identify opportunities for such reallocations.<br>• Reform features of existing numerical fiscal rules that unduly constrain governments' access to sustainable financing. |

*Source:* Original table for this publication.
*Note:* MTFF = medium-term fiscal framework; PPP = public-private partnership; SOE = state-owned enterprise

Well-prepared MTEFs can help safeguard infrastructure investments and mitigate fiscal risks from direct public provision in several ways. MTEFs take into account spending commitments on ongoing projects, make explicit the cost of planned new investments over the entire time horizon of the framework, ensure consistency of both types of investments with the projected revenue envelope over the same period, and allocate adequate resources to the operations and maintenance of existing and new infrastructures.

An MTEF helps reduce the risk that overambitious infrastructure investment plans end up not being implemented and projects are delayed for lack of adequate budgetary resources. It also helps better balance the mix of new and ongoing investments and moderate the risk of inadequate maintenance of existing infrastructure.

To help address some of the political economy factors that bias infrastructure spending toward new investments at the expense of the maintenance of existing ones, some countries have created dedicated maintenance funds, such as road funds. The evidence presented in chapter 2 suggests that such funds are effective in increasing the share of maintenance in road spending. It is essential that they be held to strict governance and transparency standards and that their accounts be fully reflected in the government's accounts.

There is significant potential to strengthen the role of government audit institutions in promoting accountability and the more effective use of budgetary resources for infrastructure investments. Doing so requires strengthening the technical capacities of such institutions and ensuring that their findings and reports are appropriately publicized and followed up by parliament and the executive.

Table 5.2 summarizes the recommendations for sustainably increasing the fiscal space for direct provision of infrastructure.

**TABLE 5.2  Recommendations for mitigating fiscal risks from direct public provision of infrastructure**

| High-level actions | Detailed actions |
| --- | --- |
| Improve the efficiency of direct public provision | • Prepare sufficiently disaggregated rolling MTFFs and MTEFs to guide the annual budget process:<br>  ◦ Incorporate the projected maintenance costs of ongoing and approved new investment projects in the MTEF.<br><br>• Strengthen project implementation process, from procurement to monitoring of the physical and financial execution of projects:<br>  ◦ Implement well-publicized open tenders, based on transparent and clear selection criteria.<br>  ◦ Conduct timely monitoring, accounting, and auditing of projects.<br><br>• Strengthen asset management:<br>  ◦ Implement asset management systems to monitor the state of existing infrastructure, and ensure that their maintenance needs are met on a timely basis, based on prespecified standards.<br>  ◦ Create dedicated maintenance funds, such as road funds. Ensure that they are held to strict governance and transparency standards and that their accounts are fully reflected in the government's accounts.<br><br>• Invest in the development of the required databases and staff capacities to undertake procurement and implementation of investment projects and asset management.<br><br>• Strengthen the role of government audit institutions, and ensure that their findings are public and followed up by parliament and the executive.<br><br>• Publicly disclose relevant data and findings of government audit institutions. |

*Source:* Original table for this publication.
*Note:* MTEF = medium-term expenditure framework; MTFF = medium-term fiscal framework.

## EFFECTIVE FISCAL AND CORPORATE GOVERNANCE OF SOEs

Reforms for mitigating fiscal risks from power and transport SOEs focus on improving incentives and strengthening transparency and accountability in their management, operations, and relations with their shareholder government.

### Limited and transparent use of quasi-fiscal activities

The most effective approach to mitigating fiscal risks arising from the imposition of uncompensated quasi-fiscal burdens on SOEs is for governments to avoid policies that can give rise to such burdens or eliminate them when they are already in place. Specific actions depend on the type of quasi-fiscal activities in a country or sector.

If the prices of goods and services provided by SOEs are set at below cost-recovery levels, they should be liberalized if SOEs operate in competitive markets or set at levels that allow efficient enterprises to earn an adequate rate of profit if SOEs operate in noncompetitive markets. Undesired distributional effects of such reforms should ideally be dealt with by providing vouchers or income transfers to affected vulnerable groups. SOEs should be subject to the same laws and regulations regarding employment and labor costs as private competitors. Local content requirements for SOEs' investments and procurement should be eliminated. The scope for interventions in the day-to-day operations of SOEs motivated by political or individual gains should be limited through reforms to corporate governance.

In competitive sectors, the government can tender public sector obligations that SOEs and private companies can compete on a level playing field to perform instead of imposing policy obligations on SOEs. For example, if air transport service cannot be operated on a commercial basis on routes that serve some remote locations, but such service provides a social and economic lifeline, tendered subsidies can be provided for such routes to underwrite the carriers' losses. Airlines' choice to operate any given route and the compensation they receive for doing so should be determined through an open-tender process to ensure competition for the routes (World Bank 2022b).

Significant political economy and other obstacles often make it difficult or impossible to eliminate quasi-fiscal burdens on power and transport SOEs. Full-cost pricing of socially sensitive goods and services, such as electricity and public transport services, is often politically infeasible, especially when weaknesses in administrative capacities do not allow the identification and compensation of vulnerable households. SOEs may be the most effective vehicle for investing in infrastructure in remote rural areas.

When governments introduce or maintain policies that place quasi-fiscal burdens on SOEs, they should provide the enterprises with clear guidelines on how to measure such burdens and ensure their timely compensation through regular and transparent budgetary transfers. Measurement of quasi-fiscal costs requires the separation of commercial and noncommercial activities of individual SOEs that may use indivisible inputs (for example, some capital investments) and enjoy economies of scale from the simultaneous conduct of the two types of activities. Box 5.1 discusses alternative methods for calculating the costs of quasi-fiscal operations. SOEs have incentives to overstate the costs of noncommercial activities. Governments have the opposite incentives, but should strive to ensure as close an approximation to the measure of the costs as the available information permits.

In regulated sectors, such as power and railways, an independent regulator determines the average tariff level commensurate with efficient cost recovery. This authority is not always

> **BOX 5.1    Calculating the costs of quasi-fiscal operations**
>
> Four types of costs can be assessed to quantify the burden of quasi-fiscal operations (QFOs): marginal costs, fully distributed costs, avoidable costs, and stand-alone costs (OECD 2010). Calculating the marginal costs of QFOs entails estimating the increase in costs as a result of the additional provision requirements. Although this method is ideal from the standpoint of an economist, the calculation requires a detailed investigation of the cost structure of the state-owned enterprise (SOE), which might be very costly and, in some cases, impossible to relate to specific QFOs.
>
> An easier method is to calculate the average cost, by fully distributing the total costs of the SOE on all its output and obtaining the unit cost of QFOs. This method tends to overestimate the costs of QFOs when there is a significant difference between the average and the marginal cost, which is especially true for infrastructure SOEs, but it is accepted as a fair method.
>
> An alternative method that tries to approximate the marginal cost of QFOs is to calculate the actual costs the SOE could avoid by removing specific QFOs. A drawback of this method is the difficulty of estimating the avoidable capital costs from additional services provided.
>
> The cost of QFOs can also be estimated by calculating the stand-alone cost of providing the QFOs in isolation. As this method ignores economies of scale and scope, it significantly overestimates the costs, especially when an SOE has large fixed costs.
>
> European countries have made significant progress in costing quasi-fiscal burdens, partly under pressure from the European Commission, which seeks to avoid both unjustifiable state aid to national SOEs and fiscal risks from the same. In EU countries that use public service agreements with their SOEs, such as France and Italy, noncommercial objectives mandated to each enterprise are identified, their cost estimated for the period covered by the agreement, and the related expected budgetary compensation specified.

respected (Foster and Rana 2020). Ideally, the ministry of finance and the regulator should work together to determine the compensation for quasi-fiscal operations, particularly operations that cap tariffs. Experience has yielded mixed results, because the regulator does not have the power to hold the ministry of finance accountable for paying the requisite compensation, leaving the approach vulnerable during periods of fiscal pressure, as in the case of Senegal's power sector in 2017. Moreover, "once established, such arrangements may be difficult to reverse and in some specific cases may even lead to sustained inefficiency in utilities as seen in Pakistan" (Foster and Rana 2020, 193).

## Stronger financial management and monitoring of SOEs

Sound financial management systems are key to good operational and financial performances of SOEs and therefore to reducing the fiscal risks posed by these enterprises. Shareholder governments should take steps to ensure that such systems are in place in their SOEs, regardless of the model of corporate governance and control chosen for the enterprises.

Governments should establish clear requirements for their SOEs on all aspects of financial management, including the preparation of multiyear business plans and annual budgets; the monitoring of execution of both; their revision, if needed; accounting and reporting; internal and external audit; and asset-liability management. They should also monitor and enforce SOE compliance with such requirements. Responsibility for these tasks is given to the ministry of finance in most countries (in a few, the ministry of planning or of state participations is charged with this responsibility). In some countries that organize their SOEs under a holding company (such as Fonafe in Peru, Temasek in Singapore, and SEPI in Spain) or similar institution (such as Sistema de Empresas [SEP] in Chile), the holding company exercises these functions, in close consultation with the ministry of finance.

The degree of specificity and detail of the requirements may vary, depending on countries' preferences regarding the degree of autonomy of the board and management in the governance and operation of the SOE, including under quasi-contractual arrangements, such as public service agreements with the government. Some reforms are broadly applicable.

SOEs' annual budgets should be prepared and presented for review and approval by the oversight authority/authorities in a standardized format, consistent with applicable accounting standards (preferably international corporate standards). Budget documentation should specify the underlying assumptions regarding relevant macroeconomic variables (for example, commodity prices, exchange rates, and interest rates) and SOE–specific factors (for example, the evolution of demand for the SOE's products; relevant regulated tariffs; the size and composition of the SOE's workforce; and specific cost determinants, such as wage increases or the prices of other key inputs). These assumptions should be subjected to sensitivity analyses and combined stress tests and the results reported in the budget documentation, along with any proposed actions to mitigate risks exceeding prudent thresholds (through, for example, hedging or insurance mechanisms). Stress tests to assess the combined impact of several different shocks on the SOE's finances are recommended, because of the frequent correlation of these shocks.[5] The budgets should also include a listing of the SOEs' explicit contingent liabilities, their maximum values, assessment of the probability of their realization, and a contingency reserve to match the combined expected value of the liabilities.

SOEs should be required to have in place systems to monitor, preferably in real time, the execution of their budgets and to transmit to the oversight authority summary monthly reports and more detailed quarterly ones. The oversight authority should be endowed with human resources and information systems that enable it to monitor and enforce the SOEs' compliance with the budgeting and reporting requirements, analyze such budgets and reports, provide timely feedback on them to the SOEs, and request and enforce appropriate corrective actions by the SOEs, when necessary.

Governments can monitor SOEs by using estimated $Z''$ scores or monitoring the components of the $Z''$ score, as discussed in chapter 3. Monitoring the four financial ratios in the $Z''$ score and the score itself may yield warnings about the deterioration of the financial health of an SOE; it can also help forecast how large the fiscal injections to support the SOE will be. Tracking these indicators can also prevent major vulnerabilities in SOEs that large shocks can exacerbate. Governments can track the $Z''$ score to create rules that trigger further scrutiny of SOE expenditures and can be used to set rules for risk management SOEs with more volatile costs that will tend to have higher $Z''$ scores, triggering preventive measures to avoid the need for a large fiscal injection in the future. Governments can also require more financial buffers (for example, larger retained earnings) for volatile SOEs or SOEs that systematically get lower $Z''$ scores.

SOEs' financial accounts are typically compiled following the national or international standards applying to private corporations. The use of such standards facilitates comparisons with private competitors or peers and meets regulatory accounting requirements for SOEs listed on domestic or foreign stock exchanges. To facilitate a comprehensive view of a country's public sector finances, SOEs' accounts should also be compiled in a public accounting format, following international standards such as the International Monetary Fund's *Government Finance Statistics Manual*, to allow their consolidation with the accounts of the general government. Governments should create a publicly available database with the relevant financial information on all SOEs.

Consolidation of governments' and SOEs' accounts is desirable for analytical and statistical purposes. Such consolidation does not necessarily imply that fiscal targets or fiscal rules should be specified in terms of the consolidated public sector (or its nonfinancial component, as is more often the case). Indeed, a case can be made that separate and different rules for the general government and the SOEs are preferable, because the government's fiscal stance should be informed by macroeconomic stabilization, as well as fiscal sustainability objectives, whereas the financial performance and borrowing capacity of SOEs should be assessed mainly in terms of profitability, liquidity, and long-term solvency.

SOEs should have in place adequate systems of internal control, including an audit committee within their boards and a dedicated unit/department within the staff with the requisite professional qualifications and experience. SOEs' annual income statements and balance sheets should be subjected to external audits by qualified domestic or international firms. Government audit institutions can also play a role in strengthening the accountability of SOE managers and their government overseers.

Many of the considerations discussed in previous sections regarding options to strengthen the management of government investments also apply to investments by SOEs, in particular concerning project appraisal and selection and the maintenance of existing infrastructure. Sound corporate and fiscal governance are key to generate the right incentives for SOEs to adopt and consistently utilize strong investment management systems and practices.

## Sound borrowing by SOEs

Like private companies, SOEs need access to financing, for both short-term liquidity purposes and investments. Fiscal rules requiring SOEs to consistently run balanced budgets put them at a competitive disadvantage vis-à-vis private firms in the same sector and can lead to serious underinvestment in key public services. Such rules may also run counter to intergenerational equity considerations, as multiple generations generally enjoy the benefits of SOEs' investments.

To mitigate fiscal risks, it is essential that SOEs' access to financing be contained within limits consistent with their debt-servicing capacity, in both the short and the long term. Governments should eliminate preferential channels or terms of access of SOEs to financing and introduce transparent, nondiscretionary, and effective systems of control of SOEs' borrowing, based on solvency and liquidity criteria.

The granting of explicit guarantees to SOEs should be strictly limited to the financing of investment projects of clear public interest. Such guarantees should be subject to a ceiling for the sector, defined by the ministry of finance and approved by the parliament in the context of the budget process. Within that ceiling, guarantees to individual SOEs should be granted only on the basis of a transparent analysis by the ministry of finance of the SOE's capacity to service the debt. Guarantees should be adequately collateralized by the SOE's liquid assets or expected revenues and accompanied by significant fees, comparable to those levied on any guarantees granted to private enterprises, as is done in Australia.

Governments should avoid policies that provide SOEs with a competitive advantage in access to financing. Examples of such policies include different prudential requirements for domestic banks' credit to SOEs and private firms, pressure on public banks to give preference to nonfinancial SOEs in lending, and preferential tax treatment of bonds issued by SOEs.

Avoiding discretion in the granting of borrowing authorization by the ministry of finance to SOEs is key to establishing an effective system of controls on SOEs' access to financing. Borrowing controls should be based on clear and prespecified objective criteria that take into account the factors determining the SOEs' capacity to service their debt over time. These factors include the size and structure of individual SOEs' liabilities, their interest burden and the profile of debt repayments, their operational profitability, the level of their contingent and known future liabilities (for example, from pension plans for their employees), the size and liquidity of their assets, and the volatility of their revenues.

Governments should design and implement a stable framework for authorizing SOEs' access to financing, based on a transparent assessment of their capacity to borrow. This framework should specify the indicators used and the value ranges considered compatible with the proposed borrowing, as well as the responsibility and procedures for the assessment. At a minimum, the indicators should include the following ratios: gross liabilities to current revenues, debt denominated in foreign currency to foreign exchange earnings, interest due to current revenues, and liquid assets to short-term liabilities. Inclusion of other relevant indicators—such as the ratio of contingent or known future liabilities to revenues and the ratio of current operational expenditures to current revenues—is desirable. All indicators should be standardized and possibly weighted to determine whether financing is approved. An alternative approach would be to rate individual SOEs on each dimension and set a threshold for each rating. This method would obviate the need to weight the indicators.

### Adequate and nondiscretionary resource extraction from SOEs

To reduce the risks from excessive extraction of resources from their SOEs, which is often dictated by short-term budgetary pressures, and ensure a level playing field for SOEs vis-à-vis domestic or external competitors, governments should implement two sets of practices. First, they should subject SOEs to the same tax regime as other enterprises operating in the sector. Similar considerations should apply to royalties or other resource-sharing arrangements for SOEs in nonrenewable natural resources (such as hydroelectric resources).[6]

Second, governments should provide clear forward-looking guidance to SOEs with regard to expected rates of return and the distribution of profits and between dividends and reinvestment in the firm. A preannounced dividend payout policy may take the form of a fixed percentage of annual profits or of a transparent link between the payout required and the desired capital structure for each SOE. Although the latter approach is more complex than the former, it is preferable, because it reduces discretion and the related risks of undercapitalizing SOEs and retains the flexibility to adjust dividend payout requirements to changing investment needs and financial market conditions.

## Summary

Table 5.3 summarizes the recommendations for mitigating fiscal risks from SOEs.

**TABLE 5.3**   **Recommendations for mitigating fiscal risks from SOEs**

| High-level actions | Detailed actions |
| --- | --- |
| Reduce the risks from quasi-fiscal activities | • Avoid the imposition of quasi-fiscal burdens on SOEs, when possible:<br>  ◦ Liberalize SOEs' prices or tender public sector obligations if they operate in competitive markets, and set regulated prices at levels that allow efficient enterprises to earn an adequate rate of profit if the SOEs operate in noncompetitive markets.<br>  ◦ Subject SOEs to the same laws and regulations regarding employment and labor costs as private companies.<br>  ◦ Avoid local content requirements for SOEs' investments and procurement.<br>  ◦ Grant SOE boards and managers adequate operational autonomy, with accountability and transparency.<br><br>• When quasi-fiscal activities cannot be avoided, ensure adequate measurement and budgetary compensation for any such activities:<br>  ◦ Provide clear guidelines on how to measure burdens from quasi-fiscal activities.<br>  ◦ If the sector is regulated and prices are set below cost-recovery level, have the ministry of finance and sector regulator work together to determine compensation.<br>  ◦ Ensure the commensurate and timely compensation of SOEs through regular and transparent budgetary transfers. |
| Strengthen SOEs' financial management and monitoring | • Establish clear requirements for SOEs on the preparation of multiyear business plans and annual budgets, the monitoring of execution of both, accounting and reporting practices, and internal and external audit:<br>  ◦ Require that SOEs prepare and present annual budgets for review and approval by the oversight authority using consistent accounting standards, preferably international standards.<br>  ◦ Require that budget documentation specify the underlying assumptions regarding relevant macroeconomic variables and SOE–specific factors, their sensitivity analyses and stress tests, and any proposed actions to mitigate risks exceeding prudent thresholds.<br>  ◦ Require that budgets include a list of the SOEs' explicit contingent liabilities, their maximum values, an assessment of the probability of their realization, and a contingency reserve to match the combined expected value of the liabilities.<br>  ◦ Compile SOEs' accounts in a public accounting format, following international standards, such as the IMF's *Government Finance Statistics Manual*.<br>  ◦ Ensure that SOEs have systems in place to monitor the execution of their budgets and submit monthly and quarterly reports to the oversight authority.<br>  ◦ Ensure that SOE boards include an audit committee and that their staffs include a dedicated unit/department with appropriate professional qualification and experience.<br>  ◦ Subject SOEs' annual income statements and balance sheets to external audits by qualified domestic or international firms and government audit institutions. |

*(continued)*

**TABLE 5.3**  *Continued*

| High-level actions | Detailed actions |
|---|---|
| | • Endow the oversight authority with adequate human resources and information systems to monitor and enforce SOE compliance with requirements. |
| | • Incorporate estimated $Z''$ scores or their components in the toolkit used to monitor SOEs' financial performance and need for fiscal injections. |
| | • Create a publicly available database with relevant financial and operational information on all SOEs. |
| Limit SOEs' access to financing based on their debt-servicing capacity | • Introduce transparent, nondiscretionary, and effective systems of control of SOEs' borrowing, focused on solvency and liquidity criteria. |
| | • Limit the granting of explicit guarantees to SOEs to the financing of investment projects of clear public interest: |
| |    ○ Establish an aggregate ceiling for guarantees for the sector, defined by the ministry of finance and approved by the parliament in the context of the budget process. |
| |    ○ Grant guarantees to individual SOEs based on a transparent analysis by the ministry of finance of the SOE's capacity to service the debt. |
| |    ○ Collateralize guarantees adequately with the SOE's liquid assets or expected revenues. Charge fees comparable to those levied on guarantees granted to private enterprises. |
| | • Remove policies that give SOEs preferential access to financing. |
| Avoid excessive and discretionary resource extraction by SOEs | • Subject SOEs to the same tax regime as other enterprises operating in the same sector. |
| | • Provide clear guidance to SOEs with regard to expected rates of return, the distribution of profits, and the allocation of dividends and reinvestment in the firm: |
| |    ○ Transparently link the payout requirement to the achievement of a desired capital structure for each SOE. |

*Source:* Original table for this publication.
*Note:* IMF = International Monetary Fund; SOE = state-owned enterprise.

## A ROBUST PPP FRAMEWORK

This section focuses on policy and institutional reforms to mitigate the fiscal risks from PPPs. These reforms focus on improving incentives and strengthening transparency and accountability in the preparation, procurement, and management of PPPs.[7]

A framework for the preparation, procurement, and management of PPPs should include procedures, decision criteria, and institutional responsibilities that are indirectly related to the fiscal management of PPPs. If well developed and applied, such procedures, decision criteria, and institutional responsibilities can reduce the risk of project failure and the related fiscal risks. A PPP framework should also include procedures, decision criteria, and institutional responsibilities that are directly related to the fiscal management of PPPs and be part of the broader public financial management framework, as discussed in the first section of this chapter.

There are many ways to set up legal and institutional frameworks for PPP projects; the best approach depends on the administrative and legal traditions in place. Countries with a common law system tend to rely more on policy statements and guidelines; countries with a civil law system tend to regulate their PPPs through overarching PPP laws and supporting implementing regulations or bylaws. As long as all elements affecting the PPP process are addressed without contradicting existing laws, any legal set-up can create an environment that is conducive to the development and implementation of PPPs.

### Fiscal management of PPPs

A robust fiscal management framework should include provisions regarding PPPs, as discussed in the first section of this chapter. These requirements should include assessment of fiscal affordability; proper accounting, reporting, and budgetary treatment of PPPs; clear and transparent decision criteria for the approval of PPPs by the relevant government institutions; and measures to ensure that appropriate funding is in place when the commitments materialize. Such provisions are designed to increase the transparency of existing commitments and avoid fiscally unsound deals.

Fiscal affordability is the ability to accommodate the fiscal implications of a PPP within the intertemporal budget constraint of the government. Assessment of fiscal affordability identifies and quantifies the long-term fiscal implications of PPPs, including their direct and contingent liabilities. The analysis starts by understanding the government commitments and exposure to risks from a PPP arrangement, including implicit and explicit risks, common risks to the specific infrastructure, and risks specific to the PPP arrangement.

Various methodologies and tools can be used to assess the fiscal costs and risks arising from PPP projects. The value-at-risk methodology (used in chapter 4 to quantify the fiscal risks from early termination of PPPs) can be used to assess risks when there are adequate data and capacity in the country. PFRAM, developed by the IMF and the World Bank Group, can be used even in environments with limited data (box 5.2). It is advisable that countries have in place a practical, comprehensive, and cohesive set of guidelines and tools to identify fiscal commitments and risks, otherwise this may lead to an inconsistent appraisal and thus ineffective control.

The ministry of finance is best positioned to determine whether a PPP is fiscally sustainable and act as a counterbalance to spending agencies, which usually handle procurement. The initial PPP approval process can have an important impact on the quality of project preparation and shape the financial structure of the PPP. A second approval by the ministry of finance before the PPP contract is signed is also necessary to ensure that the project is still fiscally affordable after any changes that may have occurred during the tendering process.

As the evidence on renegotiations of PPPs indicates, gatekeeping is required during implementation to approve renegotiations and mitigate their fiscal risks. It is good practice to have in place rules to ensure that contract variations are evaluated in terms of their fiscal implications, direct and contingent, and authorized by the ministry of finance as the fiscal gatekeeper.

The ministry of finance should be granted the legal authority to require the government entities involved in PPPs to provide any information needed to identify and analyze the risks. The absence of such authority may mean that it will have to rely on moral persuasion over line ministries and other contracting authorities, which will limit its ability to conduct robust fiscal risk management.

A complementary strategy is to create a central database with relevant information on all PPP projects and require all institutions that award PPPs to report such data. This database should be public, so that third parties can access it and undertake independent assessments and benchmarking.

---

**BOX 5.2   What is the PFRAM?**

The PFRAM is an Excel-based tool that helps identify fiscal commitments and fiscal risks arising from PPP transactions. The tool has two main components. The first is a quantitative module that analyzes the fiscal impact of PPPs from both direct commitments and common contingent liabilities based on the accounting principles from IPSAS 32. This module allows for sensitivity analysis. The second is a qualitative module that evaluates fiscal risks from PPPs through a structured questionnaire that guides the user on the analysis of common sources of fiscal risks.

The current version of PFRAM (PFRAM 2.0) is a more operationally focused and user-friendly version than its predecessor. Its quantitative module can be used to analyze the fiscal impact of a portfolio of PPP projects, showing their impact on relevant macro parameters.

PFRAM facilitates the quantification of fiscal impact and the evaluation of fiscal risks from PPPs. To make it accessible to most users, it makes some assumptions. It should therefore never be used as a substitute for a full-fledged financial model. On the quantitative analysis of contingent liabilities, it uses a maximum exposure rather than probabilistic approach, for example.

Identifying and assessing PPP-related fiscal commitments and fiscal risks is only the first step in establishing a framework for the management of PPP-related fiscal commitments and contingent liabilities. PFRAM is usually deployed in addition to technical assistance and capacity building to relevant stakeholders on, for example, developing and operationalizing guidelines for the management of fiscal commitments and contingent liabilities.

*Note:* IPSAS = International Public Sector Accounting Standards; PFRAM = PPP Fiscal Risk Assessment Model; PPP = public-private partnership.

---

Governments use different approaches to control fiscal exposure from PPPs. Some countries establish separate debt and PPP ceilings. This practice is not recommended, because it can lead to the choice of the provision modality being based on PPP fiscal space or the debt capacity instead of value for money. A better approach is to set a ceiling for government debt that includes the fiscal commitments arising from PPPs—a so-called debt plus PPP ceiling (World Bank 2022a).

For accounting purposes, IPSAS is recommended. For reporting purposes, compliance with the IMF's *Government Finance Statistics Manual 2014* (IMF 2014) and *Public Sector Debt Statistics: Guide for Compilers and Users* (IMF 2011) is encouraged. Per IPSAS 32, PPP assets are considered public assets; they should therefore be included in the government's accounts if the public partner controls them (that is, if it can define how the assets are used, who can use them, and how much should be paid for their use or availability). The government can make all of these decisions through the PPP contract. Therefore, under IPSAS, the impact of a PPP on the main fiscal aggregates is like that of publicly financed projects, preventing PPP–related assets and corresponding liabilities from being treated off the government's balance sheet (World Bank 2022a).

EU member states must comply with the European System of Accounts (ESA), which regulates how they prepare national accounts and produce comparable and homogeneous fiscal statistical information. ESA requires the public sector to account for PPP–related debt if it retains a substantial part of the risk in the PPP project. Some risk allocations underlying a PPP are thus considered off-balance sheet by ESA standards though not by IPSAS.

For accounting for contingent liabilities, the preferred approach is the accrual-based approach, which requires an upfront recognition of liabilities likely to arise from the issuance of guarantees. Most countries use a cash-based approach, which does not recognize contingent liabilities until they are called. The accrual-based approach is technically more demanding than the cash-based approach and may not be a realistic option for low-capacity environments, at least in the short to medium term (World Bank 2022a). If the cash-based approach is followed, the focus should be on enhancing the disclosure of information on contingent liabilities. The IMF's *Manual on Fiscal Transparency* (2007) requires that budget documentation include a statement indicating the purpose of each contingent liability, its duration, and intended beneficiaries; it also requires major contingencies to be quantified where possible. It would be useful to disclose the expected value of payments, as well as the magnitude and the likelihood of a liability incurred (World Bank 2022a).

Establishing adequate budgetary mechanisms for meeting payment obligations when they arise is critical. Budgeting for PPPs involves ensuring that money is appropriated and available to pay for whatever cost the government has agreed to cover for its PPP projects. Because such costs may be contingent or occur in the future, PPP budgeting can be challenging in traditional annual budget cycles. For this reason, good practice includes PPPs in MTFFs. Budgeting for a contingent liability can be particularly challenging, because payments may become due unexpectedly. To deal with this problem, some countries create a contingency line in the budget from which unexpected payments can be made. Such a contingency line can be specific to a particular liability—one considered the riskiest, for example—or cover a range of contingent liabilities (World Bank 2022a).

### Preparation and procurement of PPPs

Given the complexity, magnitude, and long-term nature of PPP contracts, the government should perform rigorous assessments to gauge the viability of infrastructure projects before deciding on PPP procurement. Sound PPP preparation starts by identifying potential infrastructure projects that could be procured as PPPs from the list of projects that have reached the appraisal stage in an integrated PIM system. Projects should be aligned with integrated infrastructure plans and strategies and selected based on robust cost–benefit analysis and assessments covering all relevant aspects of project selection and preparation, such as fiscal affordability assessment and comparative assessment to evaluate whether a PPP is the best option to deliver the project.

Governments need to conduct robust feasibility studies that assess and determine the appropriate allocation of risks and financial viability of proposed projects. The allocation of risk, particularly demand risk, is an important source of fiscal risks, as the discussion in chapters 1 and 4 pointed out. Flexible term contracts, such as the present-value-of-revenue contracts used in Chile, are a good option for allocating the demand risk to the government and alleviating the fiscal risk from renegotiation. The analysis of the determinants of early termination of PPPs in chapter 4 indicates that measures that reduce the financing risk of a project—such as providing support through capital grants, revenue subsidies, or in-kind transfers—can reduce the rates of early termination.

It is important that governments have an established methodology for each of the required assessments that can be consistently applied across potential PPP projects. A standardized methodology enhances government transparency and builds institutional capacity, because it establishes objective criteria that are uniform, publicly available, and easily applicable to multiple PPP proposals (World Bank 2020).

A procurement process that awards PPPs to the private partner that can deliver the highest value for money can help mitigate fiscal risks. The government should provide as much information as possible on the project to reduce uncertainty about the value of the project and ensure an efficient outcome. Good practice makes public the results of assessments of the feasibility and design of the project, including the environmental and social impact assessments, by including them in the request for proposals or tender document and publishing them online. Costly and time-consuming PPP tendering procedures may discourage potential bidders from preparing proposals and participating in the procurement process. Procuring authorities should try attracting as much competition as possible by reducing transaction costs and ensuring the clarity, fairness, and transparency of the procurement process (World Bank 2020).

### Contract management

Properly managing implementation of a PPP contract is key to ensuring that the project delivers the expected value for money and fiscal risks are properly mitigated. Modification and renegotiation of the contract should be regulated, with only limited reasons allowed as justification of renegotiation, in order to reduce the incentives of the private partner and the procuring authority to use renegotiation opportunistically. Approval of renegotiations by the ministry of finance is important to reduce the chances of opportunistic behavior. This approval process provides more impartial oversight over renegotiations of PPP contracts. It is advisable to keep contract amendments within certain limits. When renegotiations exceed these thresholds, or the scope of work is increased, a new tendering process should be implemented to support competition and reduce incentives for renegotiation.

Specific circumstances that may arise during the life of the contract—force majeure, material adverse government action, changes in the law—should also be regulated. Mechanisms should be in place that allow the parties to resolve disputes without adversely affecting the project. Giving lenders step-in rights when the private partner is at risk of default or the contract is under threat of termination for failure to meet service obligations can also reduce the risks of early termination. Having well-defined grounds for termination of the PPP contract and its consequences can also reduce the fiscal costs from early termination (World Bank 2020).

Since 2012, Türkiye's Ministry of Treasury and Finance has assumed foreign debt in the case of early termination of certain PPP projects. This commitment allowed the government to convert the implicit contingent liabilities associated with early termination risk to explicit ones. The practice reduced moral hazard by closely monitoring early termination risk (World Bank 2022a).

In addition to having adequate regulations, procedures, and guidelines in place, it is important that the contract management authority have adequate capacity. The contract management authority should have a system to manage implementation of the PPP contract, including risk mitigation mechanisms. Members of the PPP contract management team should meet certain qualifications to ensure successful management of PPP contracts.

### Summary

Table 5.4 summarizes the recommendations for mitigating fiscal risks from PPPs.

**TABLE 5.4** Recommendations for mitigating fiscal risks from PPPs

| High-level actions | Detailed actions |
|---|---|
| Establish PPP-specific provisions in the fiscal management framework | • Assess the fiscal affordability of PPPs by identifying and quantifying their long-term fiscal implications, including direct and contingent liabilities:<br>○ Use methodologies and tools to quantify the fiscal implications of PPPs and publish them online.<br>○ Grant the ministry of finance the authority to require relevant information from government entities involved in PPPs.<br>• Grant the ministry of finance the authority to approve PPPs and their renegotiations.<br>• Set a ceiling for government debt, including fiscal commitments arising from PPPs.<br>• Apply International Public Sector Accounting Standards as the normative accrual accounting framework and comply with the IMF's *Government Finance Statistics Manual 2014* (IMF 2014) and *Public Sector Debt Statistics: Guide for Compilers and Users* (IMF 2011).<br>• Establish adequate budgetary mechanisms for meeting payment obligations by including PPPs in MTFFs and creating a contingency line in the budget to cover specific contingent liabilities.<br>• Publish an online database with relevant information on all PPPs. |
| Implement a robust preparation framework | • Identify and appraise potential PPP projects together with all other public infrastructure investment projects.<br>• Select projects to be implemented as PPPs based on value for money and fiscal affordability considerations.<br>• Avoid allocating demand risk to the private partner when it has minimal or no control over demand. Consider flexible term contracts, such as the present-value-of-revenue contracts, for allocating demand risk to the government in such cases.<br>• Consider reducing the financing risk of PPPs by, for example, providing support through capital grants, revenue subsidies, or in-kind transfers. |
| Implement an efficient procurement framework | • Provide as much information as possible on the project to reduce uncertainty on its value and ensure an efficient outcome:<br>○ Publish the results of the assessments conduct during preparation and include them in the request for proposals or tender documents.<br>• Reduce transactions costs, and ensure the clarity, fairness, and transparency of the procurement process. |
| Implement an effective contract management framework | • Establish alternative dispute-resolution mechanisms.<br>• Clearly regulate contract renegotiations and modifications:<br>○ Regulate causes for renegotiation, limiting the reasons allowed.<br>○ Establish that when renegotiations exceed a threshold or the scope of work is increased, a new tendering process should be implemented.<br>• Regulate causes for early termination and its consequences:<br>○ Give lenders step-in rights when the private partner is at risk of default or the contract is under threat of termination for failure to meet service obligations.<br>• Develop adequate management capacity:<br>○ Establish a system for managing the implementation of the PPP contract, including risk mitigation mechanisms.<br>○ Hire members of the PPP contract management team who have adequate qualifications. |

*Source:* Original table for this publication.
*Note:* IMF = International Monetary Fund; MTFF = medium-term fiscal framework; PPP = public-private partnership.

## IN SUM

Mitigating fiscal risks from infrastructure requires removing the flaws in infrastructure governance that create perverse incentives and building adequate capacity in government to mitigate fiscal risks from infrastructure in a sustainable manner. Any reform agenda to mitigate fiscal risks from infrastructure should include four building blocks: integrated public investment management; effective fiscal and corporate governance of SOEs; robust PPP preparation, procurement, and contract management framework; and integrated fiscal risk management. All of them should be grounded in an effort to build adequate government capacity.

The content and pace of implementation of the reform agenda needs to be tailored to the sources of risk and the institutional and socio-political characteristics of each country, as well as the government capacity. Country-specific strategies therefore involve different mixes of the preventive and corrective actions presented in this chapter.

## NOTES

1. Taliercio and Estrada (2020) discuss project appraisal practices in a range of advanced and emerging economies.
2. See World Bank (2013) and Cangiano, Curristine, and Lazare (2013) for comprehensive discussions of MTEFs.
3. See, for example, Clements and others (2013) and IMF (2016).
4. Pattanayak and Verdugo-Yepes (2020) provide a comprehensive discussion of corruption risks in the various phases of the infrastructure process and possible approaches to mitigating them.
5. For instance, downturns in demand may be accompanied by pressures on foreign exchange rates. Wage pressures, political disturbances, and large natural disasters can also lead to currency depreciations.
6. Taxation (broadly defined to include royalties, production-sharing arrangements, and other compulsory payments to the government) of nonrenewable natural resources is a very complex subject that requires consideration of the special features of nonrenewable natural resource exploitation activities, including long gestation periods and high sunk costs (Daniel, Keen, and McPherson 2010). In designing the taxation regime, it is important to level the playing field between SOEs operating in these sectors and their private (domestic or foreign) competitors.
7. For an in-depth discussion of best practices and experiences in managing fiscal commitments and contingent liabilities of PPPs, see World Bank (2022a).

## REFERENCES

Allen, Richard, Mary Betley, Carolina Renteria, and Ashni Singh 2020. "Integrating Infrastructure Planning and Budgeting." In *Well Spent: How Strong Infrastructure Governance Can End Waste in Public Investment*, edited by Gerd Schwartz, Manal Fouad, Torben Hansen, and Geneviève Verdier. Washington, DC: International Monetary Fund.

Ardanaz, Martín, Eduardo Cavallo, Alejandro Izquierdo, and Jorge Puig. 2021. "Growth-Friendly Fiscal Rules? Safeguarding Public Investment from Budget Cuts through Fiscal Rule Design." *Journal of International Money and Finance* 111: 102319.

Basdevant, Olivier, Taz Chaponda, Fabien Gonguet, Jiro Honda, and Saji Thomas. 2020. "Designing Fiscal Rules to Protect Investment." In *Well Spent: How Strong Infrastructure Governance Can End Waste in Public Investment*, edited by Gerd Schwartz, Manal Fouad, Torben Hansen, and Geneviève Verdier. Washington, DC: International Monetary Fund.

Brixi, Hana Polackova, and Ashoka Mody. 2002. "Dealing with Government Fiscal Risk: An Overview." In *Government at Risk: Contingent Liabilities and Fiscal Risk,* edited by Hana Polackova Brixi and Allen Schick. Washington, DC: World Bank.

Budina, Nina, and Murray Petrie. 2013. "Managing and Controlling Fiscal Risks." In *Public Financial Management and Its Emerging Architecture*, edited by Marco Cangiano, Teresa Curristine, and Michel Lazare. Washington, DC: International Monetary Fund.

Cangiano, Marco, Teresa Curristine, and Michel Lazare, eds. 2013. *Public Financial Management and Its Emerging Architecture*. Washington, DC: International Monetary Fund.

Clements, Benedict J., David Coady, Stefania Fabrizio, Sanjeev Gupta, Trevor Serge Coleridge Alleyne, and Carlo A. Sdralevich. 2013. *Energy Subsidy Reform: Lessons and Implications*. Washington, DC: International Monetary Fund.

Daniel, Philip, Michael Keen, and Charles McPherson. 2010. *The Taxation of Petroleum and Minerals: Principle, Problems and Practice*. London: International Monetary Fund and Routledge.

de Janvry, Alain, Alejandro del Valle, and Elizabeth Sadoulet. 2016. "Insuring Growth: The Impact of Disaster Funds on Economic Reconstruction in Mexico." Policy Research Working Paper 7714, World Bank, Washington, DC.

Foster, Vivien, and Anshul Rana. 2020. *Rethinking Power Sector Reform in the Developing World*. Sustainable Infrastructure Series. Washington, DC: World Bank.

IMF (International Monetary Fund). 2007. *Manual on Fiscal Transparency*. Washington DC: International Monetary Fund.

IMF (International Monetary Fund). 2011. *Public Sector Debt Statistics: Guide for Compilers and Users*. Revised second printing 2013. Washington, DC: International Monetary Fund.

IMF (International Monetary Fund). 2014. *Government Finance Statistics Manual 2014*. Washington, DC: International Monetary Fund.

IMF (International Monetary Fund). 2016. *Managing Government Compensation and Employment: Institutions, Policies, and Reform Challenges*. Policy Paper, Washington DC: International Monetary Fund.

Kim, Jay-Hyung, Jonas Arp Fallov, and Simon Groom. 2020. *Public Investment Management Reference Guide*. International Development in Practice. Washington, DC: World Bank.

OECD (Organisation for Economic Co-operation and Development). 2010. *Accountability and Transparency: A Guide for State Ownership*. Paris: OECD Publishing.

Pattanayak, Sailendra, and Concha Verdugo-Yepes. 2020. "Protecting Public Infrastructure from Vulnerabilities to Corruption: A Risk-Based Approach." In *Well Spent: How Strong Infrastructure Governance Can End Waste in Public Investment*, edited by Gerd Schwartz, Manal Fouad, Torben Hansen, and Geneviève Verdier. Washington, DC: International Monetary Fund.

Robinson, Marc. 2013. "Aggregate Expenditure Ceilings and Allocative Flexibility." *OECD Journal on Budgeting* 12 (3).

Schaechter, Andre, Tidiane Kinda, Nina Budina, and Anke Weber. 2012. "Fiscal Rules in Response to the Crisis: Toward the 'Next-Generation' Rules. A New Dataset." IMF Working Paper WP/12/187, International Monetary Fund, Washington, DC.

Schweikert, Amy, Paul Chinowsky, Kyle Kwiatkowski, and Xavier Espinet. 2014. "The Infrastructure Planning Support System: Analyzing the Impact of Climate Change on Road Infrastructure and Development." *Transport Policy* 35: 146–53.

Taliercio, Robert, and Eduardo Andrés Estrada. 2020. "Best Practices in Project Appraisal and Selection." In *Well Spent: How Strong Infrastructure Governance Can End Waste in Public Investment*, edited by Gerd Schwartz, Manal Fouad, Torben Hansen, and Geneviève Verdier. Washington, DC: International Monetary Fund.

World Bank. 2008. *The Caribbean Catastrophe Risk Insurance Facility: Providing Immediate Funding after Natural Disasters*. Washington, DC: World Bank.

World Bank. 2013. *Beyond the Annual Budget: Global Experience with Medium Term Expenditure Frameworks*. Washington, DC: World Bank.

World Bank. 2020. *Benchmarking Infrastructure Development 2020: Assessing Regulatory Quality to Prepare, Procure, and Manage PPPs and Traditional Public Investment in Infrastructure Projects*. Washington, DC: World Bank.

World Bank. 2021. *Debt Transparency in Developing Economies*. Washington, DC: World Bank.

World Bank. 2022a. *Managing the Fiscal Implications of Public Private Partnerships in a Sustainable and Resilient Manner*. Washington, DC: World Bank.

World Bank. 2022b. *The COVID-19 Pandemic and Air Transport in Southern Africa*. Washington, DC: World Bank.

# Appendix A: Main Data Sources Used in the Report

Table A.1 identifies the major data sources used in the report.

**TABLE A.1**  Major data sources used in the report, by chapter

| Chapter | Data source | Type of analysis | Period | Countries | Description |
|---|---|---|---|---|---|
| 2 | World Bank BOOST Database | Budget execution, capital bias, budget expenditure, procyclicality of expenditures | 2006–20 | Afghanistan, Albania, Angola, Armenia, Bangladesh, Belarus, Benin, Bhutan, Bulgaria, Burkina Faso, Burundi, Cameroon, Cape Verde, Costa Rica, the Dominican Republic, Ecuador, El Salvador, Equatorial Guinea, Ethiopia, Fiji, Gabon, The Gambia, Georgia, Guatemala, Guinea, Guinea Bissau, Haiti, Indonesia, Jamaica, Jordan, Kenya, Kiribati, Kosovo, Kyrgyz Republic, Lebanon, Lesotho, Liberia, Macedonia, Malawi, Mali, Mauritania, Mauritius, Mexico, Moldova, Mongolia, Mozambique, Namibia, Niger, Papua New Guinea, Paraguay, Peru, Senegal, Sierra Leone, Solomon Islands, South Africa, St. Lucia, Tajikistan, Tanzania, Togo, Tunisia, Uganda, Ukraine | Provides panel data on budgetary items for governments participating in the World Bank's BOOST program (see the BOOST Open Budget Portal for details).[a] |
| | | Efficiency analysis | 2006–18 | Afghanistan, Bulgaria, Burkina Faso, Costa Rica, Ethiopia, Guatemala, Kenya, Kosovo, Macedonia, Mauritius, Mexico, Namibia, Niger, Paraguay, Peru, Senegal, Tanzania, Tunisia | |

*(continued)*

**TABLE A.1**   *Continued*

| Chapter | Data source | Type of analysis | Period | Countries | Description |
|---|---|---|---|---|---|
| 3 | World Bank Infrastructure SOEs Database | All | 2009–18 | Albania, Argentina, Bhutan, Brazil, Bulgaria, Burundi, Croatia, Ethiopia, Georgia, Ghana, Indonesia, Kenya, Kosovo, Peru, Romania, Solomon Islands, South Africa, Ukraine, Uruguay | Provides panel data on finances of SOEs (collected for this project) in the power and transport sectors. See appendix B for details. |
| 4 | Engel and others (2022) | Guarantees, renegotiations | 1997–2020 | Chile | Background paper published as part of this project. Provides data on PPPs in Chile. |
| | Marchesi (2022) | Guarantees, renegotiations | 2001–20 | Peru | Background case study on PPPs in Peru conducted for this project. |
| | Private Participation in Infrastructure (PPI) Database | Drivers of early terminations | 1990–2018 | All low- and middle-income countries | Provides data on main characteristics and current status of PPPs in infrastructure (see the PPI Portal for details).[b] |
| | | Estimation of fiscal risks from early termination | 1990–2021 | Albania, Argentina, Bhutan, Brazil, Bulgaria, Burundi, Ethiopia, Georgia, Indonesia, Kenya, Kosovo, Peru, Romania, Solomon Islands, South Africa, Ukraine | |

*Source:* Original table for this publication.
*Note:* PPP = public-private partnership; SOE = state-owned enterprise.
a. https://www.worldbank.org/en/programs/boost-portal/about-boost.
b. https://ppi.worldbank.org/en/ppi.

# Appendix B: The World Bank Infrastructure SOEs Database

The analyses presented in this report rely on detailed statistical work made possible thanks to the new World Bank Infrastructure SOEs Database, compiled for this project. The database was constructed using financial statements from state-owned enterprises (SOEs), obtained from SOE websites; government websites with repositories of SOE financial statements, such as the websites of ministries or the auditor general; annual reports; and other sources, such as the EMIS Intelligence database and stock exchange websites. It covers all SOE operating infrastructure assets in the power (generation, transmission, and distribution) and transportation (roads, railways, airlines, and airports) sectors in 19 countries between 2000 and 2018 (table B.1). The countries were selected based on data availability and to maximize sectoral coverage.

The database classifies an enterprise as an SOE if the state directly or indirectly owns more than 50 percent of its shares or the state is the ultimate controlling entity through majority ownership of common stock or any other mechanisms of control. This definition is in line with the European Union's definition of public undertakings in Commission Directive 2006/111/EC.

The database provides panel data on the finances of SOEs in the power and transport sectors at the SOE–year level that are consistent at the observation level and comparable across SOEs and years. To ensure consistency and reliability, the data were collected using

**TABLE B.1** Countries included in the World Bank Infrastructure SOEs Database, by region

| Region | Countries |
|---|---|
| East Asia and Pacific | Indonesia, Solomon Islands |
| Europe and Central Asia | Albania, Bulgaria, Croatia, Georgia, Kosovo, Romania, Ukraine |
| Latin America and the Caribbean | Argentina, Brazil, Peru, Uruguay |
| South Asia | Bhutan |
| Sub-Saharan Africa | Burundi, Ethiopia, Ghana, Kenya, South Africa |

*Source:* Original table for this publication.

a standardized accounting data template that was populated using the information from financial statements. To ensure that quantities like earnings before interest, taxes, depreciation, and amortization or operations subsidies in the database are comparable across SOEs and years, the World Bank team identified each item as defined by the template using the notes to the financial statements rather than relying on the way such items were presented in the SOEs' main financial tables. Data reliability was further ensured through quality assurance checks by alternate analysts and accounting experts.

The database includes fully owned SOEs (SOEs with 99.5 percent or more ownership of shares by the government or government entities) and partially privatized SOEs, which have less than 99.5 percent ownership by the government. It provides a standardized representation of the income statement, the balance sheet, and the cashflow statement of each SOE. It includes a set of selected items from the statements while maintaining consistency across the resulting financial tables. It also contains supplementary items, including currency risk, debt/loans analysis, maturity profiles of assets and liabilities, and SOE ownership structure.

# Appendix C: Methodology Used to Compare the Performance of SOEs and Similar Private Firms

To compare state-owned enterprises (SOEs) with private firms, this study followed a multistep process to create a comparison group. The team started with the SOEs in the World Bank Infrastructure SOEs Database and searched for firms in Standard and Poor's Capital IQ in the same sector and the same region. It then restricted the search to firms with similar total assets in US dollars. It compiled financial statements for firms within ±20 percent of the assets of the firms in the World Bank Database as well as in the same industry and region. A comparison set of 10–20 firms was created for each SOE in the World Bank database.

The team then eliminated companies that were easily identifiable as SOEs, leaving the potential comparison set with more than 600 firms that could be included in the matching exercise. The study focuses on 2009–18, the period for which the World Bank Infrastructure SOEs Database has better coverage and, therefore, a more balanced panel.[1]

To estimate the effect of state ownership on several indicators of the firms' performance, the team performed a matching exercise that considered the SOE sample as the treatment group and the sample of private firms as the control group. Matching techniques were needed for this exercise because the database is observational rather than randomly selected; there can therefore be systematic differences in characteristics between the treated group (SOEs) and the untreated subjects (private firms) that can cause significant imbalances between the two groups. The team used coarsened exact matching (CEM) to reduce the imbalances between groups while preserving a large comparison group of private firms rather than limiting comparisons to the nearest private firm or firms. For that purpose, it used the natural logarithm of total assets to construct strata or coarsened groups (bins) to run the comparisons. Rather than restricting the matching also by sector and region in which the firms' headquarters were located, it controlled for those variables in the regression.

The CEM procedure yielded 574 private firms (with 4,543 panel observations) matched with 85 SOEs (with 686 panel observations). The matching method also yielded nine bins and sampling weights to account for the remaining imbalance between groups.

## NOTE

1. To address the concern that the database of private firms may still include state-owned firms, the team eliminated all firms that Capital IQ codes as having public ownership and partially privatized SOEs included in the database of Lazzarini and Musacchio (2018). This step eliminated 30 firms that had minority state ownership—any firm with more than 5 percent state ownership—in the road, airport, airline, power, and railway sectors. There is still the slim possibility that firms owned by entities that are ultimately controlled by governments remained in the sample. A more specialized database that tracks ultimate ownership, such as Bureau van Dyk's Orbis, can be used to resolve this issue in the future.

## REFERENCE

Lazzarini, Sergio G., and Aldo Musacchio. 2018. "State Ownership Reinvented? Explaining Performance Differences between State-Owned and Private Firms." *Corporate Governance: An International Review*, 26(4): 255–72.

# Appendix D: Big Bang versus Frequent Small-Drip Events

The findings of this report stand in contrast to recent overviews of fiscal risk in state-owned enterprises (SOEs) that focus on large, "big-bang" events. These studies portray fiscal risk as tail risk rather than regular occurrences. For instance, Bova and others (2019) compile data on the gross fiscal costs of shocks to SOEs that exceed 0.2 percent of the gross domestic product (GDP) between 1990 and 2014. They identify 29 episodes in which SOEs were the source of contingent liabilities for the government (table D.1). Of those 29 episodes, 17 involved infrastructure SOEs broadly defined (15 in the 4 sectors covered in chapter 3). The average gross fiscal cost of these SOEs was 3.2 percent of GDP (3.0 percent for the sectors studied in this report), with a maximum gross cost of 15 percent of GDP. Most of these realizations occurred during the global financial crisis of 2008–10.

**TABLE D.1  Number and cost of bailouts of infrastructure SOEs between 1990 and 2014**

| Sector | Number of SOE bailouts between 1990 and 2014 | Percent of all SOE bailouts during this period | Average gross payout (percent of GDP) |
|---|---|---|---|
| Airline | 1 | 3 | 1.8 |
| Construction | 1 | 3 | 9.0 |
| Power | 9 | 31 | 2.7 |
| Railways | 5 | 17 | 3.6 |
| Water | 1 | 3 | 1.1 |
| Oil and gas | 4 | 14 | 4.2 |
| Non-infrastructure | 8 | 28 | 2.6 |
| All | 29 | 100 | 3.2 |
| All infrastructure SOEs excluding oil and gas | 17 | 59 | 2.8 |
| Infrastructure sectors analyzed in this report | 15 | 52 | 3.0 |

*Source:* Original table for this publication, using dataset from Bova and others 2019.
*Note:* GDP = gross domestic product; SOE = state-owned enterprise.

Table D.2 displays 42 country-year events of fiscal injections to SOEs, as measured in this study, that exceeded 0.2 percent of GDP in the World Bank Infrastructure SOEs Database. It shows that the fiscal risk from SOEs should not be thought about as tail risk but rather as more frequent occurrences of significant magnitudes (about 0.2 percent of GDP a year for infrastructure SOEs alone).

**TABLE D.2**   **Annual fiscal injections of at least 0.2 percent of GDP in the World Bank's Infrastructure SOEs Database**

| Country | Year | Sector | Sectoral fiscal injections (percent of GDP) | Total fiscal injections (percent of GDP) |
|---|---|---|---|---|
| Uruguay | 2012 | Roads | 0.14 | 0.20 |
| | | Railways | 0.06 | |
| Romania | 2013 | Railways | 0.21 | 0.21 |
| Indonesia | 2018 | Roads | 0.17 | 0.23 |
| | | Railways | 0.05 | |
| Kosovo | 2010 | Power | 0.23 | 0.23 |
| Uruguay | 2015 | Roads | 0.19 | 0.24 |
| | | Railways | 0.05 | |
| Romania | 2016 | Power | <0.01 | 0.24 |
| | | Roads | 0.09 | |
| | | Railways | 0.15 | |
| Kosovo | 2013 | Power | 0.23 | 0.24 |
| | | Railways | <0.01 | |
| Argentina | 2016 | Power | 0.18 | 0.25 |
| | | Airlines and airports | 0.01 | |
| | | Railways | 0.05 | |
| Uruguay | 2017 | Roads | 0.20 | 0.25 |
| | | Railways | 0.05 | |
| Romania | 2015 | Power | <0.01 | 0.25 |
| | | Roads | 0.08 | |
| | | Railways | 0.17 | |
| Bulgaria | 2012 | Airlines and airports | 0.05 | 0.26 |
| | | Railways | 0.21 | |
| Albania | 2016 | Power | 0.26 | 0.27 |
| | | Railways | <0.01 | |
| Uruguay | 2010 | Roads | 0.28 | 0.28 |
| Bulgaria | 2009 | Airlines and airports | 0.05 | 0.28 |
| | | Railways | 0.23 | |

*(continued)*

**TABLE D.2** *Continued*

| Country | Year | Sector | Sectoral fiscal injections (percent of GDP) | Total fiscal injections (percent of GDP) |
|---|---|---|---|---|
| Romania | 2014 | Power | 0.00 | 0.30 |
| | | Roads | 0.04 | |
| | | Railways | 0.27 | |
| Croatia | 2015 | Airlines and airports | 0.03 | 0.32 |
| | | Railways | 0.29 | |
| Uruguay | 2013 | Roads | 0.29 | 0.32 |
| | | Railways | 0.04 | |
| Indonesia | 2010 | Power | 0.33 | 0.33 |
| | | Airlines and airports | <0.01 | |
| Indonesia | 2012 | Power | 0.34 | 0.35 |
| | | Roads | 0.01 | |
| Croatia | 2014 | Airlines and airports | 0.03 | 0.35 |
| | | Railways | 0.32 | |
| Bulgaria | 2011 | Airlines and airports | 0.04 | 0.36 |
| | | Railways | 0.32 | |
| Croatia | 2018 | Airlines and airports | 0.02 | 0.37 |
| | | Railways | 0.36 | |
| Uruguay | 2009 | Roads | 0.41 | 0.41 |
| Croatia | 2011 | Airlines and airports | 0.14 | 0.42 |
| | | Railways | 0.28 | |
| Bulgaria | 2010 | Airlines and airports | 0.04 | 0.44 |
| | | Railways | 0.40 | |
| Croatia | 2016 | Airlines and airports | 0.02 | 0.45 |
| | | Railways | 0.43 | |
| Bulgaria | 2015 | Power | 0.24 | 0.48 |
| | | Airlines and airports | 0.04 | |
| | | Railways | 0.20 | |
| Kosovo | 2012 | Power | 0.52 | 0.52 |
| Indonesia | 2013 | Power | 0.66 | 0.70 |
| | | Roads | 0.04 | |
| Kosovo | 2009 | Power | 0.71 | 0.71 |
| Albania | 2014 | Power | 0.72 | 0.72 |
| | | Railways | <0.01 | |

*(continued)*

**TABLE D.2**  *Continued*

| Country | Year | Sector | Sectoral fiscal injections (percent of GDP) | Total fiscal injections (percent of GDP) |
|---|---|---|---|---|
| Bulgaria | 2013 | Power | 0.49 | 0.75 |
| | | Airlines and airports | 0.06 | |
| | | Railways | 0.21 | |
| Bulgaria | 2014 | Power | 0.53 | 0.77 |
| | | Airlines and airports | 0.04 | |
| | | Railways | 0.20 | |
| Indonesia | 2014 | Power | 0.78 | 0.78 |
| | | Roads | <0.01 | |
| Kosovo | 2011 | Power | 0.79 | 0.79 |
| Bulgaria | 2017 | Power | 0.46 | 0.84 |
| | | Airlines and airports | 0.05 | |
| | | Railways | 0.32 | |
| Bhutan | 2017 | Power | 0.89 | 0.89 |
| Indonesia | 2016 | Power | 0.94 | 0.95 |
| | | Railways | 0.01 | |
| Bhutan | 2018 | Power | 0.85 | 1.05 |
| | | Airlines and airports | 0.21 | |
| Bulgaria | 2018 | Power | 1.15 | 1.45 |
| | | Airlines and airports | <0.01 | |
| | | Railways | 0.29 | |
| Bulgaria | 2016 | Power | 2.11 | 2.32 |
| | | Airlines and airports | 0.03 | |
| | | Railways | 0.17 | |
| Croatia | 2017 | Power | <0.01 | 2.91 |
| | | Airlines and airports | 0.02 | |
| | | Roads | 2.46 | |
| | | Railways | 0.42 | |

*Source:* Original table for this publication, based on data from the World Bank Infrastructure SOEs Database and World Development Indicators.
*Note:* GDP = gross domestic product.

## REFERENCE

Bova, Elva, Marta Ruiz-Arranz, Frederik Giancarlo Toscani, and Hatice Elif Ture. 2019. "The Impact of Contingent Liability Realizations on Public Finances." *International Tax and Public Finance* 26 (2): 381–417.

# Appendix E: Methodology Used to Compare SOEs That Suffered a Negative Shock as a Result of the Decline in Oil and Gas Prices with a Control Group of SOEs

To assess the impact of a negative macroeconomic shock on state-owned enterprises (SOEs), the analysis focused on the 19 countries covered in the World Bank Infrastructure SOE Database. The analysis restricted the sample to SOEs in the power, airline, and airport sectors to maximize comparability within sectors across countries (Herrera Dappe and others 2022).

The analysis exploited the collapse in the price of oil and gas between mid-2014 and early 2015 as an unanticipated negative shock to the infrastructure SOEs in the database and examined the effects of the shock on their performance. Brent crude oil prices fell from $115 a barrel in June 2014 to $55 by the end of that year; after a short initial recovery in early 2015, prices continued to fall throughout 2015, hitting a low of $27 in early 2016. The price then bounced back to over $60 a barrel. Gas prices showed a similar pattern.

This oil shock affected countries differently, based on their oil and gas exporting status and their energy reserves. The premise is that countries that are "energy-rich" would experience a negative shock to their economies with the price collapse of these commodities vis-à-vis other countries. To categorize countries represented in the sample as energy rich and non-energy rich, the analysis set a threshold based on both exports and total reserves of crude oil and gas. Countries whose oil and gas exports were above 0.5 percent of total exports and had reserves of 1 million or more barrels of oil or more than 700 billion cubic meters of gas were categorized as energy rich. This threshold ensured that large gas re-exporters in Eastern Europe were included in the treated sample, as the price collapse had significant negative effects on their economies.

The experimental setting relied on the fact that the negative shock to the price of oil in 2014 severely affected the balance of payments of some of the major oil or gas exporters, creating a recession—precisely the negative macroeconomic shock needed for the treatment group. Countries that rely less heavily on oil or gas experienced mild to no effects.

In order to avoid potential biases, and accurately identify the effects of interest, the analysis used coarsened exact matching (CEM) to compare firms within bins in which the sector, the income level of the economy, the ratio of fuel costs to total expenses and the size as a percent of gross domestic product were similar. CEM allowed creation of bins that are balanced across the treatment and control groups using these variables. The study thus focuses on the differential treatment effect of the negative shock by comparing similar SOEs in terms of sector, country income, fuel dependence, and importance for the economy.

To identify the causal effect from the negative macroeconomic shock of the decline in oil and gas prices in the world markets, the analysis used a difference-in-differences estimation in which the variable of interest was the interaction between treatment (that is, energy rich) and posttreatment dummies.

## REFERENCE

Herrera Dappe, Matías, Aldo Musacchio, Carolina Pan, Yadviga Semikolenova, Burak Turkgulu, and Jonathan Barboza. 2022. "State-Owned Enterprises as Countercyclical Instruments: Experimental Evidence from the Infrastructure Sector." Policy Research Working Paper 9971, World Bank, Washington, DC.

# Appendix F: Methodology for Estimating Fiscal Risks from Early Termination

The value-at-risk methodology has been used to estimate fiscal risks from early termination. The fiscal risk faced by a country from its current portfolio of projects is estimated as the maximum expected loss with 99 percent confidence using the parameter and probability estimates from the following hazard regression model:

$$\ln H\left(t|X_{it}\right) = \gamma_0 + \sum_{m=1}^{2} \gamma_m z_m\left(\ln t\right) + X_{i,proj}\,\beta_{proj} + X_{it,inst}\,\beta_{inst} + X_{it,macro}\,\beta_{macro},$$

where $\ln H(t|X_{it})$ is the log cumulative hazard at time $t$ for project $i$ conditional on $X_{it} = (X_{i,proj}, X_{it,inst}, X_{it,macro})$; $X_{i,proj}$ is the vector of project-specific time-invariant covariates; $X_{it,inst}$ is the vector of country-specific time-varying institutional covariates; and $X_{it,macro}$ is the vector of country-specific time-varying macroeconomic shocks. The terms under the summation operator represent the set of restricted cubic spline terms in log time scale, $z_m(\ln t)$. The time scale is the percentage of the contract period elapsed.

Using the hazard regression, the probability of early termination for each project over a specified period of time can be calculated. It can then be used to calculate the expected loss from each project:

$$EL_i = PET_i \times EAT_i \times LGT_i,$$

where $PET_i$ is the probability of early termination for project $i$, $EAT_i$ is the exposure of the government from project $i$ at termination, and $LGT_i$ is the loss of the government from project $i$ given termination.

The value-at-risk from early termination for the PPP portfolio of country $c$ is calculated as

$$EL_{c,99\%} = \sum_i EL_i + z_{1\%} \times s.e.\left(\sum_i EL_i\right),$$

where $z_{1\%}$ is the z-score for the 99th percentile of the standard normal distribution, and *s.e.*( ) stands for the standard error of the total expected loss from early termination in a country, as estimated using the delta method based on the distribution of the parameter estimates from the hazard regression and the expected loss formula above. See Herrera Dappe, Melecky, and Turkgulu (2022) for a more detailed discussion.

## REFERENCE

Herrera Dappe, Matías, Martin Melecky, and Burak Turkgulu. 2022. "Fiscal Risks from Early Termination of Public-Private Partnerships in Infrastructure." Policy Research Working Paper 9972, World Bank, Washington, DC.